SOCIAL ACCOUNTING FOR INDUSTRIAL AND TRANSITION ECONOMIES

To Jack, Yousif and Zaki
Whose contributions have not gone unnoticed

Social Accounting For Industrial and Transition Economies
Economy-wide models for analysis and policy

S. I. COHEN
Faculty of Economics, Erasmus University Rotterdam

LONDON AND NEW YORK

First published 2002 by Ashgate Publishing

Reissued 2018 by Routledge
2 Park Square, Milton Park, Abingdon, Oxon OX14 4RN
711 Third Avenue, New York, NY 10017, USA

Routledge is an imprint of the Taylor & Francis Group, an informa business

Copyright © S. I. Cohen 2002

All rights reserved. No part of this book may be reprinted or reproduced or utilised in any form or by any electronic, mechanical, or other means, now known or hereafter invented, including photocopying and recording, or in any information storage or retrieval system, without permission in writing from the publishers.

Notice:
Product or corporate names may be trademarks or registered trademarks, and are used only for identification and explanation without intent to infringe.

Publisher's Note
The publisher has gone to great lengths to ensure the quality of this reprint but points out that some imperfections in the original copies may be apparent.

Disclaimer
The publisher has made every effort to trace copyright holders and welcomes correspondence from those they have been unable to contact.

A Library of Congress record exists under LC control number: 2002102020

ISBN 13: 978-1-138-74266-6 (hbk)
ISBN 13: 978-1-138-74262-8 (pbk)
ISBN 13: 978-1-315-18214-8 (ebk)

Contents

Preface   *vii*

Social Accounting Matrix (SAM) - Related Applications for Transition Economies

1   Comparative SAM Matrices for West and East European Countries: Construction and Structural Differences   1

2   SAM Multipliers for West and East European Countries: an Evaluation of Transitional Patterns   19

3   Growth and Distribution in Russia and China: the Difference   39

4   Policy Modelling under Fixed and Flexible Price Regimes: SAM and CGE Transition Models Applied to Hungary and Poland   57

SAM-Related Frameworks for Industrial Economies

5   SAM Analysis for the Netherlands   89

6   Inter-Temporal Analysis of Regional Multipliers   109

7   Urban Dynamics and the Circular Flow in Industrial Economies   125

8   Growth and Equity Effects of Demographic Change in Industrial Economies   145

Appendices   *167*

Bibliography   *195*

Index   *199*

Preface

In the past two to three decades, there has been an increased momentum in the design, construction and use of social accounting matrices for developing countries, this is well documented in the accompanying volume to the current volume, S.I. Cohen: *Social Accounting and Economic Modelling for Developing Countries*, Ashgate Publishing, 2002.

The construction and use of the social accounting matrix (SAM) for structural and policy analysis of industrial economies is a later development, and is the subject matter of the current volume. Most likely, the first published analysis of a SAM for an industrial economy was that for the Netherlands, cf.. Cohen (1988). Since then I have run for several years, with various team members and associates, a research programme on SAM applications for industrial countries. The topics treated included the trade-off between growth and distribution, and effective state instruments to minimise this trade-off, regionalisation of the SAM, incorporation of spatial dimensions, simulation of the effects of demographic changes and ageing, and the analysis of intertemporal changes in SAMs, SAM multipliers and their decomposition. The applications were extended to four Western European countries, namely the Netherlands, Germany, Italy and Spain.

The turnaround in the centrally planned economies of Eastern Europe, and their entry in a transitional phase in which markets would play a more dominant role, opened an important opportunity for application of social accounting in these countries. It was necessary to transform the national accounts statistics in these countries to standard uses as recommended by the United Nations and Eurostat, and to introduce modern forms of economic analysis beyond the typical input-output tables which were so popular in central planning. The SAM provided a comprehensive framework for organising national aacounts statistics. It also provided a viable framework for the analysis and shaping of economic policies in such areas as sectoral restructuring, household income distribution, maintenance of balanced government budgets and external finance. In this context, we had the opportunity of conducting and advising on SAM applications in, Chezchoslovakia, Bulgaria, Hungary, Poland, Rumania, and Russia. And lately, China has been added to this list. In this book we focus on the applications for Hungary, Poland, Russia and China.

Most of the SAM applications we treat in this volume have been published in economic journals. As usual, in such research programmes, which spread over several years and count on inputs from different persons in different settings, there are tendencies for the designs, presentations and results of the research pieces to overlap. This raises a need for the consolidation of the parts in a harmonious whole. The current volume hopes to have been successful in this endeavour. Some of the published articles had to be substantially revised to avoid overlapping. Besides, greater insight was gained as more results from more applications became available over time; and this required the upgrading of previously executed analysis, and revision of empirical results. The final outcome are eight chapters falling in two blocks. Chapters 1, 2, 3 and 4 form one block that treats social accounting and economic modelling for transition economies and reflects on the results obtained, having in mind comparative results for market economies. Chapters 5, 6, 7 and 8 develop alternative social accounting frameworks for the analysis of different policy problems in the context of Western European industrial economies.

In chapter 1 we introduce the idea of the SAM, and review the construction of such matrices for Germany, Italy, the Netherlands, and Spain, as well as for Hungary and Poland. In the way of building up acquaintance and knowledge on SAMs, the chapter is further devoted to a cross-country comparison of the structural properties of the SAMs among the six countries. We separate the Western from the Eastern European countries to allow gaining insight into the effects of systemic differences on the economic structures.

In chapter 2 we compare and assess the future courses of economies in Eastern Europe, i.e. Poland and Hungary, in relation to the four representative economies in Western Europe (WE) mentioned above, on the basis of standardised SAMs and a SAM multiplier analysis that focuses on issues of growth and distribution.

In chapter 3 SAMs of the two largest centrally planned economies around 1990, Russia and China, are displayed and the size and distribution of their multiplier effects are investigated. Even though the comparative analysis is limited to one year only, the obtained results have a durability that is supported by contrasting trends in the two countries over the past decades.

The policy problem in chapter 4 is concerned with adaptations to the introduction, during a transitional phase, of market mechanisms in the otherwise centrally planned systems of Eastern Europe. In chapter 4 we build on the postulate that with a minimum of manipulations the SAM can be converted to either a fixed-price or flexible-price model, the latter is in fact a computable general equilibrium (CGE) model. The two representations of the economy are very handy in replicating a centrally planned and a free market situation, respectively. By running one and the same policy injection in both versions, it is possible to detect the signs, sizes, and locations of the discrepancies. Furthermore, by applying sensitivity analysis, one can appraise the effectivity of different instruments in resolving the discrepancies. In this chapter we quantify and simulate SAM and CGE models for both Hungary and Poland during their early transitional phase.

Chapters 5, 6, 7 and 8 form another block that deals with in-depth national analysis of various issues of economic restructuring in industrial economies. Although the applications focus on the Netherlands, the issues dealt with are generally encountered in industrial economies, and especially in Western Europe. The applications use different configurations of social accounting matrices for multiple years.

In chapter 5 the conceptual framework of the SAM is introduced and tabulated for the Netherlands. The matrix is then put to an analysis of multipliers, thereby permitting the investigation of the structural properties of the Dutch economy. Key sectors that drive growth will be identified, as well as the distribution of growth incidence on household groups. The multipliers will also be decomposed in transfer, open-loop and closed-loop effects and analysed.

In chapter 6, making use of the social accounting framework, answers are sought for several questions relating to regional development. How can internally structuring forces and externally intervening forces, working together in the economy-wide circular flow, explain regional development during the 1980s in the Netherlands? When and where were the externally intervening forces more significant than the internally structuring forces? And in which direction would these forces be shaped in the future? The hypothesis we pose is that while the external forces are statistically more significant than the internal forces in generating growth and distributionary effects at the regional level, the combination of the two forces is different for different regions.

In chapter 7 a social accounting matrix was specially designed to examine the underlying factors behind the growth and decline of household groups belonging to metropolitan cities, large and small towns, and suburban and rural municipalities, and how these developments link with the economy-wide circular flow. It will be seen, for instance, that large towns and the services sector are experiencing negative growth bias in terms of both internal and external influencing forces. Taking into account the working of the circular flow, the social accounting model employed here suggests that a deconcentration of cities towards towns, rural municipalities, dormitory towns and small towns goes simultaneously with enhanced growth for the sectors of mining, banking and public utilities at the cost of light industry, construction and services.

The policy problem in chapter 8 is concerned with the long range effects of demographic change on economic growth and income distribution in Western Europe and the appraisal of alternative policies to mitigate negative effects. In chapter 8 the impact of changing demographic structures in industrial economies is studied by developing a social accounting framework that includes households by size. The functioning of the economy is investigated under a past economic demographic situation (Netherlands, 1981) and under a future simulated situation (2010) featuring a more differentiated demographic structure with a significant increase of the share of the one- and two-person households. Comparing the multiplier results of both SAMs, we shall find out that the income bias of the recent past towards the three- and more-person households tends to continue in the future. However, in the reconstructed SAM for 2010 there is a tendency towards a more progressive income distribution. The model simulates also the effects of the demographic changes on sectoral performance over time.

The completion of the research programme was made possible by the joint cooperation of a number of associates and co-authors. I like to acknowledge contributions of M.C. Braber, E. Gavrilenkov, Wu Gupei, F.N. Lafeber, T. Revesz, J.M.C. Tuyl, E. Zalai, M. de Zeeuw, L. Zienkowski, and Z. Zolkiewski. Typing and retyping were carefully done with the assistance of Annet van Loon and Jane Dolgova.

As was stated above, I have drawn in part on some of my published articles in economic journals and bundles. Appreciation goes to the following journals for the granted permission to employ the material: De Economist, Socio-Economic Planning Sciences, Journal of Policy Modelling, Economic Modelling, Acta Oeconomica.

The SAM research on Eastern Europe was partly supported by a generous grant from the Action for Cooperation in the field of Economics (ACE), a programme of the European Union. The work on the SAM for Russia was supported by the Dutch Science Foundation (NOW). That on China was supported by the Foundation for Economic Research Rotterdam (SEOR). We are grateful for the support from all three sources.

Chapter 1

Comparative SAM Matrices for West and East European Countries: Construction and Structural Differences

1. Introduction

By way of introduction it can be stated that the social accounting matrix, SAM, is compiled according to the same accounting principles as input-output tables, each transaction being recorded twice so that any ingoing in one account must be balanced by an outgoing of another account. However, the SAM contains a complete list of transactions describing income, expenditure and production flows among sectors, factors of production and groups of households. These transactions are usually grouped into several sets of accounts belonging to various economic agents, as will be elaborated later.

The SAM itself is nothing more or less than the transformation of the circular flow in the national economy into a matrix of transactions between the various agents. In a first phase an aggregate SAM is structured entirely from published data of the national accounts, corresponding with the circular flow; as such the SAM is no more than a presentation of available national statistics in a matrix form. In a second phase, the disaggregation of the SAM takes place depending on the purpose of the analysis and on available data sources.

The idea of a social accounting matrix, SAM, can be traced back to Quesnay's Tableau Economique in 1758. The idea was revived only 200 years later. Hicks coined the term social accounting in 1942; the realisation of a SAM was the work of Stone in 1947; and it was associates of Stone, working in the context of developing countries, who presented the first comprehensive publication of a SAM, cf. Pyatt and Roe (1977).

In the past two to three decades, there has been a noticeable shift of interest from the basic input-output matrix to the social accounting matrix, as evident from the increased momentum in the design, construction and use of social accounting matrices in developing countries, see Cohen (2002).

There have been several considerations working in favour of extending the input-output towards the social accounting framework. First, the SAM is a helpful tool in setting up integrated statistical accounts of households, firms and government, in addition to those of activities, in transparent and consistent manners. The advantage of forcing national statistics into a social accounting framework is that the statistician can discover inconsistencies and gaps, which went, unnoticed before. Second, SAM facilitates the initialisation of corresponding economy-wide models. The discipline of building an explicit SAM assures that the initial values of the variables in the modelled system are internally consistent. Third, once a SAM is available it can be used to give a quantitative diagnosis of the structure of the whole economy, which is hardly feasible in the conventional presentation of national statistics. Fourth, there has been an increasing requirement by policy-makers and the larger public in developing countries to appraise development in terms of both growth and equity objectives. The SAM simultaneously integrated disaggregated data on production, income and expenditure, thereby allowing a systematic recording of circular transactions that are necessary for the study of growth and its distribution. Especially in the context of developing countries, the SAM has demonstrated its ability to analyse the underlying growth and equity properties of these economies. Fifth, the availability of SAMs for different countries and for more years allowed for the fruitful use of cross-country and inter-temporal comparisons on the structure and performance of economic systems, and investigates the economic mechanisms behind superior and inferior performances.

The construction and use of social accounting for developed economies is a later development and is the main concern in this volume. One of the first publications on the construction and use of the SAM for an industrial economy was for the Netherlands, Cohen (1988). The analysis contributed to a better understanding of the driving power of different sectors in causing economic growth and redistributionary incomes on earning households. The analysis evaluated also the growth and redistribution effects of state injections in sectoral activities and transfers among households. More SAM applications to the Netherlands and other industrial economies such as Germany, Italy and Spain followed suit. Chapters 5, 6, 7 and 8 will highlight various refinements that were incorporated in social accounting and economic modelling in the context of industrial economies.

The turnaround in the centrally planned economies of Eastern Europe, and their entry in a transitional phase in which markets would play a more dominant role, opened an important opportunity for application of social accounting in these countries in recent years. In countries that are undergoing a transition from a planning-oriented economy towards a more market-oriented economy, the system of national accounts statistics had to be overhauled, and the SAM offered new and wider perspectives for such redesigns. More knowledge on the differences between planning and market systems and the functioning of the two systems as a whole can give much insight into the transformation process. As will be shown in a couple of chapters in this book, economy-wide models, like SAM, are very useful in identifying the content and direction of, and reaction to, basic economic changes in the transition phase from one to the other system. Chapters 1, 2, 3 and 4 of this volume will deal primarily with social accounting and economic modelling in transitional economies, even though in chapters 1 and 2 we shall apply comparative evaluations between Eastern and Western European countries.

Being the first chapter, the aim of this chapter is to briefly describe the main features of the SAM, explain how it is constructed, and review procedures for tabulation of standardised SAMs for countries that belong to different economic systems and that use basically different systems of national accounts statistics. Once the SAMs for Western and Eastern European countries are standardised, we shall reflect in this chapter on the structural differences between market- and planning- oriented economic systems as being represented by the selected six Western and Eastern European countries. We shall start with more analytical uses of the SAM from the next chapter onwards.

2. Construction of Standard SAMs for Four Western European Countries

As was just stated the SAM itself is nothing more or less than the transformation of the circular flow in the national economy of figure 1.1 into a matrix of transactions between the various agents as in tables 1.1 and 1.2, which will be shortly reviewed. In the lower bound of figure 1.1, households supply labour and capital to firms who are organisers of production activities; households are paid back in return for the use of their labour and capital factors.

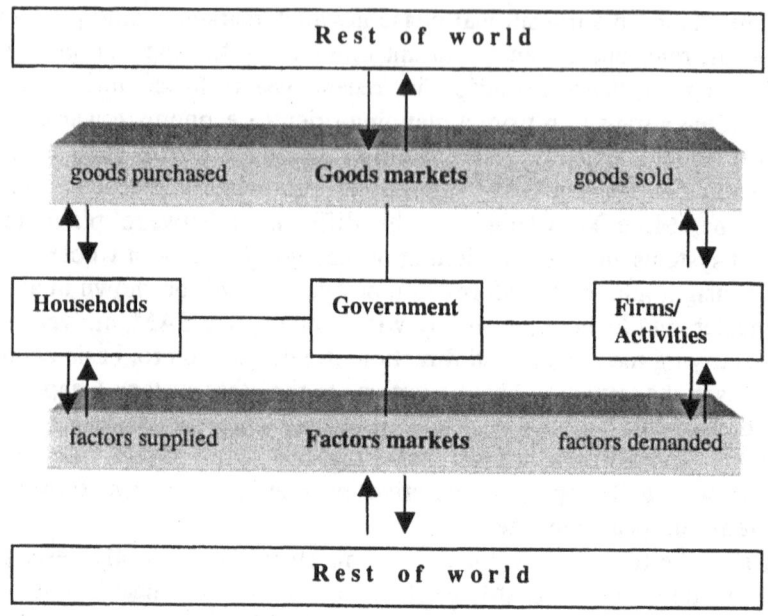

Figure 1.1. Circular Flow

In the upper bound, households spend their incomes on products that are delivered by the firms/activities. In the centre there is the government, which is involved in transfers to and from households and firms/activities. Furthermore, there are the economic relations between the country and the rest of the world.

A SAM contains the following list of accounts:

- Want accounts; indexed as 1.
- Factor of production accounts; indexed as 2.
- Institution accounts; indexed as 3. A distinction is made between current and capital transactions. Current transactions are disaggregated by whether they belong to households, firms, and government. Capital transactions are aggregated for all institutions in one national capital account.
- Activity accounts, and rest of the world accounts, indexed as 4.

The content of the SAM can be introduced further by means of table 1.1. The first set of accounts represents the want accounts. It is not obligatory to include these accounts in the SAM, but by incorporating the want accounts, we increase focus on a whole range of goods and services which are representative of levels of well being. These will usually include expenditure on food, housing, clothing, health, education, transport and other goods and services. It is informative to know, for instance, how much each specific household group spends on food and how this expenditure flows to agriculture and the non-agricultural sectors.

The factor of production accounts are meant to show how the value added generated in the various production activities are allocated over the production factors, and subsequently how these factor incomes are distributed to the current institutions. The SAMs constructed here make a distinction between the two major factors of production, namely labour and capital; either may be disaggregated further.

The institution current accounts are split up into accounts for households, firms and government. For any institution, by adding the different sources of incomes in the rows, we find the total incomings of that institution. In the columns we see how the institutions pay out some of their incomings as direct taxes and transfer payments, spend on consumer goods, and transfer their savings to the combined national capital account.

The capital transfers between the separate institutions - flow of funds - are netted and can therefore be left out from the SAM. It follows that domestic and foreign savings should be spent on capital goods. As a result, the national capital account shows total savings equal total investment.

The activity accounts show on the row the money receipts of the producing sectors from the sale of private and public consumption goods, investment goods, intermediate goods and exports. Column-wise, the sales revenue of the producing sectors go in part as value added to factors of production, indirect taxes, depreciation costs, and purchase of intermediate goods and imports. The sales revenue of each production activity is taken up in part by purchases of raw materials which may be either domestically produced or imported, these besides indirect taxes and subsidies and depreciation costs. Part of the production costs takes the form of value added paid out to the factors of production labour (wages) and capital (profits).

Table 1.1. Sam Entries

	(1) Wants	(2) Factors	(3) Institutions				(4) Activities		Totals
			Households	Firms	Government	Capital	Production sectors	Rest of World	
Wants			households spendings						Wants expenditure
Factors							Domestic value added	Foreign factor payment	Factors income
Institutions									
Households		Households factor income			Public transfer to households			Transfers	Households income
Firms		Firms factor income			Public debt servicing				Firms income
Government		Public enterprise profit	Households direct taxes	Firms direct taxes			Indirect taxes	Transfers	government income
National capital			Households savings	Firms savings	Public savings		Depreciation	Deficit balance of payments	Gross capital formation
Activities									
Production sectors	Private consumption				Public consumption	Investment goods	Intermediate goods	Exports	Gross production
Rest of World			Transfers		Transfers		Imports		Outgoings
Totals	Wants receipts	Factors income	Households income	Firms income	Public income	Gross capital formation	Gross production	Receipt rest of world	Grand total

Finally, in the rest of the world account, imports and exports are matched with incoming and outgoing foreign transfers. Intermediate goods, consumer goods, investment goods and exports. The row gives the distribution of imports on consumption goods, investment goods, intermediate goods and transit imports for re-exports. The column gives the expenditure of the external world in the form of net factor incomes from abroad, net household and government transfers, net capital inflow and export and transit balances of goods and services.

We show as an example the aggregate SAM of Germany in table 1.2, those of the other Western European countries are in the appendix. These are no more than a presentation of available national accounts statistics in a matrix form. Table 1.3 displays the example of the obtained SAM for Poland; the SAM of Hungary is in the appendix.

Table 1.2 SAM for Germany (1984, billion marks)

	1	2	3	4	5	6	7	8	9	Total
1 Wants				1003.6						1003.6
2 Labour								950.5	3.5	954.0
3 Capital								393.4	10.6	403.9
4 Households		954.0	343.0			299.0			-12.1	1583.8
5 Firms			81.7			4.0			-0.5	85.2
6 Government	87.8		-20.7	489.8	37.8		19.7	79.8	-17.2	671.0
7 Capital				90.5	47.3	23.8		222.0	-22.3	361.2
8 Activities	823.3					350.2	310.6	1508.5	476.9	3469.5
9 ROW	92.5						30.9	315.4	60.6	499.4
Total	1003.6	954.0	403.9	1583.8	85.2	677.0	361.2	3469.5	499.4	9037.6

Table 1.3. SAM for Poland (1987, billion zlotys)

	1	2	3	4	5	6	7	8	9	Total
1 Wants				8736						8736
2 Labour								8332		8332
3 Capital								7431		7431
4 Households		6740	851			1561			375	9526
5 Firms			5616			316				5932
6 Government		1592	964	180	2616			72	57	5481
7 Capital				610	3316	-164		1130	-8	4884
8 Activities	8371					2937	4425	19373	3516	38623
9 ROW	365					831	458	2286	109	4049
Total	8736	8332	7431	9526	5932	5481	4883	38623	4049	92994

Once the matrix was constructed, each account within it was disaggregated on the basis of additional data from surveys of the labour force, household income and expenditure, input-output deliveries, finance, government, trade and other statistics to give the disaggregated SAM, which is really what we are after. The disaggregated SAM tables are found in the appendix at the end of the book with notes on their construction and data sources.

With the comparative analytical purposes in mind, as set out in the introduction above, the individual SAMs have been standardised to give the following details.

1. The wants account is subdivided in six groups of products: foodstuffs, housing, clothing and footwear, medical care and hygiene, recreation and culture and transport, and other goods and services with few exceptions regarding Italy.
2. The factors account distinguishes between labour and capital.
3. The households are classified by income deciles, with the exception of Spain for which directly available data are more aggregate.
4. The classification of activities covers five sectors: agriculture, industry, trade, transport and services.

All SAMs were calculated and stored in spreadsheet format, which has the advantage that row and column totals can be checked simultaneously while changing any cell in the matrix. Additional matrix operations can also be easily performed in a spreadsheet.

3. Reconstructing Statistics and SAM Tabulations for Eastern European Countries

There are several problems connected with the construction of standard SAMs for Eastern Europe comparable to those of Western Europe. The System of National Accounts (SNA), held in Western Europe, and the Material Product System (MPS), held in Eastern Europe, differ (a) in the ways detailed items are defined or assigned and (b) how balances are consolidated. With regard to (a), appendix 2 at the end of this book contains a discussion of the treatment of several detailed items in both systems. Adjustment for all these detailed items is not feasible. On the other hand, the differences lose their relevance and significance in the context of the broad classification of the SAM followed. With respect to (b), the consolidation of balances, appropriate supplementation of the data and conversions have been applied to conform to SNA.

The conventional SAM accounting scheme is sufficiently flexible to accommodate for the P-system as it does for the M-system. The main difference between the two systems lies in the principle that, in the extreme, the P-system property belongs to the state with minor private ownership, while in the M-system property is both publicly and privately owned. As far as statistics are concerned, there are differences in degree and not in substance. In practice, in the P-system there can be a significant share of the so-called 'other income', which originates mainly from the operation of private farms, small unincorporated enterprises, handicrafts and household production, while in the M-system state ownership is no less significant. In the factor account, all incomes are distributed over labour and capital, the bulk of which in the M-system is transferred to households and small parts are retained by firms and government and in the P-system it is largely retained by the firms and government.

In principle, with a view to the transition, a distinction by type of firms, whether public or private, can be useful. Such a distinction is also feasible. For example, for Poland it was possible to distinguish between socialised firms, private firms, private farms, banking and insurance companies. It is to be noted that the size of the private sector outside agriculture and the number of so-called commercial banks in Poland and Hungary was in both 1981 and 1990 not yet important, but started to grow faster from 1990 onwards. For the moment, only one account for all firms combined is used, with a possibility of elaboration in the future.

The *government* sector in P- and M-systems has similar tasks, but with different emphasis. The different degrees of emphasis on government versus social security expenditures in the two systems makes it desirable to classify the government sector into government and social security, separately. Besides, the social security funds in the P-system are often covered on budget rather than on insurance basis. For the aggregated comparison in this chapter we do not separate social security from government, as yet.

The main transactions relating to the *capital accumulation* account are savings (in cash or in the bank) and credits. Although both activities are performed in P- and M-systems, there are large differences between the two economic systems in the field of finance. Covering these differences would require a further disaggregation of the capital accumulation account in the form of flow of funds tables. This was not done in the present research, due to the scarcity of consistent data on financial flows.

Considering the *activities* account, the main feature of the MPS, and perhaps the most wellknown, is the consideration of material productions as being the sole production activities. Marxist economists, in conformity with the classical economists, regard services as non-productive activities. As a result, in official statistics, the non-material services were excluded from the national accounts and input-output tables. Both intermediate deliveries between material and non-material sectors of activity and the consumption of non-material services were often recorded as direct transfers between firms or between firms and government. As GDP and input-output tables are now available according to SNA principle: (at least partly), the content of the activities account does not differ much any more between Eastern and Western European countries. For the level of aggregation used in the SAM, it was possible to use an almost identical classification for the six countries.

Transactions with the *Rest of the World* take the form of income and capital transfers, and value of imports and exports of goods and services. There are no differences between the two types of economies in the above respect, except that statistical sources may be incomplete for Poland and Hungary in the case of transfers, causing some bias.

4. Structural Differences in the Six SAMs

A comparison of structural parameters of the SAMs for countries belonging to different economic systems can be useful in reviewing basic structural differences behind the systems. The purpose of this section is to use the SAMs for gaining insight into the structural differences between market- and planning-oriented economic systems, while reserving the more analytical tasks to subsequent chapters. One way of presenting the underlying structure of the SAM is to express each entry as a percentage of the grand total of matrix. Examples are presented in tables 1.4 and 1.5 for Germany and Poland, taking as 100% the matrix total found at the bottom of last column and last row. The appendix contains tables for the other countries. Expressing the entries in terms of the grand total of the matrix has the advantage of providing a comparable basis for evaluating the relative importance of individual flows in the various countries. Alternative presentations are when the total of individual columns or individual rows are taken as 100%.

Already on the basis of the aggregated SAM and such calculated percentages as mentioned above, one can observe important structural differences between the two economic systems as represented by the six selected countries. Table 1.6 presents some key percentages derived from the SAMs in the appendix. Rows 1 to 4 give gross output, intermediate deliveries, labour income and capital income as percentages of the matrix total. The share of the gross output is about the same in all six countries with Poland on the higher side and the Netherlands on the lower. Poland is probably higher due to an inflated share of intermediate deliveries typical of most P-systems. The reasons are mainly system-specific. As regards the Netherlands, the low figure is likely due to the large welfare transfers that occur via the government and social security system. The grand total is pushed up, leading to a reduced share of most items in the SAM, and hence the gross output, too.

The third and fourth rows give distribution of value added in labour and capital incomes. As can be seen, there is no clear distinctive pattern in distribution of labour and capital incomes between P- and M-systems.

Table 1.4. SAM Structure for Germany 1984

		1	2	3	4	5	6	7	8	9	Total
1	Wants				11.1						11.1
2	Labour								10.5		10.6
3	Capital								4.4	0.1	4.5
4	Households		10.6	3.8			3.3			-0.1	17.5
5	Firms			0.9						-0.0	0.9
6	Government	1.0		-0.2	5.4	0.4		0.2	0.9	-0.2	7.5
7	Capital				1.0	0.5	0.3		2.5	-0.2	4.0
8	Activities	9.1					3.9	3.4	16.7	5.3	38.4
9	Rest World	1.0						0.3	3.5	0.7	5.5
	Total	11.1	10.6	4.5	17.5	0.9	7.5	4.0	38.4	5.5	100.0

Table 1.5. SAM Structure for Poland 1987

		1	2	3	4	5	6	7	8	9	Total
1	Wants				9.4						9.4
2	Labour								9.0		9.0
3	Capital								8.0		8.0
4	Households		7.2	0.9			1.7			0.4	10.2
5	Firms			6.0			0.3				6.4
6	Government		1.7	1.0	0.2	2.8			0.1	0.1	5.9
7	Capital				0.7	3.6	-0.2		1.2	-0.0	5.3
8	Activities	9.0					3.2	4.8	20.8	3.8	41.4
9	Rest World	0.4					0.9	0.5	2.5	0.1	4.4
	Total	9.4	9.0	8.0	10.2	6.4	5.9	5.3	41.5	4.4	100.0

However, there are differences in the distribution of operating profits of corporate and state enterprises, the share of premiums for social security in the compensation of employees, and the relative importance and ways of registration of incomes from small unincorporated enterprises. We will elaborate on this later in the section.

The share of household transactions in the matrix total is smaller in the P-system, 13%, than in the M-system, 17%. The share of government transactions is about the same in both systems, around 7%. The share of firms' transactions appears to be higher in the P-system, with Poland on top with a figure that is more than twice as much as the other countries. As the firms account still consists mainly of state enterprises, the high share for Poland should be evaluated in the light of the relatively low share of the movement. Then, together, firms and government make up for a larger share in the economy in the P-system than in the M-system.

The Rest of World Account has a lower share in the P-system, 5.0%, as compared to the M-system, 5.8%, which is equivalent to a difference of 16%. But there are wide differences among countries of the M-system. A small open economy as the Netherlands has a ratio about twice that of Italy, Germany or Spain.

Table 1.6. Key Variables Expressed as Percentages of Matrix Total

	Poland	Hungary	Average	Spain	Italy	Netherlands	Germany	Average
Gross output	37.8	32.6	35.2	33.6	33.7	25.2	31.6	31.0
Intermediate delivery	20.8	17.9	19.4	17.5	15.8	9.9	16.7	15.0
Labour income	9.0	11.5	10.3	7.6	11.0	10.3	10.6	9.9
Capital income	8.0	3.2	5.6	8.5	4.9	5.0	4.5	5.7
Households	10.2	12.9	11.6	15.8	18.0	17.1	17.5	17.1
Government	5.9	8.3	7.1	5.3	6.7	8.1	7.5	6.9
Firms	6.4	2.4	4.4	2.9	2.8	1.4	0.9	2.0
Rest of World	4.4	5.5	5.0	3.8	4.4	9.5	5.5	5.8
Consumption	13.4	12.6	13.0	15.1	14.8	13.9	14.0	14.5
Investment	5.3	4.7	5.0	4.4	3.3	3.7	4.0	3.9

Source: Appendix

Finally, as can be expected, the policy orientations of the P-system lead to a lower consumption share and a higher investment share as compared to the M-system.

The percentage distribution of final demand, value added and primary income is presented in table 1.7. To be noted is the lower share of primary inputs, that is the GDP, in total output in the P-system, 44%, as compared to an average of 49% for the M-system, which confirms the general observation that more resources are used to create a certain level of GDP in the P- than in the M-system. Also notable are the already observed lower share of consumption and the higher share of capital formation in the final demand distribution in countries with the P-system as compared to countries with the M-system.

Table 1.7. Main Variables as Percentage of GDP

	Poland	Hungary	Spain	Italy	Netherlands	Germany
Total output	*100*	*100*	*100*	*100*	*100*	*100*
-Intermediate inputs	56	56	53	53	46	53
-Primary inputs (GDP)	44	44	47	47	54	47
Value added	*100*	*100*	*100*	*100*	*100*	*100*
-Labour income	49	65	40	62	58	58
-Capital income	50	26	45	30	39	37
-Government	1	9	15	8	3	5
Final demand	*100*	*100*	*100*	*100*	*100*	*100*
-Consumption	74	71	81	83	78	77
-Capital formation	29	25	24	19	19	21
-Net exports	-3	4	-5	2	3	2

Source: Appendix

In the remaining part of this section, we will elaborate on other typical differences between M- and P-systems that can be illustrated by means of the structures of the aggregated SAMs. Respectively, we will deal with the share of capital and labour income received by households, the transfers from the government to the households, and the sources of financing the government budget.

With the ownership of firms entrusted collectively to the state, households in the P system get very little capital income in the form of profits and/or dividends. Table 1.8 shows that capital income forms only 0.5% of the matrix total in the P-system as compared to 4.1% in the M-system. The share of labour income is also lower in the P-system than in the M-system. As a result, households in the P-system obtain only 8.5% of the matrix total to spend, as compared to 13.45 in the M-system. Table 1.8 shows Hungary to be closer than Poland to the M-system.

Table 1.8. **Share of capital and labour income to households as a percentage of matrix total**

	Poland	Hungary	Spain	Italy	Netherlands	Germany
-capital income	0.9	0.2	5.4	3.0	4.0	3.8
-labour income	7.3	8.6	7.6	11.0	8.0	10.6
-total	8.2	8.8	13.0	14.0	12.0	14.4

Source: Appendix

There are typical differences in the field of financing the government expenditures between the two groups of countries, as is shown in table 1.9. The share of the government is high in more advanced countries with an M-system such as Germany or the Netherlands. Especially the size of the social security system is often larger than in a P-system. Correspondingly, the household contributions to the government budget in the form of social security premiums and direct taxes are more important in the M- than in the P-systems. The only exception to the above is the case of Spain when compared with Hungary, which may be attributed to the lower level of economic development of Spain in 1980 than at present.

In table 1.9 it is shown that the value added tax, VAT, in Hungary is already an important source of revenue, and its share is equivalent to that in the Western European countries. However, in most countries with a P-system, as is shown for Poland, no VAT system and no personal income tax system has yet been introduced. As a result, and visible in the table, operating profit and turnover tax of firms are taxed heavily in a P-system.

The same table shows low shares of transfers from the government to households in Poland among the P-countries and Spain among the M-countries, indicating that these two countries have the least developed social security systems.

Table 1.9. Share of Government Income, Total and by Origin; and Social Security Transfers to Households (each expressed as Percentage of Matrix Total)

	Poland	Hungary	Average	Spain	Italy	Netherlands	Germany	Average
Government income	5.9	8.3	7.1	5.3	6.7	8.1	7.5	6.9
Originating from								
-factors	2.7	2.6	2.7	0.1	0,1	2.0	-0.2	0.6
-households	0.2	2.0	1.1	1.7	4.7	3.7	5.4	3.9
-firms	2.8	1.6	2.2	0.6	0.5	0.7	0.4	0.6
-indirect tax*	0.1	1.6	0.8	2.7	1.4	0.8	1.1	1.5
-vat	0.0	1.3	0.7	0.2	0.0	1.0	1.0	0.6
Government & social security transfers to households								
All households	1.7	3.2	2.5	2.6	4.0	5.3	3.3	3.8

Source: Calculated from the SAMs in appendix. * Net of price lowering subsidies

In the appendix the disaggregated SAMs for all six countries are presented. With these SAMs, it is possible to compare the structure of the disaggregated SAMs for the row and column totals of wants, households and activities. This allows us to compare the incomes and expenditures per income decile group, the consumption expenditures by products (wants), and the relative importance of the different sectors of activities in the selected economies. Tables 1.10 and 1.11 present the percentage distribution.

Examining expenditure by wants in table 1.10, it is observed the share of expenditures for food in the P-system of Poland and Hungary is remarkably high (50.4% and 37.1%). The M-system spends no more than 25% on food. As a result, most other product groups show higher shares for the M-system.

The different expenditure patterns in M- and P-systems are more explainable in terms of differences in levels of economic wellbeing and economic development than the differing economic systems.

Considering the income distribution among household groups, table 1.10 shows the income distributions in the P- and M-system re remarkably similar, with a slightly more equal distribution for Poland and Hungary.

The highest 40% has on average about 24% of income in the P-system as opposed to 20% in the M-system. The highest 20% receives around 35% in the P-systems and slightly below 40% in the M-systems.

Table 1.10. Distribution of Expenditure by Want Category and Income by Decile Group (percentage share)

	Poland 1987	Hungary 1990	Spain 1980	Italy 1984	Netherlands 1987	Germany 1984
Expenditures by wants						
Food	50.4	37.1	23.5	n.a.	16.7	23.8
Housing	18.9	15.7	13.7	n.a.	25.4	30.9
Textiles	11.7	6.1	6.7	n.a.	7.1	8.9
Hygiene/Med.care	2.6	2.1	17.7	n.a.	14.1	4.9
Culture/Transpport	10.1	15.2	8.8	n.a.	29.3	25.1
Other goods	6.3	23.8	29.8	n.a.	7.4	6.4
Income by decile group						
1st group	3.8	4.7	n.a.	3.5	3.0	2.3
2nd group	5.3	6.2	n.a.	5.1	4.5	3.6
3rd group	6.4	7.0	n.a.	6.4	5.7	5.3
4th group	7.4	7.7	n.a.	7.1	6.9	6.7
5th group	8.6	8.5	n.a.	8.1	8.2	8.4
6th group	9.6	9.3	n.a.	8.9	9.7	10.2
7th group	10.9	10.4	n.a.	10.1	10.8	11.9
8th group	12.4	11.7	n.a.	11.9	12.7	13.7
9th group	14.7	13.7	n.a.	14.5	15.2	17.5
10th group	20.9	20.8	n.a.	24.4	23.3	20.4

Next is table 1.11. The distribution of output by activity shows the generally observed feature of an underdeveloped status of the service sector (including trade) in Poland and Hungary, which cannot be attributed only to differences in the level of economic development. System-specific factors that manifest themselves in central planning, a limited role for financial markets, and a dogmatic attitude towards services as a non-productive activity, have played an important role in attaching low priority to the development of services. The higher shares of the agriculture sector in Poland and Hungary are more related to the level of economic development.

By definition, sectoral shares in the value added are higher than sectoral shares in the total output, shown also in table 1.11. More insight is gained when the sectoral shares in total output are divided by sectoral shares in value added. This gives the sectoral ratios in the bottom part of table 1.11. The lower the sectoral ratio the more efficient is that sector in running its operations. The results in table 1.11 are mixed. Countries with the M-system show lower ratios for industry. But the P-system shows lower ratios for transport.

Table 1.11. Sectoral Shares in the Total Output and Total Value Added (in percentages)

	Poland 1987	Hungary 1990	Spain 1980	Italy 1984	Netherlands 1987	Germany 1984
Output share						
Agriculture	10.2	15.8	7.4	5.3	4.6	2.2
Industry	66.0	52.2	54.4	55.1	47.5	51.8
Trade	7.5	9.1	13.4	8.5	13.7	8.0
Transport	6.1	5.8	4.8	4.1	5.9	4.5
Services	10.3	17.1	20.0	27.1	28.3	33.5
Value Added share						
Agriculture	10.6	14.6	8.4	5.6	4.2	1.8
Industry	57.9	42.1	37.2	32.8	32.2	41.4
Trade	10.5	12.9	19.6	12.2	16.1	12.8
Transport	6.9	8.1	6.8	6.5	7.2	5.9
Services	14.0	22.3	28.0	43.0	40.4	38.0
Output/value added						
Agriculture	104	92	114	106	91	81
Industry	88	81	68	60	68	80
Trade	141	142	146	143	118	160
Transport	114	140	141	160	122	131
Services	136	130	140	159	143	114

5. Concluding Remarks

In this chapter, the methodological and technical issues of constructing SAMs for Western and Eastern Europe were discussed. Social Accounting Matrices can be a useful instrument for international comparisons especially when they are standardised, represented as relative structural patterns, and the countries compared are classified in meaningful groups based on levels of economic development and types of economic systems; as was done in this chapter. Of course, the problems that apply to all international comparisons, especially those between different economic systems, are also pertinent for SAMs. In subsequent chapters we turn to more analytical uses of social accounting matrices and related models.

Chapter 2

SAM Multipliers for West and East European Countries: an Evaluation of Transitional Patterns

1. Introduction

The economies of Eastern Europe (EE), under communist rule for more than four decades, have developed specific traits which are in variance with structural patterns of economic development. Communist priorities are known to have favoured investment in heavy industries over final consumption, the so-called productive sectors over services, large scale firms over small ones, state owned over private firms, etc. Besides, the height and distribution of remuneration as well as the size and pattern of consumption were superficially maintained at levels imposed by state authorities without due consideration of agent responses. Now that these economies are turning back to *normal* market conditions, there is a need for more insight into the gap between the imposed and normal structural patterns.

Studies of structural patterns have been the subject of intensive empirical analysis by Clark in the 1940s, Kuznets in the 1950s and 1960s, and Chenery and associates in the 1970s and 1980s, cf. Chenery, Robinson and Syrquin(1986). They attempted to specify normal structural patterns of the economy for varying levels of economic development, country size and other specific characteristics. These approaches have been criticised for their dominant assumptions of universal tendencies and for lacking an analytical framework that reflects on mechanisms behind observed differences in structural patterns among countries observed. The issue of structural patterns can be approached differently through modelling economies along the structure of the social accounting matrix, SAM. Using a comparative analytical framework, the SAM can be helpful in deriving normalised patterns and indicating prospective patterns for economies in transition. The SAM multiplier analysis can give insight as to which economic mechanisms need to be strengthened to push a specific economy closer to its prospective patterns, see among others Cohen (1989) and Pyatt (1991).

The purpose of this chapter is to compare and assess the future courses of economies in Eastern Europe, i.e. Poland and Hungary, in relation to representative economies in Western Europe (WE), on the basis of standardised SAMs for a particular year. SAMs for Poland and Hungary, next to those of Germany, Italy, Netherlands, and Spain have been reported upon in chapter 1. We shall first review, in section 2, the comparative form of the SAMs for these six countries. We will then employ, in section 3, the SAM as a model of the economy. Sections 4 and 5 discuss the size and distribution of different multipliers. The chapter ends in section 6 with summary and conclusions.

2. The Construction of Comparative SAMs

The SAM is the transformation of the circular flow of products and factors between production and household activities into a matrix of transactions between the various actors and/or accounts. A particular row gives receipts of the account while columnwise we read the expenditure of the actor.

The previous chapter reported on the construction of SAMs for six countries, following rules that apply for the United Nations System of National Accounts. The six SAMs were adjusted and standardised to give the following common classification of accounts.

1. Wants are classified into six groups of products: food, housing, clothing and footwear, medical care and hygiene, recreation and culture, transport and other goods and services.
2. Factors are classified into labour and capital.
3. Institutions are classified into household groups, firms and government. Each of these has a current account. All households, firms and government have a combined capital account.
4. Activity accounts are subdivided in five sectors: agriculture, industry, trade, transport and services. Next to these there is a-rest-of-the-world account.

3. The Comparative Analysis of Multiplier Properties

The use of SAM as a model that generates multipliers can be demonstrated from a very simple example. Take the simplest Keynesian model, which contains an equation relating consumption to income via a propensity to consume, and an equation defining income as consumption plus an exogenous investment. This is thus a model of two equations in two endogenous variables of consumption and income. The model can be written as a square matrix which is then inverted to give a Keynesian multiplier showing the impact of a change in investment on income. Similarly, in an input-output analysis, an endogenous vector of sectoral production, q, can be predicted from a matrix of input-output coefficients, L, and a vector of exogenous final demand, f. That is,

$$q = L q + f = (I - L)^{-1} f = M_l f$$

where M_l is the Leontief multiplier matrix.

Now, the interesting case arises when the SAM is also a square matrix, and, as such, represents a model of the economy. By appropriate manipulations of this square matrix, it is also possible to derive SAM-multipliers that are more comprehensive than those of Keynes and Leontief together. The SAM-multipliers are more comprehensive because the underlying matrix contains the whole circular flow of the economy.

To transform the social accounting matrix into an economy-wide model requires performing several steps. Assuming proportional relationships for the cells in terms of their column totals, a SAM coefficient matrix that relayes variables to each other is obtained. The variables and coefficients can be rearranged to give a model of the economy consisting of six equations. In these equations the endogenous variables and related coefficients are placed on the left-hand side, and the exogenous variables and related coefficients are placed on the right hand side.

The endogenous variables in this model include production, income, consumption, investment, among others. We take for the exogenous variables the layouts of government and rest of world.

A SAM-based model can take the form of eqs. (1) to (6), below, whereby the following notations hold:

V_v = value of production of sector v,
W_w = factor incomes of factor type w which can be wages, profits, etc.,
Z_z = receipts of household group z,

$F =$ receipts of firms,
$K =$ capital formation,
$Y =$ national income,
$X =$ purchases of government and/or exports, both of which are assumed exogenous, and
$T =$ transfers from government and/or rest of the world, both assumed exogenous.

$$V_v - \sum_{v'} a_{v'v} V_{v'} \quad - \quad \sum_z c_{vz} Z_z \quad + \quad e_v K \quad = \quad i_v X \quad (1)$$

$$Y \quad - \quad \sum_w W_w \quad = \quad 0 \quad (2)$$

$$-\sum_v a_{wv} V_v \quad + \quad W_w \quad = \quad 0 \quad (3)$$

$$- \sum_w b_{zw} W_w \quad - \quad \sum_{z'} c_{zz'} Z_{z'} + Z_z \quad = \quad i_z T \quad (4)$$

$$- \sum_w b_{fw} W_w \quad + \quad F \quad = \quad i_f T \quad (5)$$

$$-\sum_v a_{kv} V_v \quad - \quad \sum_z c_{kz} Z_z \quad - \quad d_k F \quad + \quad K \quad = \quad i_k T \quad (6)$$

Eq. (1) gives the sectoral balance by sector v, consisting of intermediate delivery $\sum_{v'} a_{vv'} V_{v'}$, consumption expenditure $\sum_z c_{vz} Z_z$, capital formation $e_v K$, and a variable for the sectoral receipts from both government expenditure and exports, $i_v X$. The coefficient i_v gives the share received by sector i.

Eq. (2) defines national income, consisting of factor incomes.

Eq. (3) determines factor incomes by factor w as originating from value added coefficients and production by sector $\sum_v a_{wv} V_v$.

Eq.(4) determines household receipts by household group z, consisting of portions of factor income $\sum_w b_{zw} W_w$, inter-household transfers $\sum_{z'} c_{zz'} Z_{z'} + Z_z$, and transfers from government and rest of the world $i_z T$. The coefficient i_z gives the share received by household group z.

Eq. (5) determines firm receipts, including portions of factor income and transfers from government and the rest-of-the-world.

Eq. (6) shows the different sources of capital formation to consist of depreviation summed over sectors, savings summed over households, reinvested savings of firms and capital transfer from government and the rest of the world.

The coefficients a,b,c are proportions of the total receipts (outlays) for the columns corresponding to V, W, Z respectively, where $\Sigma a = 1.0$, $\Sigma b = 1.0$, $\Sigma c = 1.0$.

In this model we have as endogenous variables the column totals of output by activity, product by activity, and disposition by factors, households, capital and firms, and they appear on the left hand side. The endogenous variables can be generally denoted by y. Government and rest of the world are exogenous variables, they appear on the right hand side.

The exogenous variables can be generally denoted by x. As was stated before, the model assumes proportional relationships between individual cells and column totals that are brought together in the SAM coefficient matrix. This matrix can be generally denoted by A.. The system can thus be described generally by $y - Ay = x$. Solving gives:

$$y = (I - A)^{-1} x = M_a x \qquad (7)$$

where M_a stands for the SAM matrix of system multipliers.

On the design and interpretation of multipliers, two points should be made. First, government and rest-of-the-world injections work differently in their multiplier effects, depending on whether they are expenditure allocations or transfer payments. To appreciate these differences, injections in x will be interpreted to mean either an exogenous expenditure of dollar units to the receipts of sector v, or an exogenous transfer of dollar units to the receipts of household z. As a result, x should be read as either a sectoral expenditure x_v or a household transfer x_z. Second, the impact of the exogenous impulses will be traced on such endogenous variables as the output by sector V_v and the income by household group Z_z. Note that V_v and Z_z are variables belonging to the endogenous vector y in eq. (7).

	Injections in sector v'	Transfers to households z'
output multipliers by sector v	$M_{a,vv'}$	$M_{a,vz''}$
income multipliers by household z	$M_{a,zv'}$	$M_{a,zz'}$

Summarising, analysis can be restricted to four types of multipliers. These are the output and income multipliers by two types of injection:

expenditure and transfers, as is shown above. By output multipliers we mean $M_{a,vv'}$ and $M_{a,vz'}$. By income multipliers we mean $M_{a,zv'}$ and $M_{a,zz'}$.

There are several uses of these multipliers. For years directly before and after the year of computation, the SAM multipliers can be employed to show economic effects of exogenous additional demand for sectoral activities emanating from either government allocations or foreign trade. Two economic effects are prominent: first, the growth of output and its distribution on sectors, denoted by v, and, second, the generation and distribution of income by household groups, denoted by z. These two effects will be called, respectively, the output and income effects.

In a similar way, one can assess the effect of institutional transfers (by government) on the generation and distribution of both output and income.

For assessment purposes, the income multiplier is a more relevant concept than the output multiplier. There are two reasons for this. Earned income is closer to the *efficiency notion* of value added than is gross output. Besides, earned income by household groups is a better indicator of *social welfare* than is gross output. Although this is generally true, there may be minor exceptions.

To balance our exposition, we conclude this section by making explicit four general limitations of the SAM-multiplier approach as well as our counterpart arguments in defence of the approach for current purposes.

(1) Cell entries of the SAM are amounts, i.e. products of prices × quantities. However, quantities and prices are not explicitly disentangled. In the fixed price multiplier model, supplied amounts are supposed to adjust to demanded amounts. They will, but if there is restricted capacity the result is inflation. This may require a revision downward in the real sizes of multipliers. Of course, if the size of the injection is relatively small, which is usually the case, the fixed price multiplier results can still be seen to represent realizable quantity effects. It is also feasible to check in a single way within the SAM framework whether the capacity limits will be violated or not. The supply side can simply be modelled as a relationship between the investment rate and economic growth via an incremental capital output ratio κ, as in $K/Y = \kappa(\Delta Y/Y)$. From the SAM, we obtain multiplier effects for K and Y. If division of the multiplier effects of K by those of Y gives values equal to or above K/Y for the base period, this implies that the SAM solves for sufficient investment to meet the projected capacity increase. It is noted that multiplier results show that this condition is fulfilled for the six countries studied.

(2) Many linear relationships are assumed: constant shares of factor remunerations in total output, of household incomes in the various factor

payments, of commodities in household expenditure, and of sectors in commodity production. While average consumption propensities can be easily replaced by marginal ones, doing the same for other coefficient sets does not produce stable or meaningful statistical values. Taking one portion of the coefficients as marginal and the rest as average introduces estimation bias. Following the uniform proportional assumption in cross-country comparisons is an advantage in contrast with incomparable specifications for individual countries. Of course, individualised specifications are suitable for other purposes.

(3) The size of the multiplier depends to some degree on the level of aggregation. This argument is not relevant in the context of a uniform aggregation for the compared countries. Moreover, the differences in multipliers due to alternative aggregations tested do not go beyond the 8% for the individual countries studied here.

(4) Last, and not least, evaluation of the multipliers of the SAM-model cannot be done in isolation from the closure rules applied. The size of the multipliers depends on the choice of the exogenous and endogenous variables, which, in turn, depends on the problem studied. In the context of the comparative analysis of economic systems, there is an established rationale for considering government policy and rest of world conditions as exogenous and taking the functioning of the rest of the economic system as endogenous. This is also what is postulated in the SAM model.

4. Size and Distribution of Multipliers of Sectoral Injections

This section will examine selected results from cross-country comparisons of SAM models applied to the six countries under study here. Results on SAM multipliers of injections in activities can be examined in table 2.1.

In general, the size of the multipliers of an inverted matrix is relatively high if the leakage is relatively low. The leakage may take two forms: external outflow of effects and internal outflow of effects.

The first form of leakage is that of an outflow of effects beyond the system, as when the endogenously inverted share of the SAM is low because of a high exogenous share. For instance, this outside leakage is higher for Hungary (endogenous share is 87.3%, exogenous is 13.8%), than for Poland (endogenous share is 89.2%, exogenous is 10.2%). As a result, the SAM multipliers are lower in Hungary than Poland, 3.01 vs. 4.65 for output multipliers and 0.77 vs. 0.92 for income multipliers, respectively. Similarly, the Netherlands has higher exogenous shares than

Table 2.1: Income and Output Multipliers Resulting from Injections in Alternative Activities; Exogenous Shares and other Indicators

	Poland 1987	Hungary 1990	Spain 1980	Italy 1984	Netherlands 1987	Germany 1984	Average Western Europe
1.Income multipliers of injections in:							
Agriculture	1.06	0.81	1.44	1.34	0.85	1.24	1.22
Industry	0.82	0.64	1.28	1.12	0.67	1.16	1.06
Trade	0.76	0.78	1.62	1.57	0.88	1.48	1.39
Transport	0.93	0.77	1.70	1.86	0.89	1.38	1.46
Services	1.06	0.86	1.61	1.63	0.97	1.35	1.39
2.Average income multiplier	0.92	0.77	1.53	1.50	0.85	1.32	1.30
3. High/Low	1.39	1.34	1.33	1.66	1.45	1.28	1.43
4.Output multipliers of injections in:							
Agriculture	5.16	3.27	4.54	3.64	2.54	3.63	3.59
Industry	4.58	2.95	4.41	3.55	2.24	3.36	3.39
Trade	3.98	2.93	4.74	3.82	2.22	3.37	3.54
Transport	4.72	2.89	4.91	4.57	2.23	3.39	3.78
Services	4.81	3.03	4.54	3.89	2.22	3.50	3.54
5. Average output multiplier	4.65	3.01	4.63	3.89	2.29	3.45	3.57
6. High/Low	1.30	1.13	1.11	1.29	1.14	1.08	1.16
7. Income/output multiplier a	0.20	0.26	0.33	0.39	0.37	0.38	0.37
8 Other indicators b							
Population	37.7	10.6	37.4	57	14.7	61.2	
Income per capita($)	1930	2590	5400	6420	11860	11130	

a Row 2/Row 5. b Refers to SAM year and taken from World Bank Development Reports

do Germany, Italy or Spain, resulting in lower multipliers for the first than for the latter. Taken as a whole, the EE and WE countries show equal endogenously inverted share of the SAM, so that the external leakage should be on average about the same.

The exogenous share in the SAM consisting of government and rest of the world will generally depend on the population size of the country, its location, politico-economic system, and the level of its economic development. Small population countries like the Netherlands or Hungary tend to have higher shares of transactions with rest of the world, other things remaining the same; this may in turn lead to a greater role of the government in maintaining specific infrastructures for the preservation of foreign trade. The politico-economic regime in planning oriented economies, in short, P-systems implies a dominant share of the state in the economy. But the share of the public sector in market-oriented economies, i.e., M-systems, can be as high or higher due to large income redistributions that take place through social security. Furthermore, the politico-economic system has an important influence on the openness of the economy and the share of exports in the economy; this share is lower in EE than in WE. Finally, the level of economic development contributes positively to the openness of the economy to foreign trade. Economic theory predicts at higher levels of economic development higher shares of government and exports. There is, therefore, a general tendency for the exogenous share to be lower, and for the output multiplier to be higher, in a country with a lower economic development level.

The exogenous shares in Hungary and Poland are 10.2% and 13.8%, respectively. These fall in the range of the average exogenous share for WE, which amounts to 12.7 percent. So, on average the external leakage is about the same, though it differs appreciably by individual country. This and the previous paragraph suggest that the exogenous in the EE context is influenced more by system-specific factors that enhance the exogenous share than by a lower level of economic development that downplays the exogenous share.

The second form of leakage, the internal leakage, will also be seen to be very much influenced by system-specific factors. Taking the SAM multiplier performance of the WE countries as the norm the following can be stated.

The average income multiplier for the M-countries was found to be 1.30 that was achieved with an average endogenous share of 87.3. This implies a multiplier of 0.015 for each endogenous percentage point. Applying this norm to Hungary, which has a 86.2% endogenous share, would result in an income multiplier of 1.28 as compared to the observed income multiplier of 0.77. This is a significant gap. A similar calculation for Poland would give a normalised income multiplier of 1.33 as compared to the observed income multiplier of 0.92. The lower performance of EE countries reflects a lower effectiveness of the (internal) circular flow and should be fully accounted for by the specific politico economic regime.

The lower effectiveness occurs in contexts of low forward and backward linkages between economic activities and restricted rolling of the circular flow over more agents that are more typical of P-systems as compared to M-systems. The endogenous inverted share of the SAM in a typical P-system will be less extensively and intensively filled than in a M-system. Due to the lack of a capitalistic drive and the absence of market competition the introduction of new innovative activities with higher multipliers is limited in P-systems, so that the circular flow in a P-system does not undergo major structural changes. Such an economy tends to show stationary tendencies as can be manifested in multiplier effects that vary within a narrow range. In contrast, an M-system which experiences frequent exits and entries of new activities would show more variation in multiplier effects, whereby the new activities with higher multipliers would pull old activities with lower multipliers, and contribute to a higher overall multiplier effects. These tendencies can be gathered from table 2.1. The highest/lowest ratio for income multipliers is lower in both Poland and Hungary (1.39 and 1.34, respectively) when compared with the average of 1.43 for the M-systems studied here. The range for the output multipliers shows Poland to be high (1.30), Hungary low (1.13) and the average for WE countries in between (1.16).

There are other mechanisms in P-systems that result in relatively lower multiplier performances when compared to M-systems. Consider the size of the multipliers from injections in alternative sectors. The results for the M-countries show services, transport and trade to have the highest income multipliers, and, often, the highest output multipliers. For the P-systems, agriculture is still more prominent. To guarantee a shift of emphasis in Poland and Hungary towards the tertiary sectors and away from the primary sectors will thus require introduction of differently oriented investments in infrastructure and technology.

Furthermore, the ratio of income to output multipliers is 0.20 and 0.26 in Poland and Hungary, respectively. These are far below the average of 0.37 in the M-countries. The contention of a very low efficiency in factor use in P- as compared to M-countries is thus supported.

Besides comparing the levels of multipliers, it is also important to study the distribution of the multiplier effects across the respective sectors and households and to discover the underlying structural bias. In order to do so, a Relative Distributive Measure of sector-sector effects, $RDM_{vv'}$ is defined in eq. (8):

$$RDM_{vv'} = \frac{M_{a,vv'} - d_{vv'}}{\sum_v M_{a,vv'} - 1} \bigg/ \frac{Output_{v,o}}{\sum_v Output_{v,o}} \qquad (8)$$

where v denotes activities, i.e. sectors, and $d_{vv'}$ is the Kronecker-symbol that equals 1 if $v=v'$ and 0 in other cases, and which is subtracted to obtain the share of v in the multiplier effects of v' on all sectors after deducting the initial injection. The result is divided by the actual output share of sector v in all sectors in year o, i.e. the year to which the SAM refers. For values of $RDM_{vv'} > 1, < 1$, and $= 1$, there are positive, negative and neutral redistributive effects, respectively. For instance, values of $RDM_{vv'} = 1$ mean that sectoral injections would reproduce exactly the sectoral distribution pattern of the base year.

Similarly, a relative distributive measure, $RDM_{zv'}$ for the multiplier effects of sectoral injections on institutional income, $M_{a,zv'}$, can be calculated as in eq. (9), where z stands for the institutions, i.e. household groups.

$$RDM_{zv}' = \frac{M_{a,zv}'}{\sum_z M_{a,zv}'} / \frac{Income_{z,o}}{\sum_z Income_{z,o}} \qquad (9)$$

Values of $RDM_{zv'} = 1$ mean that sectoral injections would reproduce exactly the share that hoeshold group z had in the base year in total income. A higher value would mean an increase in its income share, while a negative value would mean deterioration.

RDMs have been calculated for the six countries under study in table 2.2. Given are the relative distributions of the output multipliers across sectors as well as those for the income multipliers on household groups. A few comments are now given regarding the results.

Taking first the distributionary pattern of the output multipliers, most RDMs show little difference between the P- and M-countries. Thus, note a large positive bias towards agriculture, trade and transport, a small positive bias towards industry and a strong negative bias towards services, especially in Poland. A display of more or less the same bias for M- and P-countries would be acceptable for Poland and Hungary if the economic structures of both countries were indeed consistent with prospective patterns that go with higher levels of economic development.

Table 2.2. RDMs for Households Resulting from an Overall Injection in Activities

	Poland 1987	Hungary 1990	Spain 1980	Italy 1984	Netherlands 1987	Germany 1984
1. % distribution of multipliers						
1st decile	3.5	3.4	*	1.6	0.6	0.9
2nd decile	4.9	5.0		3.9	1.7	2.0
3rd decile	5.8	6.0		5.3	3.3	3.7
4th decile	6.8	6.8		6.4	5.6	5.2
5th decile	8.0	7.7		7.7	7.7	7.1
6th decile	9.4	9.0		8.7	10.1	9.2
7th decile	10.6	10.4		10.2	11.2	11.3
8th decile	12.5	12.3		12.7	14.3	14.0
9th decile	15.7	14.8		16.0	17.0	20.3
10th decile	22.8	24.5		27.7	28.5	26.1
2. Actual % shares	3.8	4.7	*	3.5	3.0	2.4
1st decile	5.3	6.2		5.1	4.5	3.7
2nd decile	6.4	7.0		6.4	5.7	5.3
3rd decile	7.4	7.7		7.1	6.9	6.7
4th decile	8.6	8.5		8.1	8.2	8.4
5th decile	9.6	9.4		8.9	9.7	10.1
6th decile	10.9	10.4		10.1	10.8	11.7
7th decile	12.4	11.7		11.9	12.7	13.6
8th decile	14.7	13.7		14.5	15.2	17.5
9th decile	20.9	20.8		24.5	23.3	20.5
10th decile						
3. RDMs (rows 1-3)						
1st decile	0.91	0.73	*	0.45	0.10	0.37
2nd decile	0.93	0.81		0.77	0.38	0.55
3rd decile	0.91	0.87		0.82	0.57	0.70
4th decile	0.91	0.89		0.90	0.81	0.78
5th decile	0.93	0.91		0.95	0.93	0.85
6th decile	0.97	0.96		0.98	1.05	0.91
7th decile	0.97	1.00		1.01	1.03	0.96
8th decile	1.01	1.04		1.06	1.13	1.03
9th decile	1.06	1.08		1.10	1.12	1.16
10th decile	1.09	1.18		1.13	1.22	1.28

* The disaggregation of household groups for Spain is not done in terms of deciles

Table 2.3. RDMs for Activities Resulting from an Overall Injection in Activities

	Poland 1987	Hungary 1990	Spain 1980	Italy 1984	Netherlands 1987	Germany 1984
1. % distribution of multipliers						
Agriculture	12.9	19.9	8.7	7.1	4.5	3.3
Industry	69.2	50.2	57.8	58.7	47.9	53.2
Trade	8.5	9.7	14.1	9.5	16.6	9.4
Transport	6.5	6.9	5.0	4.7	7.0	5.4
Services	2.9	13.3	14.5	20.0	24.0	28.6
2. Actual % shares						
Agriculture	10.2	15.8	7.4	5.3	4.6	2.2
Industry	66.0	52.2	54.4	55.1	47.5	51.8
Trade	7.5	9.1	13.4	8.5	13.7	8.0
Transport	6.1	5.8	4.8	4.1	5.9	4.5
Services	10.3	17.1	20.0	27.1	28.3	33.5
3. RDM*						
Agriculture	1.27	1.26	1.18	1.36	0.96	1.51
Industry	1.05	0.96	1.06	1.06	1.01	1.03
Trade	1.14	1.06	1.05	1.12	1.22	1.18
Transport	1.07	1.19	1.03	1.15	1.19	1.20
Services	0.28	0.78	0.73	0.74	0.85	0.85

* For example, for Polish agriculture, the RDM of 1.27 = 12.9/10.2

To take Hungary first, it is noted that the actual share of agriculture, which was 15.8% in 1990, should be expected to fall in the longer run to levels comparable to the M-countries, say about 5%. Contrary to this, the endogenous mechanisms of the SAM multipliers show a distributionary share going to agriculture of 19.9%. This is a bias towards more agriculture, which is contrary to the normed track. Similarly, in Poland, there is a share of agriculture of 10.2% that should fall in the longer run. However, the SAM multipliers, with a 12.9% share going to agriculture, obstruct achievement of the prospective patterns. This is even more apparent in the case of services (Poland has an actual share of services of 10.3%, which should grow to 30% by Western standards. However, the SAM multipliers produce a share of only 2.9%).

In bringing both Poland and Hungary on the right track with respect to prospective patterns, it will be necessarily to implement two steps. Mobilise the exogenous forces through government expenditure and exports in such a way as to curb the prospects of agriculture and industry to the advantage of services. And, reshape the mechanisms of SAM multipliers through appropriate investments in the transition phase so as to favour services vs. agriculture and industry.

The first alternative seems unattractive for both economies because there are many healthy prospects for export of agricultural and industrial goods. The second scenario thus looks to be the more effective. The question to be raised is where and which actions must the countries take to modify the distribution bias of the SAM multipliers. A decomposition of these multipliers in the so-called transfer, open- and closed-loop effects, and other types of decompositions, will give insight into the more significant mechanisms. This area of analysis is elaborated in chapter 4.

As regards the distributionary pattern of the income multipliers, i.e. the percentage distributions of the multiplier benefits on each household group, the results in table 2.3 show that, for all countries, that RDMs are higher for richer household groups. This is an indication of regressive redistributions of primary income. It is generally due to the exogenous influences of government transfers; that is, some incomes of higher deciles are redistributed to lower deciles so as to reproduce the more equal distributions that are actually observed in these countries.

The degree to which these tendencies occur in the P- and M-countries are clearly different. Poland and Hungary are much less regressive in primary income distribution than the M-countries. The role of the government budget is, therefore, less of a redistributionary instrument in the P- than M-countries. This role may have to change if they approach the

M patterns. The prospects may be that of reduced government intervention in the factor market and in the formation of primary incomes and their distribution. However, there is a more significant role for the state in the redistribution of secondary income transfers. In this way, the state corrects the regressive mechanisms of the primary income formation. The results show that the burden of such a shift in emphasis is likely to be higher in Poland than in Hungary.

5. Size and Distribution of Multipliers of Household Transfers

We may now treat the multiplier effects of household transfers. Table 2.4 gives income and output multipliers of transfers to different household groups classified by income deciles. Taking up first the income multipliers, the results show that the average level in Poland and Hungary is quite similar to that in Germany and the Netherlands. The average multiplier is 1.78 in both Poland and Germany, and approximately 1.50 for Hungary and the Netherlands.

Table 2.4. Income and Output Multipliers Resulting from Transfers to Different Household Groups

	Poland 1987	Hungary 1990	Spain 1980	Italy 1984	Netherlands 1987	Germany 1984
1. Income multipliers of transfers to:						
1st decile	1.78	1.53	*	2.22	1.60	2.00
2nd decile	1.78	1.53		2.09	1.57	1.93
3rd decile	1.78	1.53		2.06	1.54	1.82
4th decile	1.79	1.52		2.03	1.53	1.78
5th decile	1.79	1.52		2.00	1.51	1.75
6th decile	1.79	1.51		2.00	1.49	1.73
7th decile	1.79	1.50		2.01	1.49	1.71
8th decile	1.78	1.50		2.00	1.48	1.70
9th decile	1.78	1.49		1.99	1.46	1.70
10th decile	1.78	1.48		1.90	1.43	1.69
2. Average	1.78	1.51	2.30	2.03	1.51	1.78
3. Output multipliers of tranfers to:						
1st decile	4.22	2.20	*	3.30	1.53	2.62
2nd decile	4.23	2.17		2.97	1.47	2.45
3rd decile	4.23	2.16		2.89	1.40	2.17
4th decile	4.24	2.15		2.81	1.38	2.07
5th decile	4.24	2.13		2.76	1.33	1.99
6th decile	4.24	2.10		2.75	1.29	1.92
7th decile	4.24	2.08		2.79	1.30	1.88
8th decile	4.24	2.04		2.74	1.26	1.86
9th decile	4.24	2.02		2.72	1.23	1.85
10th decile	4.23	1.98		2.53	1.14	1.84
4. Average	4.23	2.10	4.02	2.83	1.33	2.06

However, the differences in multipliers between the decile groups are much smaller in P-countries than in the M-countries. The differences are small in Poland and Hungary because the multiplier by decile group is dependent on how much is leaking away from the system in the form of direct taxes and social premiums, and these leaks are uniform for all groups. On the other hand, in Germany, the Netherlands and Italy, transfers to lower income groups are found to generate more income than transfers to higher income groups, because of the higher propensity to spend among the lower income groups which works positively on the circular flow.

Higher income groups in the M-countries must pay a relatively higher share of taxes and premiums, leading to lower multipliers. This progressive taxation system is less developed in Hungary and almost absent in Poland. Similar observations hold for the output multipliers of household injections.

Table 2.5. RDMs of Households and Activities Resulting from an Overall Transfer to Households

	Poland 1987	Hungary 1990	Spain 1980	Italy 1984	Netherlands 1987	Germany 1984
1. Households						
1st decile	0.91	0.73		0.45	0.20	0.36
2nd decile	0.92	0.81		0.77	0.38	0.54
3rd decile	0.91	0.87		0.82	0.57	0.70
4th decile	0.91	0.89		0.90	0.81	0.78
5th decile	0.93	0.91		0.95	0.93	0.85
6th decile	0.98	0.96		0.98	1.05	0.92
7th decile	0.98	1.00		1.02	1.03	0.97
8th decile	1.01	1.04		1.07	1.13	1.04
9th decile	1.07	1.08		1.10	1.12	1.16
10th decile	1.09	1.18		1.13	1.22	1.26
2. Activities						
Agriculture	1.15	1.14	1.04	1.14	0.68	1.07
Industry	1.04	0.96	1.01	1.04	0.81	0.96
Trade	1.45	1.28	1.30	1.34	1.50	1.44
Transport	0.98	1.08	0.94	0.94	0.96	1.03
Services	0.27	0.82	0.79	0.79	1.14	0.95

Along similar lines as in tables 2.2 and 2.3, *RDMs* of transfers to households have been calculated in eqs. (10) and (11).

$$RDM_{zz}' = \frac{M_{a,zz}' - d_{zz}'}{\sum_z M_{a,zz}' - 1} / \frac{Income_{z,o}}{\sum_z Income_{z,o}} \qquad (10)$$

$$RDM_{vz}' = \frac{M_{a,vz}'}{\sum_v M_{a,vz}'} / \frac{Output_{v,o}}{\sum_v Output_{v,o}} \qquad (11)$$

The results for the six countries are in table 5.2. Here we find the relative distributions of (1) the output multipliers on the sectors, and (2) the income multipliers on household groups. A few comments will be made on the results obtained.

Taking first the distributionary pattern of the output multipliers, positive biases exist for agriculture and trade, rather low and mixed biases for transport and industry, and a strong negative bias for services. The Netherlands is the country deviating most from this pattern with negative biases for agriculture and industry and a positive bias for services. Other results are similar to those already discussed for injections to activities. In general, *RDMs* indicate little difference between the P- and M-countries.

As regards the distributionary pattern of the income multipliers, the results show that for all countries, that *RDMs* are again higher for richer household groups, which is an indication of regressive redistributions of primary income.

6. Conclusions

Four decades of central planning in Eastern European countries have had the effect of substantially changing the structure of these economies from their *normal* paths, broadly proxied by the neighbouring Western European countries. In identifying normal structural patterns, and studying effective mechanisms to approach them, the comparative analysis of the SAM, as a multiplier model across Eastern and Western European countries, is shown to be a helpful and an easily implementable tool. It can be used to simulate the economic effects of exogenous additions in sectoral activities and in institutional transfers.

System-specific factors influence multiplier results significantly, after allowing for exogenous leakage. Both, the ratio of income to output multipliers, and the levels of multipliers relative to the endogenous share of the circular flows, were thus very low in Poland and Hungary when compared with Western Europe.

To a certain extent, and more so for Poland than for Hungary, it could be shown that there are growth biases in the economy towards primary sectors. The size and share of multipliers of the services sectors were thus found to be relatively low. In bringing both Poland and Hungary on the right track with respect to prospective patterns, the results suggest that it will be necessary to do one or more of the following. First, mobilise the exogenous forces through government expenditure and exports in such a way as to curb the prospects of agriculture and industry to the advantage of services. Second, reshape the mechanisms of SAM multipliers through appropriate investments in the next few years so as to favour services vs. agriculture and industry. The first solution is unattractive for both economies because there are many healthy prospects for export of agricultural and industrial goods. The second solution is the more effective one.

As far as distribution bias is concerned, Poland and Hungary are much less regressive in primary income distribution than are the selected Western European countries. The role of the government budget is, therefore, less of a redistributionary instrument in planning than it is in market-oriented systems. By WE standards, this role is bound to change in the transitionary phase, and thereafter. The future prospects are those of reduced government intervention in the factor market and in the formation of primary incomes and their distribution, and a more significant role for the state as a redistributor of secondary income transfers to correct for the regressive mechanisms of primary income formation. Our results showed that the burden of such a shift in emphasis will be higher in Poland than in Hungary. More analysis is required to determine where and which actions to take in modifying distribution bias of the SAM multipliers. Decomposition of SAM multipliers can assist in such analyses.

The SAMs of Poland and Hungary analysed here served as bench marks for the simulation of general equilibrium models during the early years of economic transition. These will be dealt with in chapter 7. The results of chapter 7 will be seen to reinforce those obtained here.

Chapter 3

Growth and Distribution in Russia and China: the Difference

1. Introduction

The Social Accounting Matrix, SAM, brings the aggregate national accounts of a country together and breaks them down into production sectors, production factors, earning households expenditure categories, government, and the rest of the world; the whole within a consistent and statistically closed matrix. Assuming linear relations and constant prices, the SAM is convertible in a model that gives the functioning of the economy and its performance. The objective of this chapter is to analyse the structures and performances of Russia and China making use of the SAM as a framework for the comparative analysis of their systemic differences.

Table 3.1 is helpful in giving a quick insight into the empirics of different performances between Russia and China. Russia's GDP grew between 1979 and 1989 by 43.2% and then decreased between 1989 and 1997 by about 60% according to official Russian statistics. China's GDP has been increasing at an annual average rate of 9.5 % since 1979. Even if a more modest estimate of 8% were used, that would mean a total increase between 1979 and 1997 of 4 times. Taking as a benchmark estimates of the World Bank Development Indicators and putting China's GDP in 1997 at 100 gives the indices in rows 3 and 4. These show China's GDP in 1997 to be 2.25 times as large as that of Russia.[1]

---

[1] Using purchasing power parity, the World Bank estimates the GNP per capita of Russia for 1997 at US$ 4880 and that of China at US$ 2920.

Table 3.1. Indices of GDP of Russia and China

		1979	1989	1997
Russia	(GDP for 1979 = 100)	100	143	85
China	(GDP for 1979 = 100)	100	216	400
Russia	(China's GDP for 1997 = 100)	52	75	44
China	(China's GDP for 1997 = 100)	32	67	100

The relative sizes of the two economies have reversed position in historically unmatched terms during less than two decades. The contrast between the effect of reforms in both countries can also be seen from a comparison of output of some ten major goods in physical terms; as is shown in table 3.2. Unweighted average gives an increase of 45% over five years for China and a decrease of 61% for the same years for Russia.

Table 3.2. Output of Major Goods in China and Russia

Item	China 1990	1995	Percent change	Russia 1990	1995	percent change
Electric Energy (bln kwh)	620.0	1000.0	61	1082.0	862.0	-20
Steel (mln ton)	63.5	94.0	48	89.6	51.3	-43
Synthetic fibres (mln ton)	1.6	2.9	81	0.6	0.2	-66
Mineral fertiliser (mln ton)	18.7	24.5	31	16.0	7.5	-53
Tractors (000)	39.0	63.0	62	214.0	21.0	-90
Television sets (mln)	26.8	34.7	29	4.7	1.0	-79
Washing machines (mln)	6.6	9.4	42	5.4	1.3	-76
Textile fabrics (mln ton)	18.8	21.0	12	8.4	1.7	-80
Grain (mln ton)	355.0	417.0	17	107.8	63.5	-41
Meat (mln ton)	25.1	42.0	67	9.8	3.4	-65
Unweighted average			45			-61

Sources: Russian Statistical Yearbook, several years; Economics of Transition, Vol.4, No. 1, 1996, p. 289; China Statistical Yearbook, several years; World Economic and Social Survey 1994, United Nations, p. 259

De Melo, Denizer, Gelb and Tenev (2001) explain the opposite performances in terms of differences in initial conditions, system structures and the types and timing of government policies. Nolan (1995), among others, emphasise the difference in pursued policies. The intensification of the gap between the two countries over many years suggests that the causes are more related to structural differences in the two systems than to economic policy. Here we shall attempt to separate the two effects.

Turning from economic growth to income distribution, Russian data show an increase in the skewness of income distribution from 1988 onwards, together with a surge in the proportion of the population at and below the poverty line, Silverman and Yanowitch (1997). The transition in China was initially believed to be accompanied by more equitable income redistribution than in Russia, Walder (1996), but more recent evidence suggests that China's income distribution is catching up in terms of regressive tendencies. Contrasting performances in growth and distribution between these two major countries have been persistent for a long time.

The contrast remained intact even in the periods of reform suggesting that the differences in the structures and mechanisms behind these performance trends are endurable and can be subjected fruitfully to comparative systemic analysis. The Social Accounting Matrix, SAM, provides a very suitable analytical framework in this context. The SAM brings the national accounts of a country together and breaks them down into activity sectors, production factors, earning households, expenditure categories, government and the rest of the world, the whole within a consistently accountable square matrix. Assuming linear relations and constant prices, the SAM is convertible in a model which describes the functioning of the economy. The model can be solved to give SAM-multipliers that show the economic impact of changes in exogenously assumed inputs in the economy such as the final demand categories of government expenditure, investment, and exports; and income transfers. Basically differently functioning economies will show contrasting multipliers.

This chapter reports on the SAMs of the two largest centrally planned economies around 1990 and compares their SAM multipliers. Even though the comparative analysis is limited to one year only, the obtained results have a durability that is supported by contrasting trends in the two countries over the past decades. In this chapter section 2 introduces the SAMs of Russia and China; section 3 derives SAM multipliers; section 4 analyses the *growth* effects of injections in final demand and income transfers; section 5 does the same for *redistributionary* effects; section 6 concludes.

2. The SAMs of Russia and China

The circular flow of expenditure on, and payment for the purchase and production of, goods and services is basic to all economies. National account statistics tabulate the various aspects of this circular flow. The social accounting matrix, SAM, is nothing more or less than the transformation of the well-known circular flow into a matrix of transactions between the various agents, as in table 3.3. This is a matrix which refers to Russia, 1991. In the rows of such a matrix we find: first, the products account; second, the factors account, consisting of labour income and other income from profit, interest, etc.; third, the separate institutional current accounts for respectively households, firms and government, and the aggregate institutional capital account; fourth, the production activities account, and the rest of world account. The columns are ordered similarly. Transactions between the holders of these accounts take place at the filled cells and in correspondence with the circular flow. A particular row gives receipts of the holder while column-wise we read the expenditure of the holder. For example, row 7 is equivalent to the sum total of the input-output table, giving from left to right receipts of the production activities from private consumption 483.9 billion roubles (br), public consumption 307.6 br, intermediate deliveries 1441.8 br. and exports to rest of world 178.9 br. Column 8 gives the expenditure of rest of world, i.e. receipts for Russia, in the form of a foreign capital outflow of -16 br., and the above mentioned exports of 178 br.

Table 3.3 giving, thus, the aggregate national accounts for Russia in 1991 is exclusively constructed from the definite and published estimates of the national accounts for 1991. These accounts have been disaggregated further into four products, five factors, five household groups classified by income ranges, firms, government, aggregate capital account, three production activities and rest of world, together resulting in a SAM of 21 rows by 21 columns, as found in the Appendix.[2]

The required data for disaggregating the SAM of table 3.2 into the extended SAM in the Appendix includes: (a) the household budget survey for breaking up the household account into the income groups and

---

[2] There is an extended version of the SAM for Russia with 38 rows by 38 columns, but we refrain from discussing this here. This paper focuses on achieving a comparable base for Russia and China. Such a comparable base is obtained with the SAM for Russia of 21x21 and for China of 19x19. The two SAMs are reported upon in Braber and Gavrilenkov (1994) and Cohen and W. Gupei (1995).

specifying their incomes by source and expenditures by type of product; (b) the input-output table for disaggregating the production activities; and (c) an initial converter table for transforming a products classification into a sectoral classification.

Table 3.3. SAM of the Russian Federation, 1991 (in billion Rouble)

	Products	Factors	Households	Firms	Government	Capital	Activities	Rest World	Total
1 Products			541.2	*					541.2
2. Factors							1166.6		1166.6
3. Households		562.8		23.8	202.8				789.4
4. Firms		404.3		92.6					496.9
5. Government		199.5	66.5	99.4			30.0		395.4
6. Capital			181.7	281.1	-115.0		104.0	-16.0	435.8
7. Activities	483.9				307.6	414.9	1441.8	178.9	2827.1
8. Rest World	57.3					20.9	84.7		162.9
Total	541.2	1166.6	789.4	496.9	395.4	435.8	2827.1	162.9	7114.3

The above-mentioned data are used as follows. The household budget survey provides distribution structures of receipts and expenditures by household groups. These are multiplied by the number of households and evenly adjusted to fit the aggregate household account in table 3.3, to give the greater details of the extended SAM in the Appendix. Regarding the data in the input-output table these are aggregated to suit the classification into three sectors. The absolute values thus obtained fit directly within the disaggregated SAM. Regarding the converter matrix between products and sectors, this was constructed in a preliminary way from the codes of the household budget survey and the input-output and later subjected to several adjustments to assure consistency of the grand totals of its rows and columns, which is solved by applying the RAS method.

The comparable aggregate SAM for China 1989 is displayed in table 3.4. The disaggregated SAM for China is reproduced in the Appendix, resulting in a 19x19 matrix. It consists of about the same accounts as for Russia except that there is less disaggregation in the factor and household accounts.

Table 3.4. SAM for China, 1989 (in billion Yuan)

	Products	Factors	Households	Firms	Government	Capital	Activities	Rest World	Total
1. Products			610.7						610.7
2. Factors							1125.1		1125.1
3. Households		637.1			4.2				641.3
4. Firms		483.1							483.1
5. Government		4.9	6.2				247.7		258.8
6. Capital			24.4	483.1			45.2	28.7	581.4
7. Activities	610.7				254.6	581.4	1584.9	176.8	3208.4
8. Rest World							205.5		205.5
Total	610.7	1125.1	641.3	483.1	258.8		3208.4	205.5	7114.3

3. Deriving SAM Multipliers for Russia and China

In the input-output analysis an endogenous vector of sectoral production, q, can be predicted from a matrix of input-output coefficients, L, and a vector of exogenous final demand, f, as in eq. (1).

$$q = L q + f = (I - L)^{-1} f = M_l \, f \qquad (1)$$

where M_l is the Leontief multiplier matrix.

The SAM can be used similarly with the obvious difference that the SAM contains more variables and relationships. To transform the social accounting matrix into an economy-wide model along the above lines requires performing several steps.

First, the accounts of the SAM need to be subdivided into exogenous and endogenous and regrouped in such a way that the expenditure and receipts of the exogenous accounts would fall respectively to the right and bottom of the endogenous accounts. The choice regarding subdivision into exogenous and endogenous accounts can lead to lengthy discussions on alternative closure rules. This is avoided here by following an established convention, which coincides with the step-wise closure of demand models and assumes, *initially* the expenditure accounts of capital, government and rest of world in centrally planned economies as exogenous. This can be modified *later* by endogenising the capital account, as the economic system becomes more market oriented. These closure rules were followed in the previous chapter and will be followed in other chapters that deal with market economies.

Applied to the Russian SAM, the closure rules would mean that columns 16, 17 and 21 would be shifted further to the right. The corresponding receipts of these exogenous accounts, rows 16, 17 and 21 are shifted to the bottom of the matrix. As a result, the remaining accounts which are endogenous accounts, would for the Russian SAM count the following categories:

- Products, rows and columns 1 to 4
- Factors, rows and columns 5 to 9
- Households 10 to 14, and firms row and column 15
- Production activities, rows and columns 18 to 20

These endogenous accounts form an 18*18 submatrix within the regrouped SAM, containing all the flows from endogenous to endogenous accounts.

The same procedure applied to the Chinese SAM results in the three exogenous expenditure accounts of capital, government and rest of world, and a 16*16 submatrix of endogenous to endogenous accounts.

Secondly, the flows in the endogenous accounts need to be expressed as average propensities of their corresponding column totals. Thus each flow in the SAM is divided by its respective column total to give the matrix of average propensities, denoted by A. As a result of the above manipulations an economy-wide model in the form of table 3.4 is obtained. The row totals of the endogenous accounts, *i.e.* the endogenous variables, are represented by the y vector; the exogenous variables are represented by the x vector. Note that the A matrix, which relates the y and x vectors to each other, appears in a partitioned form to facilitate a decomposition of multiplier effects.

The vector of endogenous variables y can now be solved from eq. (2)

$$y = Ay + x \; (I - A)^{-1} x = M_a x \qquad (2)$$

where M_a is the SAM multiplier matrix.

For Russia M_a is a matrix of 18*18, while for China M_a is 16*16. For reasons of space we shall select only a few parts of this matrix for comment. For instance, a distinction can be made between two types of exogenous impulses: demand injections into the activities account x_4, and transfer injections to the institutions account x_3. The impact of either impulse can be traced on the four types of endogenous accounts y: (1) expenditure by product, (2) earnings by factor, (3) income by household group h, and (4) output by sectoral activity s. We are interested in the latter two endogenous accounts.

Table 3.5. SAM in the Form of $A_y + x = y_E$

Expenditures Receipts	1. Wants	2. Factors	3. Institutions	4. Activities	Government, capital and rest of the world	Totals
Endogenous						
1. Wants			A_{13}		x_1	Y_1
2. Factors				A_{24}	x_2	Y_2
3. Institutions		A_{32}	A_{33}		x_3	Y_3
4. Activities	A_{41}			A_{44}	x_4	Y_4
Exogenous	R e s i d u a l b a l a n c e s					
Totals	y_1	y_2	y_3	y_4		

We shall limit the analysis to the impact of sectoral demands and institutional transfers on output by activity and income by household. The effects on expenditure by product and earnings by factor are of less interest here given the focus of the paper on growth and distribution. This means that the four parts of the multiplier matrix indicated in table 3.6 will be further analysed.

Table 3.6. Selected Multipliers for Further Analysis

Endogenous Accounts	1. product	2. factors	Types of exogenous impulses x	
			3 transfers to household h	4 injection to sector s
1. products				
2. factors				
3. income of household h			$M_{a,hh}$	$M_{a,hs}$
4. output of sector s			$M_{a,sh}$	$M_{a,ss}$

4. Growth Multipliers in Russia and China

To start with, table 3.7 gives the growth multiplier effects of final demand injections on variables of income $M_{a,hs}$ and output $M_{a,ss}$. The results are obtained from the inversion of the SAM as explained in eq. (2). The results show for Russia that, on average, a demand injection in the sectors, of say one billion roubles (br) has a multiplier effect on output of 2.81 br, and a multiplier effect on income of 0.62 br. An income transfer of 1.0 leads to a combination of an output multiplier of 2.09 with an income multiplier of 1.40.

The corresponding results for China in table 3.8 show demand injections lead to output and income multipliers of 3.26 and 1.26, while transfer injections lead to output and income multipliers of 2.84 and 1.66. China's performance is higher than Russia's in all four respects.

This section will further examine selected results from the two country comparisons. The section will elaborate on the interpretation of differences in multipliers of demand injection by sector of activity. Later on we consider differences in multipliers of transfer injections.

In general, the size of the multipliers of an inverted matrix is relatively high if the inverted SAM coefficient matrix, i.e. the endogenous part, represents a large share of the economy, and correspondingly the exogenous part represents a small share. Multipliers are relatively low if the endogenous share is small and the exogenous share is large, as this exogenous share is not ploughed back in the economy. The exogenous share in the SAM, consisting of investment, government and rest of the world, will generally depend on the economic system, the development level and the size of the country.

Table 3.7. SAM Multipliers for Russia 1991

Multipliers of demand injections into sectors			Multipliers of transfer injections to household groups		
sectors:	Income effects	Output effects	household groups:	Income effects	Output effects
Agriculture	0.76	2.95	Hh. < 250 Rbl. per month	1.47	2.44
Industry	0.52	3.05	Hh. 250-300 Rbl.p.m.	1.43	2.26
Services	0.59	2.44	Hh. 300-350 Rbl.p.m.	1.41	2.15
			Hh. 350-400 Rbl.p.m.	1.39	2.08
			Hh. > 400 Rbl. p.m.	1.29	1.52
Average	0.62	2.81	Average	1.40	2.09
Highest/ Lowest	1.46	1.25	Highest/Lowest	1.14	1.61

The share of investment and government is expected to be greater in planning oriented economies especially among those with a larger defence budget. Economic theory predicts also a greater share of investment, government and rest of world at more advanced levels of economic development. Countries with a larger population tend to have lower shares of transactions with rest of the world, other things remaining the same.

Given the above it is not surprising that the exogenous share as defined here, should be higher in Russia than in China. This is also evident from the SAMs that show a higher exogenous share for Russia than China, with respectively 19.6% and 14.7% of the economy considered exogenous. The correspondingly endogenous shares are 80.4% and 85.3% for Russia and China, respectively, implying a lesser circular flow in Russia than China.

As a result, the SAM multiplier should be expected to be lower in Russia than China, which is the case as tables 3.7 and 3.8 indicate.

However, there is the additional question of which of the two countries is more successful in generating more output, and more income, per one percentage point of the endogenous share. It can be calculated, on average, that in the case of Russia a demand injection gives an output multiplier of 2.81 for an endogenous share of 80.4%, implying an output multiplier of 0.035 for each endogenous percentage point. China's performance is higher in this respect, (i.e. 3.26/85.3%=0.038), as it is able to achieve from an equivalent demand injection an output multiplier of 0.038 for each endogenous percent. The difference amounts to a positive edge of about 10 percent, (i.e. .038/.035). This edge can be interpreted as a more efficient use of the circular flow of the economy.

Table 3.8. SAM Multipliers for China 1989

Multipliers of sector injections:			Multipliers of household transfers:		
sectors	Income effects	Output effects	households	Income effects	Output effects
Agriculture	1.66	3.70	Rural Farm	1.77	3.30
Industry	0.89	3.07	Rural Non-farm	1.72	3.08
Services	1.06	3.00	Urban Employed	1.73	3.12
			Urban Self-employed	1.43	1.85
Average	1.20	3.26	Average	1.66	2.84
Highest//Lowest	1.87	1.23	Highest/Lowest	1.24	1.78

Why China surpasses Russia in the efficient use of the circular flow? Three related reasons can be given. First, a better-knitted economy, in the sense of having more extensive and intensive transactions between its agents is characterised by more transactions and a more filled SAM. The more that the SAM cells are filled the greater the multiplier effect. The extreme situation of an autonomous sector which produces and supplies exclusively for its own employed labour households who buy exclusively from this sector will show very low multipliers. Centrally planned economies tend to save on transactions and emphasise autonomy. This is in contrast to free market economies which propagate more transactions and a higher turnover of circulating funds. While both Russia and China share features of a command economy there is general agreement in the empirical literature that the Russian system has been less forthcoming than the Chinese system in creating multi-channels for the flow of goods and services, and creating a more flexible framework for resolving imbalances.

Secondly, while there may be specific flows with higher multiplier effects than others yet in the longer run an economy which manifests little structural change will tend to show less variation in multiplier effects of alternative injections. In contrast, a rapidly moving economy undergoes frequent structural changes and the variation in multipliers is bound to be greater. The introduction of a new activity or flow extends the circular flow by that activity and links with other activities, resulting in a widening of the variation between multipliers as well as higher overall multipliers. Russia has been less successful than China in modernising its economy and extending the circular flow, this is associated with a lower range of multiplier values in Russia as compared to China. We tried to demonstrate these tendencies for Russia and China in tables 4 and 5. The highest/lowest ratio of output multipliers shows about the same value for Russia (1.25) and China (1.23). However, the disparity in the income multipliers for Russia is lower (1.46) than for China (1.87), suggesting more replicability of the status quo in Russia as compared to a rapidly changing China.

Thirdly, the Russian economy's focus on industry foregoes important multiplier effects elsewhere, i.e. agriculture and services. Comparative SAM multiplier results for advanced countries, cf. Cohen (1993), show the sectors of services and agriculture to have the highest output and income multipliers, while industry lags behind in its multiplier effects. This is also true for multiplier analysis of developing countries. These results are due to the high expenditure on food and services and greater earnings flows in services as compared to industry. While the results for China are in general agreement with the findings for other countries, those for Russia differ as they show a predominance of the output multiplier for demand injections in industry. These results are due to a restricted circular flow in Russia that tends to downgrade the role played by the sectors of agriculture and services and foregoes, as a result, potentially higher multiplier effects.

For assessment purposes, the income multiplier is a more relevant concept than the output multiplier for two reasons. First, earned income is closer to the *economic efficiency* notion of value added than gross output. Second, earned income by household groups is a better indicator of *social welfare* than gross output. Assessment of the income multipliers of Russia and China leads to two remarks. First, the average income multiplier from demand injection for Russia is found to be 0.62 that is achieved at an endogenous share of 80.4%, implying a multiplier of 0.0077 for each endogenous percentage point. Applying this norm to China should result in an income multiplier of 0.66, but China is able to secure a SAM income multiplier of 1.20, which is almost the double. A similar calculation for Russia on the basis of China would give a normalised income multiplier for Russia of 1.3 as compared to the SAM income multiplier of only 0.62. The conclusion is that China fairs better than Russia in aggregate income multiplier effects as well. Calculating the ratio of income to output multipliers gives 0.22 and 0.37 for Russia and China, respectively; supporting the hypothesis of greater leakages of value added and/or a lower efficiency in factor use in Russia as compared to China.

Attention can now be directed to the multiplier effects of *transfer injections*. These are generally consistent with the preceding results for demand injections showing output and income multipliers of transfer injections to household groups to be lower in Russia, 2.09 and 1.40 resp., than in China where they reach 2.84 and 1.66 resp., even though the performance edge tends to be narrowed to the extent that the income/output ratio of transfer injections is reversed in favour of Russia, reaching 0.67, as compared to China 0.58. In the light of the preceding results this outcome can be interpreted to mean that transfer payments to household groups in Russia occur in an economy with a relatively less intensive and extensive circular flow and with more emphasis on the direct rather than indirect effects, and hence converting transfer payments directly into higher income rather than higher output effects. The Chinese economy, in contrast, allows the transfer payment, to be turned over more intensively and extensively permitting more output and more income.

5. The Distributionary Impacts in Russia and China

Besides comparing the levels of the multipliers, it is also important to study the distribution of the multiplier effects on the respective sectors and households and assess the underlying structural bias in the two countries. For instance, one should ask how the output multipliers of an injection in sector s' distribute themselves on the individual sectors s. A Relative Distributive Measure of sector on sector effects, ss', is developed for this purpose, denoted by $RDM_{ss'}$. The indicator was defined in the previous chapter, but is repeated here to facilitate exposition.[3]

$$RDM_{ss'} = \frac{(M_{a,ss'} - d_{ss'})}{(\sum_s M_{a,ss'} - 1)} / \frac{Output_{s,0}}{\sum_s Output_{s,0}} \qquad (3)$$

where the individual multiplier effect of s' on s, $M_{a,ss'}$, is divided by the column sum of multipliers of s after deducting the initial injection. Here we use $d_{hh'}$ for the Kronecker symbol that equals 1 if h=h' and o in other cases. The result is divided by the actual output share of sector s in year 0, as found in the SAM for the base year. For values of $RDM_{ss'}$ >1, <1, and = 1, there are positive, negative and neutral redistributive effects. For instance, values of $RDM_{ss'}$ = 1 mean that sectoral injections would reproduce exactly the sectoral distribution pattern of the base year.

Similarly, a relative distributive measure for the multiplier effects of sectoral injections s' on income of household group h, that is $RDM_{hs'}$, can be calculated as in eq. (4)

$$RDM_{hs'} = \frac{M_{a,hs'}}{\sum_h M_{a,hs'}} / \frac{Income_{h,0}}{\sum_h Income_{h,0}} \qquad (4)$$

Values of $RDM_{hs'}$ =1 mean that sectoral injections would reproduce exactly the initial distribution pattern of the base year. A positive value for a household group h would mean an increase in its income share relative to the base year, a negative value would mean a deterioration.

---

[3] Note that in the previous chapter v and z represented activities and institutions, respectively. In this chapter we use s and h for sectors and household groups, correspondingly. The notations are consistent given the understanding that s is a subset of v, and h is a subset of z. In terms of account numbers, we have assigned accounts number 4 to activities including sectors, and accounts number 3 to institutions including households.

In correspondence with the above, two types of *RDM* for transfer injections can be formulated, giving $RDM_{sh'}$ and $RDM_{hh'}$:

$$RDM_{hh'} = \frac{(M_{a,hh'} - d_{hh'})}{\sum_h M_{a,hh'} - 1} / \frac{Income_{h,0}}{\sum_h Income_{h,0}} \qquad (5)$$

$$RDM_{sh'} = \frac{M_{a,sh'}}{\sum_s M_{a,sh'}} / \frac{Output_{s,0}}{\sum_s Output_s} \qquad (6)$$

Table 3.9 shows all four measures for Russia. The effect of sectoral demand injections on the sectoral distribution of output show that for all sectoral injections there is a highly positive growth bias towards the agricultural sector, the value of *RDM* being between 1.06 and 1.89. In contrast, the results show a negative growth bias for the services sectors, *RDM* between 0.69 and 0.74: and a uniform replication of the share of industry with *RDM* being about 1.0.

Considering the effects of sectoral injections on income distribution the results show injections in the various sectors to have the same effect of high regressiveness. The poorest household group comes badly off with *RDM* around 0.7. Most benefits go to the richest groups, which are calculated to enjoy *RDM* of 1.05 or more.

Next we may consider the *RDM* of transfer injections. The pattern is the same as found for demand injections. Among the sectors the share of agriculture ends better off, services worse off and industry is unaffected. Among the household groups the poorest are unflavoured, *RDM* = 0.7, while the richest are favoured with *RDM* = 1.05. That, nevertheless, the actual income distribution in Russia shows more equality than what the SAM multipliers demonstrate, is due to the positive effect of annually repeated initial injections to the poorest household groups.

The results for China can be now reviewed from table 3.10. On the average, demand injections in China favour both industry and agriculture, but industry more so than agriculture, these in contrast with Russia which does the opposite. Both countries disfavour services.

Income redistribution effects are uniform for alternative demand injections. The effects favour rural households *RDM* > 1.0, and disfavour urban households *RDM* < 1.0, and to the extent that the poorest population lives in rural areas the multiplier effects can be interpreted to promote more equality. It was observed before that the results for Russia show the opposite *RDM* effects as regards income distribution.

These results reveal sector earning and household expenditure patterns and mechanisms, which redistribute income towards the richer household groups in Russia as opposed to a redistribution towards poorer household groups in China.

Table 3.9. RDM's Russia 1991

	Demand injections into sectors:		
	Agriculture	Industry	Services
$RDM_{hs'}$ Impact on income of five household group categories:			
Hh. < 250 Roubles p. m.	0.67	0.74	0.73
Hh. 250-300 Roubles p.m.	0.91	0.93	0.92
Hh. 300-350 Roubles p.m.	0.97	0.99	0.99
Hh. 350-400 Roubles p.m.	1.01	1.01	1.01
Hh. > 400 Roubles p. m.	1.06	1.05	1.05
$RDM_{ss'}$ Impact on output of three sectors:			
Agriculture	1.89	1.31	1.06
Mining and Industry	0.99	1.10	1.17
Services	0.74	0.74	0.69

	Transfers to households:		
	Hh. < 250	Hh. 250-300	Hh. 300-350
$RDM_{hh'}$ Impact on income group of five household group catagories:			
Hh. < 250 Roubles p.m.	0.72	0.72	0.72
Hh. 250-300 Roubles p.m.	0.92	0.92	0.92
Hh. 300-350 Roubles p.m.	0.98	0.98	0.98
Hh. 350-400 Roubles p.m.	1.01	1.01	1.01
Hh. > 400 Roubles p.m.	1.05	1.05	1.05
$RDM_{sh'}$ Impact on output of three sectors:			
Agriculture	1.50	1.41	1.37
Mining and Industry	1.15	1.16	1.16
Services	0.60	0.61	0.62

Table 3.10. RDM's China 1989

	Demand injections into sectors:		
	Agriculture	Industry	Services
RDM_{hs}			
Impact on four household group categories:			
Rural farm	1.37	0.91	0.76
Rural non-farm	1.37	0.91	0.76
Urban employee	0.46	1.13	1.35
Urban self-employed	0.47	1.15	1.38
RDM_{ss}			
Impact on three sectors:			
Agriculture	1.30	0.91	0.97
Industry	1.03	1.17	1.15
Services	0.71	0.70	0.70

	Transfer injections to household group categories:			
	Rural farm	Rural nonfarm	Urban employer	Urban self employed
RDM_{hh}				
Impact on four household group categories:				
Rural farm	1.17	1.18	1.17	1.17
Rural non-farm	1.17	1.18	1.17	1.17
Urban employee	0.76	0.74	0.75	0.75
Urban self-employed	0.77	0.75	0.76	0.76
RDM_{sh}				
Impact on three sectors:				
Agriculture	1.45	1.46	1.45	1.44
Industry	0.93	0.95	0.95	0.96
Services	0.82	0.76	0.78	0.76

6. Concluding Remarks

The use of the SAM as a framework for the comparative analysis of systemic differences in economic performance serves as an important tool in outlining and checking the differences and gives valuable insight in the patterns and mechanisms that cause the differences in performance. The SAM was applied to a comparative analysis of the difference in growth and equity between Russia and China. Even though the comparative analysis is limited to one year only, the obtained results indicate a durability that is supported by contrasting trends in the two countries over the past decades. The results of the analysis are consistent with the observed economic trends of recession with inequity in Russia during the transition phase as compared to a strengthened growth with restrained redistribution in China. The SAM analysis was able to reflect on several structural differences in the two economic systems that lie behind these differing performances.

There are limitations of the SAM multiplier approach as followed here. These were discussed in the previous chapter. They relate to the assumption of excess capacity, linear relationships, aggregation errors, and closure rules. Of special relevance for the comparative validity of the results between Russia and China is the assumption of excess capacity. The SAM is a fixed price multiplier model, and hence supplied amounts are supposed to adjust to demanded amounts if the full potential of the multiplier effect is to be realised. If there is restricted capacity the result is immediate or repressed inflation. This may require a revision downward in the real sizes of multipliers. Applied to Russia and China, and given the relatively greater shortages in Russia than China around 1990, the realisable multiplier effects are likely to be lower than the potential for Russia, as compared to China.

Chapter 4

Policy Modelling under Fixed and Flexible Price Regimes: SAM and CGE Transition Models Applied to Hungary and Poland

1. Introduction

The proper approach to the transformation of the planning-oriented economies to market-oriented economies is a very controversial subject. Some economists have used the term shock therapy to emphasise the necessity of a change in mentality among consumers and producers. Others advocate a gradual approach to economic restructuring. Some support a combination of the two approaches. There are momentarily no operational frameworks that are able to appraise such choices against each other, or are able to monitor the actual results of any choice made. This is rendered most difficult in situations of hectic price changes and unstable relations that preclude the possibility of a reliable aggregation of data and empirical modelling during transition.

Less ambitious, but nevertheless helpful in reflecting on performance aspects of the transformation process, is a comparative static analysis based on social accounting matrices, SAM, and computable general equilibrium models, CGE. The SAM can be seen as a baseline measurement of the general equilibrium interactions in the economy for a particular year. With a minimum of manipulations the SAM is convertible to either a *fixed*-price or *flexible*-price model, cf. Cohen (1989), Pyatt (1991), and Dervis, de Melo, and Robinson (1982), Piggott and Walley (1985). These two versions are very handy in replicating a centrally planned and a free market situation, respectively. By running one and the same policy injection in both versions, it is possible to detect the signs, sizes, and locations of the discrepancies. Furthermore, by applying sensitivity analysis, one can appraise under which structural changes the discrepancies can be more effectively resolved.

The SAM displays the transactions of the economy with regard to receipts and expenditures of production activities, factors, and institutions (whether households, firms, government, or rest of the world) in a matrix form. Because of its algebraic properties, the SAM can be viewed as a model of the economy. It can be broken down in an endogenous and an exogenous part; the latter can be recalculated as a matrix of proportional coefficients in terms of column totals, which can then be inverted to give multipliers that show the impacts of changes in the exogenous part on sectoral output, household incomes, and so forth.

The impact multipliers in a fixed-price SAM model assume relative prices unchanged so that all impacts go into quantity changes. As such this version of the SAM can be seen to represent a truly centrally planned economy in which prices are fixed by the state and quantities carry the burden of the adjustment. The impact multipliers of an imposed injection, to be fully realised in quantity changes, assume the availability of sufficient production capacity. Especially of relevance in this context is the relative size of the injection to the available capacity.

On the other hand, a free market economy is commonly modelled as a computable general equilibrium model. As is well known, the rules of the game in a CGE model are different from those in a fixed-price SAM model. In the CGE model producers maximise their profits and consumers maximise their utility in markets in which the demand for and supply of products and factors are cleared at flexible equilibrium prices. Because the SAM for a particular year can be seen as a baseline measurement of the general equilibrium interactions in the economy, the matrix can serve as a modular framework for replicating a free market situation with endogenous prices. We aim in the second formulation to switch the regime towards a CGE model. The same policy simulation applied to the fixed-price SAM model can be now inserted in the flexible price CGE model to give alternative results.

The SAM-CGE can be seen as the opposite poles between the central planning model and free market model. In this chapter, we review applicability of SAM-CGE to the modelling of economies in transition from a pure centrally Planned Economy (PE) to a pure free Market Economy (ME). Two countries serve as case studies: Poland and Hungary.

The chapter is structured as follows: In the next section the fixed-price SAM model and its applicability to centrally planned economies will be discussed. In Section 3 the CGE model will be presented. Two demonstrative simulations are performed with both models for two different countries - Poland and Hungary - for two different base periods.

The simulation results for the Polish economy will be examined in Section 4; the Hungarian results will be reviewed in Section 5. Finally, in Section 6, a summary and some concluding remarks will be given.

2. The Fixed-Price SAM Model

The SAM multiplier model is a linear model of the form:
$$y = (I - S)^{-1} x = Mx$$
where:
M = matrix of multipliers,
S = matrix of average expenditure propensities for endogenous accounts,
y = endogenous variables,
x = exogenous variables.

Endogenous variables represent SAM totals to be explained by the model, while exogenous variables are aggregate injections into the endogenous part of the economy. The distinction between endogenous and exogenous parts of the economy (respectively, accounts of SAM) should reflect behavioural features of the economy and the objectives of modeller. To be consistent with the specification of the CGE model presented in the next section, the accounts of social security, government and the rest of the world are considered exogenous here. The procedure of transforming the SAM into a multiplier model has been presented in literature many times and will not be discussed here in detail.

Formally, the fixed-price SAM model closely resembles the Leontief input-output model, LM, which is well anchored in the planning procedures of the former Soviet Union. In that sense, the LM is a mathematical formulation of the so-called 'material balances' planning technique widely used in CPEs. Five basic assumptions underlying the LM can be listed.

1. planners aim at achieving consistency between resources and uses,[1]
2. planners know all the relevant technological coefficients,
3. all technologies are characterised by fixed input proportions and constant returns to scale,

---

[1] The other way to think of modelling planners' behaviour is to assume that they optimise some social welfare function. The extensive discussion of different modelling approaches to central planning can be found in Bennett (1989).

4. primary resources (capital stock, labour force) are outside the model,
5. prices are fixed.

The LM simulates a planning procedure in which planners fix net output targets (consumption, investments, and exports) and then determine gross outputs and intermediate inputs necessary for achieving those targets. Thus, mutually consistent figures of net output (exogenous), gross outputs, and intersectoral deliveries form the production plan obtained by the LM. Because primary resources are not explicitly dealt with in the model, one should assume that planners are able to adjust production capacities to the requirements of the plan. This is consistent with the highly centralised nature of investment processes in CPEs on the one hand and with relatively large labour resources during the industrialisation phase of the 1950s and 1960s on the other hand.[2] As mentioned above, it is assumed as well that reallocation of resources does not change prices. This reflects the minor economic function of prices in CPEs where prices are under the control of planners and are kept relatively isolated from supply/demand and efficiency considerations.

The arguments for considering the LM and the fixed-price SAM model as simple models of a CPE lie in assumptions 1 and 2 listed above. What differs in both models is the extension of the production relationships typical of the Leontief model to cover the full circular flow of the economy, typical of the SAM. In the SAM the central planner takes into account primary incomes generation, their distribution and then redistribution among institutions, and finally its uses for consumption and savings purposes. The SAM applications for Poland and Hungary relate to the years 1987/88 and 1990, just before and somewhat halfway into the transition. The benchmark SAMs for these years are adapted versions of the SAMs compiled and published in Cohen (1993).[3]

3. The Flexible-Price CGE Model

The CGE model applied in this paper portrays an idealised free market economy, which corresponds otherwise with the same discussions of the constructed SAMs for Poland and Hungary. All markets distinguished in the model, namely, five goods markets, the labour market, and the market

---

[2] This interpretation refers rather to early stages of CPEs.
[3] A full explanation of the original SAM and its multiplier properties can be found in Cohen (1993).

for foreign exchange, are fully competitive. Demand and supply are equalised at all markets by instantaneous adjustment of all prices.

Next to production activities the model distinguishes five types of actors: firms, households, social security, public sector and the rest of the world. Activities supply and demand goods and services and such factors as labour and capital.[4] The producing firms maximise profits subject to a technological production constraint, taking all prices as given. Households are suppliers of labour and capital and are demanders for goods and services. They maximise utility subject to their budget constraint, again taking all prices as given. The social security agency is a passive body that accumulates and transfers funds. The public sector levies taxes and premiums, and it redistributes income over households. The public sector is also a demander and supplier of goods and services. The rest of the world is engaged in trade and financial transfers with the domestic economy.

The equilibrium described by the model is of a static nature without intertemporal effects. The equilibrium solutions can be altered by the government through changes in its expenditures and tax rates.

The flexible-price CGE model we use in this paper will apply the following notational conventions: Real variables are represented by lower-case characters. All price variables are represented by a capital P and a subscript identifying the corresponding real variables. Capitals represent nominal variables. Greek characters stand for parameters and coefficients. Activities are indicated by the subscripts i and j; want categories by k. Households (and firms), social security, government and the rest of the world are indicated by h, s, g, and f, respectively. Dollar signs denote variables expressed in foreign currency. Exogenous variables are denoted by overbars. The complete model is specified as follows.

Real output is determined from a two-level production structure. At the lowest level, sectoral real value-added v_i is derived by a Cobb-Douglas function from labour l_i and capital k_i; therefore smooth substitution possibilities exist at this level. The sectoral amount of capital is assumed to be fixed in the short run.

$$v_i = \bar{v}_{io} \ l_i^{\beta_i} \ \bar{k}_i^{1-\beta_i} \tag{1}$$

---

[4] Because part of the intermediate inputs are imported, this demand implicitly generates a demand for foreign exchange.

At the highest level real value-added is combined in fixed proportions with domestic and imported intermediate inputs to arrive at real output.

$$x_i = v_i \bigg/ \left(1 - \sum_j \alpha_{ji} - \mu_i \right) \qquad (2)$$

By definition nominal output is equal to real output times the output price.

$$X_i = P_{x_i} x_i \qquad (3)$$

Value-added prices P_{vi} can be derived by deducting indirect tax rates σ_i and unit costs of intermediate inputs from output prices. Imported intermediate goods are valued at exogenously fixed foreign prices $P_{mi}^\$$, which are transformed into domestic currency by multiplying with the exchange rate ER.

$$P_{v_i} = (1 - \sigma_i) P_{x_i} - \sum_j \alpha_{ji} P_{x_j} - \mu_i\, ER\, \overline{P}_{m_i}^\$ \qquad (4)$$

Each sector is assumed to consist of many similar firms that all maximise profits in perfectly competitive product and labour markets. The latter implies that wage and prices are given for the individual firm, and this allows us to treat each sector as one large price-taking firm. Following first-order conditions for profit maximisation, firms will hire labour l_i until the wage rate P_l, equals the value of its marginal product.

$$P_l\, l_i = \beta_i\, P_{v_i}\, x_i \qquad (5)$$

The remuneration of capital is the residual nominal value-added after labour is paid its share. Because the volume of capital is fixed, remuneration rates P_{ki} have to adjust to be equal to the value of marginal product of capital. Consequently, remuneration rates of capital may differ among sectors.

$$P_{k_i}\, k_i = (1 - \beta_i)\, P_{v_i}\, x_i \qquad (6)$$

Total demand for labour is equal to the exogenous supply. The wage rate is solved from this equilibrium equation.

$$\sum_i l_i = \bar{l} \qquad (7)$$

Primary income of institutions Y^p consists of factor remunerations, which are distributed, in fixed proportions. Primary income of government comprises also indirect taxes.

$$Y_h^p = \omega_h \, P_l \, \bar{l} + \pi_h \sum_i P_{k_i} \, \bar{k}_i \qquad (8a)$$

$$Y_s^p = \omega_s \, P_l \, \bar{l} + \pi_s \sum_i P_{k_i} \, \bar{k}_i \qquad (8b)$$

$$Y_g^p = \omega_g \, P_l \, \bar{l} + \pi_g \sum_i P_{k_i} \, \bar{k}_i + \sum_i \sigma_i \, P_{x_i} \, x_i \qquad (8c)$$

Households and firms pay (direct) tax to the government. Direct tax is levied over taxable income Y^t. Taxable income comprises primary income and income transfers received from government, from social security, and from abroad. Income transfers paid by government and social security are exogenous in real terms. Nominal transfers are pegged to the consumer price index CPI to maintain purchasing power of households at the benchmark level. The consumer price index is chosen as numeraire of the model and is fixed exogenously. Transfers from abroad are fixed in foreign currency and are transformed to domestic currency by multiplication with the exchange rate ER. Transfers to firms are zero in the SAM; so for firms taxable income is implicitly equal to primary income.

$$Y_h^t = Y_h^p + \bar{o}_{hg} \, \overline{CPI} + \bar{o}_{hs} \, \overline{CPI} + \bar{o}_{hf} \, ER \qquad (9)$$

Disposable income of households and firms Y_h^d is defined as taxable income minus direct taxes and social security contributions paid. Both social security contributions and direct taxes are fixed proportions (τ_{sh} and τ_{gh}, respectively) of taxable income.

$$Y_h^d = (1 - \tau_{sh} - \tau_{gh}) Y_h^t \qquad (10)$$

Most outlays by social security are fixed in real terms. Nominal transfers paid to domestic and foreign households are pegged to the consumer price index, as the objective of the government is to maintain purchasing power of transfer payments. Because savings of social security s_s are a provision for future fluctuations in the number of transfers, they are pegged to the consumer price index also. Incomings are primary income and social security contributions paid by households. The budget is balanced by adjusting the net transfers paid to the government O_{gs}.

$$Y_s^p + \sum_h \tau_{sh} Y_h^t = \overline{s}_s \, \overline{CPI} + \sum_h \overline{o}_{hs} \, \overline{CPI} + \overline{o}_{fs} \, \overline{CPI} + O_{gs} \qquad (11)$$

The government budget deficit is defined as incomings minus expenditures. Also for the government expenditures are fixed in real terms. In addition to spending on transfers, government also spends on consumption, of which the volume c_{ig} is fixed exogenously. Incomings are primary income and direct taxes paid by households and firms.

$$S_g = \sum_h \tau_{gh} Y_h^t + Y_g^p - \sum_i \overline{c}_{gi} \, P_{x_i} - \sum_h \overline{o}_{hg} \, \overline{CPI} - \overline{o}_{fg} \, \overline{CPI} + O_{gs} \qquad (12)$$

Consumption expenditure of households is distinguished by want categories W_{kh}. For simplicity it is assumed that consumption behaviour is determined by Cobb-Douglas utility functions, which generate the following constant budget shares consumption demand functions:

$$W_{kh} = \gamma_{kh} Y_h^d \qquad (13)$$

Wants are composed of domestic goods, distinguished by sector of origin, and imported goods, of which the volume shares v_{ik} and v_{fk} in the composite are fixed. Thus, no substitution is possible between domestic and imported goods.

Consumption expenditure on imports M_k follows from:

$$M_k = \overline{P}_{mk}^\$ \, ER \, v_{fk} \sum_h \frac{W_{kh}}{P_{wk}} \qquad (14)$$

Total consumption expenditure by sector Q_i can be derived in a similar way:

$$Q_i = P_{x_i} \sum_k V_{ik} \sum_h \frac{W_{kh}}{P_{wk}} \qquad (15)$$

The price index of wants P_{wk}, is a weighted average of all component prices. The weights are the respective shares of the components in the composite.

$$P_{w_k} = v_{fk} \, \overline{P}^\$_{m_w} \, ER + \sum_i v_{ik} P_{x_i} \qquad (16)$$

The closure of the model is neo-classical, which implies that domestic investment expenditure Z is determined by the sum of domestic and foreign savings. Total domestic savings are the sum of savings by government, social security, and households and firms; the latter is defined as disposable income minus consumption expenditure. Net foreign savings consist of an exogenous flow $F^\$$, which is fixed in foreign currency, and an endogenous flow that is equal to the government budget deficit, as it is assumed that the government finances its total budget deficit by foreign borrowing. As the endogenous part of foreign savings cancels out against net government savings both are excluded from equation 17.

$$Z = \overline{F}^\$ \, ER + \overline{s}_s \, \overline{CPI} + \sum_h Y^d_h - \sum_h \sum_k W_{kh} \qquad (17)$$

It is assumed that there exists only one type of investment good, which is a composite of domestic goods, again distinguished by sector of origin, and imported goods. The volume shares of the delivering sectors in the composite ξ_i are fixed. Nominal investment expenditure by sector of origin I_i can specified as follows:

$$I_i = P_{x_i} \, \xi_i \, \frac{Z}{P_z} \qquad (18)$$

The price index of the composite investment good P_z, is a weighted average of domestic output prices P_{x_i} and the price index of a composite of imported investment goods $P^\$_{mz}$. The weights are the respective shares of the components in the composite.

$$P_z = \xi_f \, \overline{P}^\$_{mz} \, ER + \sum_i \xi_i \, P_{x_i} \qquad (19)$$

Domestic products are assumed to compete on the world market with goods produced abroad, which differ by country of origin. This product heterogeneity implies that the world market demand for domestic products depends partly on domestic prices. Then, the value of exports E_i can be expressed as follows:

$$E_i = P_{x_i} e_i = P_{x_i} \left[\frac{\overline{P}^{\$}_{e_i}}{P_{x_i}/ER} \right]^{\delta_i} \overline{e}_{io}$$

where e_i is the volume of exports, $P^{\$}_{ei}$ is the weighted average of the fixed prices of competitors on the world market and δ_i is the world market demand elasticity for domestic products of sector i. $\overline{e}_{io}$ is a constant term reflecting total world market demand for output of sector i and the domestic market share if P_{xi}/ER is equal to $P^{\$}_{ei}$. If it is assumed that the export demand elasticity is equal to one, we get:

$$E_i = \overline{P}^{\$}_{e_i} ER \, \overline{e}_{io} \tag{20}$$

The balance of payments equation gives on the left-hand side the capital account balance. On the capital account a distinction is made between the inflow of foreign capital needed to finance the government budget deficit S_g and other capital flows $F^{\$}$, which are fixed in foreign currency. The right-hand side gives the current account balance, which consists of imports of investment goods, intermediate goods and consumption goods, exports and net income transfers to abroad.

$$\overline{F}^{\$} ER + S_g = \overline{P}^{\$}_{mz} ER \, \xi_f \frac{Z}{P_z} + \sum_i \overline{P}^{\$}_{m_i} ER \, \mu_i \, x_i + \sum_k M_k$$
$$- \sum_i E_i + \left(\overline{o}_{fg} + \overline{o}_{fs} \right) \overline{CPI} - \sum_h \overline{o}_{hf} ER \tag{21}$$

Equation 22 gives the product balances. According to Walras' Law only four equations have to be specified, equilibrium on the four markets guarantees equilibrium of the fifth. Output prices P_{xi} can be solved from these equations.

$$X_i = \sum_j P_{x_i} a_{ij} x_j + Q_i + I_i + E_i + \bar{c}_{ig} P_{x_i} \qquad (22)$$

The consumer price index is taken as numeraire of the model. The weights are the proportions of the respective products in aggregate household expenditure. This specification implies that changes in household income can be interpreted as changes in real household income.

$$\overline{CPI} = \sum_k \rho_k P_{wk} \qquad (23)$$

To finish this section we will discuss the comparability of the CGE and SAM model. The CGE model described above employs, except for prices, wage, and exchange rate, the same assumptions as the SAM model reported in the previous section.

In the SAM model government, social security, and the rest of the world are exogenous. Exogenity implies in this context that payments by these actors to endogenous actors are fixed. Because prices are fixed, this specification corresponds to the specification in the CGE model. Here government expenditure is fixed in real terms. The same is true for transfers paid by the rest of the world. Exports are determined by relative prices only, so that in the case of price fixation they would become fixed as well.

Incomings of exogenous actors are not constant in the SAM model, but are proportional to expenditures by endogenous actors. Thus, incomings of government depend among others on tax payments by activities, households, and firms. Incomings of social security are a fixed share of the total wage sum, while incomings of the rest of the world are payments for imports, which are proportional to domestic activities, consumption, and investment.

In the aggregate, total incomings of the exogenous sectors will be equal to total expenditures, including policy injections. For individual accounts this does not have to be the case, because increased expenditure by the government leads to higher receipts by social security and the rest of the world through higher social security contributions and higher imports. To achieve that the three exogenous accounts are not only in equilibrium in the aggregate but also separately, two additional assumptions are made in the SAM model. First, the budget surplus of social security is fixed, and every increase in receipts by this institution will be compensated by an increase in its contribution to the government. The same closure of the social security budget is chosen in the CGE model. Second, the remaining increase of the government budget deficit will be financed by the rest of the world. Also this assumption is applied in the CGE version.

The capital account is taken endogenous in the SAM model. This is consistent with the savings-driven investment specification in the CGE model.

Finally, it may be remarked that in the case of fixed-prices, all equations that assume substitution are reduced to fixed coefficient specifications similar to those that are used in the SAM model. For instance, the factor demand equations 5 and 6 will be reduced to Leontief-type specifications if it would be assumed that price indices remain at their benchmark levels, which are unity. So, the difference in price regime and the accompanying assumptions about the constraints on total supply of labour, capital, and foreign savings form the only ground for differences in simulation results between the CGE model and the SAM model.

4. The Results of Simulations: the Polish Case

4.1. Introduction

To demonstrate the different consequences of government policy under the two opposite regimes of central planning (fixed-prices) and free market (flexible prices), two government policy measures are simulated under both price regimes. One is aimed at shifting the production structure towards services, the other is aimed at changing the income distribution in favour of the poorest households. In the first, Experiment S, government demand for services is increased by 1% of total government expenditure. The measure can be interpreted as been taken to reduce the bias against the underdeveloped service sector inherited from the old planning system. In the second, Experiment H, the same amount is transferred as welfare payments to the lowest decile household group, which can be interpreted as a measure to reduce the adverse effects of transition for the poorest households.

The exogenous impulse of 1% of total government expenditure was equal to 31.197 bill.zl in 1987 and 1.144 th.bill.zl in 1990. The results of the simulations are presented in tables 12.1 to 12.4. The results will be discussed for each simulation (S and H) and each price regime (fixed-price SAM model and flexible price CGE model) separately and for both years simultaneously.

4.2. Variant S: Increase in Government Demand for Services

The SAM model. As can be expected, additional expenditures of government in services lead to increased output of services (by 0.66% in 1987, table 12.1, row 5 and 0.67% in 1990, table 12.3, row 5). Output of other activities adjusts complementarily according to input-output ties with no limits for factor supplies. Construction, which has the strongest forward linkage, responds most. Factor incomes grow with increasing output at approximately the same rate (0.39% in 1987 and 0.40% in 1990). Labour incomes are affected slightly more than capital, because of the shift in branch output composition towards labour-intensive branches. On average, factors reacted more than activities, because branches that expanded were more value-added intensive than the economy on average. With rising factor incomes, institutions increased their income: households by 0.32% in 1987 and 0.31% in 1990, firms by 0.37% in 1987 and 0.39% in 1990. Thus, firms profited more than households despite the fact the labour factor incomes grew more than capital. Two reasons may be given to explain these results. First, there is a relatively large leakage from the labour account to exogenous accounts (over 20% in both years). Second, household incomes are substantially dependent on exogenous sources (about 22% in 1990). Among households, the rich gain much more than the poor, which may be explained by much more dependency of the latter on exogenous incomes. For example, transfers constituted 85.4% of total income of the 1st decile group, while it comprised only 4.8% of total income of the 10th decile group in 1990. As far as outlays of institutions are concerned, savings increased more than consumption (i.e., 0.40% vs. 0.31% in 1990). This can be explained by (1) higher income growth of firms than households, and (2) higher propensity to save of firms than households can (viz., 53.6% vs. 21.8% in 1990). Direct taxes grow – by definition – by the same rate as the incomes of institutions and indirect taxes by the same rate as output. Increasing tax revenues provide the budget with resources for financing additional expenditures for services.

Generally, the initial impulse results in GDP growth of 0.39% in 1987 and 0.40% in 1990, see tables 4.1 and 4.3, row GDP, with investments growing faster than individual consumption (viz., 0.79% vs. 0.32% in 1987, and 0.40% vs. 0.41% in 1990).

Table 4.1. Results of the Simulations for 1987 (SAM totals in percentage deviations)

Accounts	SAM model		CGE model		CGE-SAM	
	S	H	S	H	S	H
Activities						
Agriculture	0.31	0.43	0.22	0.34	−0.09	−0.09
Light industry	0.31	0.42	−0.23	0.01	−0.54	−0.41
Heavy industry	0.28	0.30	−0.95	−0.69	−1.23	−0.99
Construction	0.36	0.35	1.31	1.04	0.95	0.69
Services	0.66	0.28	1.57	0.80	0.91	0.52
Average	0.37	0.36	0.09	0.09	−0.28	−0.27
Factors						
Labour	0.40	0.35	0.91	0.69	0.51	0.34
Capital	0.38	0.35	0.82	0.64	0.44	0.29
Average	0.39	0.35	0.87	0.66	0.48	0.31
Institutions						
1st decile	0.29	8.83	0.66	9.07	0.37	0.24
2nd decile	0.30	0.26	0.67	0.51	0.37	0.25
3rd decile	0.29	0.25	0.66	0.50	0.37	0.25
4th decile	0.29	0.25	0.66	0.50	0.37	0.25
5th decile	0.30	0.26	0.67	0.50	0.37	0.24
6th decile	0.31	0.27	0.70	0.53	0.39	0.26
7th decile	0.31	0.27	0.70	0.53	0.39	0.26
8th decile	0.32	0.28	0.73	0.55	0.41	0.27
9th decile	0.34	0.30	0.76	0.58	0.42	0.28
10th decile	0.35	0.30	0.78	0.59	0.43	0.29
Average	0.32	0.61	0.72	0.87	0.40	0.26
Firms account	0.37	0.33	0.79	0.61	0.42	0.28
Capital account	0.37	0.36	0.98	0.78	0.61	0.42
Macro indicators						
GDP	0.39	0.35	0.87	0.66	0.48	0.31
Investment	0.37	0.36	0.96	0.78	0.59	0.42
Domestic savings	0.16	0.11	0.59	0.43	0.43	0.32
Ind. Consumption	0.32	0.61	0.72	0.87	0.40	0.26
Imports	0.34	0.39	−4.06	−3.10	−4.40	−3.49

Table 4.2. Results of the Simulations for 1990 (SAM totals in percentage deviations)

Accounts	SAM model		CGE model		CGE-SAM	
	S	H	S	H	S	H
Activities						
Agriculture	0.27	0.42	−0.18	0.08	−0.45	−0.34
Light industry	0.28	0.40	−0.31	0.00	−0.59	−0.40
Heavy industry	0.25	0.27	−0.86	−0.57	−1.11	−0.84
Construction	0.36	0.37	0.94	0.78	0.58	0.41
Services	0.67	0.32	1.57	0.79	0.90	0.47
Average	0.36	0.34	0.05	0.08	−0.31	−0.26
Factors						
Labour	0.41	0.34	0.65	0.46	0.24	0.12
Capital	0.39	0.33	0.52	0.39	0.13	0.06
Average	0.40	0.34	0.57	0.42	0.17	0.08
Institutions						
1st decile	0.06	5.46	0.09	5.47	0.03	0.01
2nd decile	0.16	0.14	0.26	0.18	0.10	0.04
3rd decile	0.23	0.20	0.37	0.26	0.14	0.06
4th decile	0.26	0.22	0.41	0.29	0.15	0.07
5th decile	0.30	0.26	0.47	0.33	0.17	0.07
6th decile	0.32	0.27	0.48	0.34	0.16	0.07
7th decile	0.35	0.30	0.53	0.38	0.18	0.08
8th decile	0.37	0.31	0.55	0.39	0.18	0.08
9th decile	0.38	0.32	0.57	0.41	0.19	0.09
10th decile	0.38	0.32	0.57	0.41	0.19	0.09
Average	0.31	0.59	0.47	0.67	0.16	0.08
Firms account	0.39	0.33	0.52	0.39	0.13	0.06
Capital account	0.40	0.38	0.76	0.59	0.36	0.21
Macroindicators						
GDP	0.55	0.47	0.57	0.42	0.02	−0.05
Investment	0.58	0.55	0.76	0.59	0.18	0.04
Domestic savings	0.49	0.47	0.04	0.00	−0.45	−0.47
Ind consumption	0.43	0.90	0.46	0.73	0.03	−0.17
Imports	0.44	0.53	−2.54	−1.77	−2.98	−2.30

Table 4.3. Results of the Simulations for 1987 (price and quantity variables in percentage deviations)

	CGE model						CGE-SAM	
	VA prices		Output prices		Real output		Real output	
Activities	S	H	S	H	S	H	S	H
Agriculture	0.81	0.67	0.42	0.36	−0.21	−0.02	−0.52	−0.45
Light industry	0.71	0.68	−0.05	0.02	−0.18	−0.01	−0.49	−0.43
Heavy industry	0.09	0.09	−0.32	−0.23	−0.63	−0.46	−0.91	−0.76
Construction	1.71	1.33	0.74	0.58	0.57	0.46	0.21	0.11
Services	1.53	0.94	0.84	0.50	0.72	0.30	0.06	0.02

Table 4.4. Results of the Simulations for 1990 (price and quantity variables in percentage deviations)

	CGE model						CGE-SAM	
	VA prices		Output prices		Real output		Real output	
Activities	S	H	S	H	S	H	S	H
Agriculture	0.48	0.41	0.17	0.17	−0.36	−0.10	−0.63	−0.52
Light industry	0.30	0.40	0.08	0.04	−0.23	−0.04	−0.51	−0.44
Heavy industry	−0.24	−0.14	−0.37	−0.24	−0.49	−0.33	−0.74	−0.60
Construction	1.50	1.17	0.50	0.42	0.43	0.36	0.07	0.01
Services	1.39	0.78	0.92	0.51	0.65	0.28	−0.02	−0.04

The CGE model. As in the SAM model, additional government demand for services is satisfied by an increase in the output of services (by 1.57% both in 1987 and 1990). Because total factor supplies are given, part of the increase in demand disappears into a rise in the price index (0.84% in 1987, table 4.2, row 5, column 3, and 0.92% in 1990, table 4.4, row 5, column 3). As a result, the real increase in the output of services is much smaller: 0.72% in 1987 and 0.65% in 1990. Moreover, as factor supplies are given, the rise in output of services can now be realised only through reallocation of factor supplies from other activities; this is restricted to the allocation of labour, because capital is immobile.

The mechanism goes along the following lines: The government budget deficit rises through the increase in spending. It is assumed that the credit-worthiness of the government is sufficient to enable it to finance the deficit by foreign borrowing. This leads to an increase in the supply of foreign currency, inducing an appreciation of the zloty: The exchange rate has to decrease by − 4.13% in 1987 (1990: − 2.69%) to restore equilibrium on the balance of payments. The appreciation deteriorates the competitive position of Polish exporters, and exports will decrease. So, exports carry the burden of the macroeconomic adjustment and have to give in to make the expansion of government consumption possible.

On the sectoral level it is heavy industry, which is to a large extent reliant on exports, that suffers most from the adjustment. Real output decreases by − 0.63% in 1987 (− 0.49% in 1990). The decrease in the production levels of agriculture and light industry is less pronounced. Both sectors have a more diversified demand structure and are less vulnerable to changes in the pattern of final demand. Surprisingly, construction does not suffer at all from the expansion of services, production has increased by 0.57% in 1987 (1990: 0.43%). This is caused by the boost in investment expenditure that amounts to 0.96% in 1987 (0.76% in 1990).

An important additional effect of the appreciation of the zloty is a strong improvement in the terms of trade, which is manifested by high value-added prices. This leads, in spite of fixed resources, to a considerable increase in the total value-added or GDP, namely by 0.87 % in 1987 and 0.57% in 1990. See tables 4.1 and 4.3, row GDP.

The rise in factor payments results in an increase in household income averaging 0.72% (1990: 0.47%). The rise in household income is smaller than the rise in factor payments, because part of household income stems from fixed income transfers. The income distribution becomes more unequal in 1990 than in 1987, which can be explained by the fact that the share of transfers, which are fixed in real terms, in the income of the poorest households has increased significantly in three years time.

Private consumption increases through the rise in household income by 0.72% in 1987 (1990: 0.48%). Higher household and firm incomes result in higher tax receipts by the government. This mitigates the initial increase in the budget deficit, so that in the end the increase in private and foreign savings dominates the decrease in government savings. The neo-classical closure of the model implies that investment will rise at a rate equal to the increase in total savings: 0.96% in 1987 and 0.76% in 1990.

It can be concluded that private consumption, investment, and government demand have increased at the expense of exports, or, to put it differently, the Polish economy has benefited from the government policy at the expense of the rest of the world.

4.3. Variant H: Additional Government Transfer to 1st Decile Household Group

The SAM model. The results show that the additional transfer to the lowest income decile raises this decile's income by 8.83% in 1987 and by 5.46% in 1990. Incomes of other decile groups grow only a little because of the low share of the 1st decile group in the total of household incomes (viz., 3.8% in 1987 and 6.1% in 1990) and the absence of direct transfers among household groups. On average, household income grows only by 0.61% in 1987 and by 0.59% in 1990. Increased incomes together with an altered decile distribution generated increased consumption with a changed pattern. As might be expected, foodstuffs and other necessities increased most. Increasing consumption demand has been covered by growing output: mainly by light industry (viz., 0.42% in 1987 and 0.40% in 1990) and agriculture (viz., 0.43% in 1987 and 0.42% in 1990). Increasing output requires additional factor inputs. As a consequence, factor incomes increase by 0.35% in 1987 and by 0.34% in 1990, with labour and capital growing at approximately the same rate, as agriculture is relatively labour-intensive while light industry is relatively capital-intensive.

Generally, the economy reacts to additional government transfers to lowest household group by moderate growth of all its macroindicators. GDP increases by 0.35% in 1987 and by 0.34% in 1990.

The CGE model. In the CGE model, additional government transfers to the lowest decile household group results in significant increases in incomes of those households (by 9.05% in 1987 and 5.47% in 1990). Other households' incomes also increased, which are the consequence of the improvement in the terms of trade resulting from the appreciation of the zloty. As in the previous experiment, the appreciation is caused by an increased inflow of foreign capital to finance the government budget deficit. It should be remarked here that these mechanisms are incorporated in the model and that the appreciation and accompanying improvement in terms of trade do not arise from the fact that the government implements the injection. A transfer by the rest of the world to the poorest households would have given almost exactly the same results.

Total consumption expenditure increases by approximately the same rate as the average of household incomes, but its pattern changes towards a larger share of foodstuffs and other necessities. Consumption demand has increased more than in the previous experiment, which follows from the fact that in the current experiment household incomes are affected directly by the government impulse, while in the previous experiment incomes were only indirectly influenced. The large increase in consumption, and the consumption of foodstuffs in particular, has a favourable effect on the production of agriculture and light industry. However, this impact is not enough to offset the decrease in these activities' export earnings so that real production in agriculture and light industry decreases by − 0.02% and − 0.01%, respectively, in 1987 (1990: − 0.10% and − 0.04%, respectively). Services expand by 0.30% in 1987 (0.28% in 1990), mainly through trade, which increases with consumption and investment. The increase in investment also causes a sharp rise in the production level of construction: 0.46% in 1987 and 0.36% in 1990. Heavy industry undergoes the largest decline in production, resulting from its strong dependence on exports.

Also in the case of an additional government transfer from the government to the lowest decile household group, consumption and investment increase, this time the increase in the former slightly larger than in the latter. Again, exports have to give in to realise the increase in domestic demand.

4.4. Flexible versus Fixed Prices: A Comparison

To analyse the impact of the switch in price regime on the real output of activities changes in price and quantity variables are presented separately in tables 4.2 and 4.4. It can be seen that heavy industry is performing much worse under a flexible price regime. Depending on the type of experiment and year the change in output is − 0.60 to − 0.91 percentage point lower than under a fixed-price regime. Agriculture and light industry are also performing worse under the flexible-price regime. The change in real output is for agriculture up to − 0.63 and for light industry up to − 0.51 percentage point lower. Generally construction is performing better under a flexible-price regime. Services are performing better under a flexible-price regime in 1987 and better under a fixed-price regime in 1990.

Despite the fact that total resources are given under the flexible-price regime, the increase in household income generated by government injections is higher than under the fixed-price regime. Average household income in 1987 is 0.40 percentage point higher in the services experiment and 0.26 percentage point in the transfer experiment. Under the flexible-price regime the price changes, more in particular a decrease in the exchange rate, are responsible for the increase in real household income. However, because total resources are fixed, price changes cannot generate a rise in income for all actors in the system; they can only redistribute income between actors. In this model the rest of the world pays for the increase in domestic incomes. Of course, the favourable impact of the increase in foreign borrowing only holds for the short term. In the long run, debts have to be amortised and interest has to be paid. However, the same argument holds under the fixed-price regime, where also a foreign capital inflow is needed to compensate for the imbalance on the current account, because imports increase proportional to domestic expenditures while exports are fixed.

For 1990 the difference in impact on household income between both price regimes is less pronounced. This holds for both experiments. This smaller difference can be explained by the smaller change in the exchange rate in 1990. The lower exchange rate results from the increase in exports relative to imports between 1987 and 1990. Higher exports facilitate the adjustment to balance of payments equilibrium, because the adjustment takes place mainly through changes in exports, because imports are non-competitive and thus do not react directly to changes in the exchange rate.

So, in conclusion we can say that the level of exports relative to imports plays an important role in determining the effect a transition will have on household incomes. Apart from this, the effect does depend on the assumed substitution elasticities. For the current simulations, we have chosen specifications that allowed all parameters to be calibrated by the SAM, which implicitly means that the substitution elasticity was zero for import demand and unity for export demand. For future simulations it will be useful to use substitution elasticities with greater empirical relevance.

5. The Results of Simulations: the Hungarian Case

5.1. Introduction

The SAM and CGE models were also calibrated on SAMs for Hungary on a pre-transition and a transition year, (Cohen, 1993). Because no SAM for 1987 was available, the 1988 SAM was chosen as a pre-transition SAM, and the 1990 SAM was chosen as a transition SAM.

Because the format of the Hungarian SAM deviates from the format of the Polish SAM, some minor adjustments in the CGE model were necessary.[5]

The two experiments undertaken with the Polish model were repeated for Hungary. In the first experiment (Variant S) government's demand for services was increased by 1% of total government expenditure, while in the second experiment (Variant H) the transfers to the poorest household group were increased by the same amount. The impulse was equal to 5.668 billion forints in 1988 and to 9.065 billion forints in 1990. The simulation results for 1988 can be found in tables 4.5 and 4.6, and results for 1990 are shown in tables 4.7 and 4.8.

In both models, 1% increase in government expenditure (in real terms) leads to a fall in government saving. In the SAM multiplier model, this is very trivial: A unitary exogenous injection always generates a one-unit increase in spending on exogenous accounts (leakages), which are the taxes (government) and imports (ROW) in our model. So, because the injection leaks partly to imports, government income increases less than expenditures, and this implies lower savings. In the CGE model a similar result can be found: tax revenues are proportional to the (intermediate and final) consumption of the individual agents; so domestic consumption should increase by 1% (in real terms too) in order to maintain the original level of government saving. However, real output and real value-added are fixed in average in the CGE model due to resource constraints. So domestic real income and real consumption can increase only if the domestic currency appreciates significantly to make imports cheaper (the

---

[5] The adjustments are the following:
1. Capital income in Hungary is not distributed directly to the households as a total proportion of capital income, but flows to the firms and is distributed over the households as a fixed proportion of firm income;
2. Government sector also comprises social security;
3. Firms are allowed to buy consumption goods;
4. Indirect taxes are levied not only on production but also on consumption and imported investment goods.

export part of the revenues is proportional to the domestic price due to the special assumptions for the calibration of the model).

The fall in government savings (the 'growing deficit') induces a counterbalancing decrease in the flow of savings to abroad (debt repayments by the government are reduced). In the SAM model this only implies that accumulation grows slower than other items (because this part of the savings is constant). However, in the CGE model it leads to a drop in real accumulation (even nominal accumulation is decreasing in all but one CGE simulation). The decrease in debt repayments reduces the demand for foreign currency; the exchange rate appreciates, and this reduces the domestic value of foreign currency in fixed savings. Non-government domestic savings are proportional to the income of the corresponding agents; the increase in this variable is insufficient to counterbalance the fall in the domestic value of foreign savings. In CGE simulations the growing domestic consumption is counterbalanced by the fall in export, which is reached by the appreciation of the exchange rate. The simulation results will be discussed in detail below.

Table 4.5. Results of the Simulations for 1988 (SAM totals in percentage deviations)

Accounts	SAM model S	SAM model H	CGE model S	CGE model H	CGE-SAM S	CGE-SAM H
Activities						
Agriculture	0.43	0.48	−0.03	0.20	−0.46	−0.28
Light industry	0.39	0.45	−0.54	−0.10	−0.93	−0.55
Heavy industry	0.29	0.24	−1.02	−0.58	−1.31	−0.81
Construction	0.46	0.31	0.20	0.15	−0.26	−0.16
Services	1.22	0.47	1.70	0.72	0.48	0.24
Average	0.56	0.40	−0.02	0.04	−0.59	−0.36
Factors						
Labour	0.64	0.41	0.95	0.59	0.31	0.19
Capital	0.60	0.40	0.79	0.53	0.19	0.13
Average	0.63	0.40	0.90	0.57	0.27	0.17
Institutions						
1st decile	0.37	13.36	0.55	13.47	0.18	0.10
2nd decile	0.41	0.26	0.60	0.38	0.19	0.12
3rd decile	0.44	0.28	0.64	0.40	0.20	0.12
4th decile	0.45	0.29	0.66	0.41	0.21	0.13
5th decile	0.46	0.30	0.68	0.43	0.22	0.13
6th decile	0.48	0.31	0.70	0.44	0.23	0.14
7th decile	0.50	0.32	0.73	0.46	0.24	0.14
8th decile	0.52	0.33	0.76	0.48	0.24	0.15
9th decile	0.53	0.34	0.78	0.49	0.25	0.15
10th decile	0.56	0.36	0.83	0.52	0.27	0.16
Average	0.49	0.91	0.73	1.05	0.23	0.14
Firms account	0.60	0.40	0.79	0.53	0.19	0.13
Capital account	0.37	0.31	−0.32	−0.12	−0.69	−0.43
Macro-indicators						
GDP	0.63	0.40	0.90	0.57	0.27	0.17
Investment	0.37	0.31	−0.32	−0.12	−0.69	−0.43
Domestic saving	−.26	−0.33	−0.35	−0.35	−0.09	−0.03
Ind. consumption	0.50	0.95	0.73	1.09	0.23	0.14
Imports	0.45	0.44	−2.44	−1.38	−2.88	−1.82

Table 4.6. Results of the Simulations for 1990 (SAM totals in percentage deviations)

Accounts	SAM model		CGE model		CGE-SAM	
	S	H	S	H	S	H
Activities						
Agriculture	0.46	0.55	−0.18	0.16	−0.64	−0.39
Light industry	0.41	0.49	−0.76	−0.21	−1.17	−0.70
Heavy industry	0.34	0.29	−1.12	−0.61	−1.45	−0.90
Construction	0.52	0.39	0.27	0.24	−0.25	−0.15
Services	1.23	0.50	1.49	0.62	0.26	0.11
Average	0.62	0.45	−0.09	0.01	−0.71	−0.44
Factors						
Labour	0.72	0.46	0.89	0.56	0.18	0.10
Capital	0.71	0.45	0.79	0.52	0.09	0.06
Average	0.71	0.46	0.87	0.55	0.15	0.09
Institutions						
1st decile	0.39	13.95	0.49	14.00	0.09	0.05
2nd decile	0.44	0.28	0.54	0.34	0.10	0.06
3rd decile	0.47	0.30	0.58	0.37	0.11	0.07
4th decile	0.48	0.31	0.59	0.38	0.11	0.07
5th decile	0.49	0.32	0.61	0.38	0.12	0.07
6th decile	0.52	0.33	0.64	0.40	0.12	0.07
7th decile	0.54	0.35	0.67	0.42	0.13	0.08
8th decile	0.56	0.36	0.70	0.44	0.13	0.08
9th decile	0.58	0.37	0.72	0.46	0.14	0.08
10th decile	0.64	0.41	0.79	0.50	0.15	0.09
Average	0.54	0.99	0.67	1.07	0.13	0.08
Firms account	0.71	0.45	0.79	0.52	0.09	0.06
Capital account	0.46	0.41	−0.19	0.00	−0.66	−0.41
Macro-indicators						
GDP	0.71	0.46	0.87	0.55	0.15	0.09
Investment	0.46	0.41	−0.19	0.00	−0.66	−0.41
Domestic Savings	−0.14	−0.21	−0.48	−0.40	−0.34	−0.19
Ind. Consumption	0.54	1.05	0.67	1.12	0.12	0.07
Imports	0.48	0.49	−2.88	−1.64	−3.36	−2.13

Table 4.7. Results of the Simulations for 1988 (price and quantity variables in percentage deviations)

	CGE model						CGE-SAM	
	VA prices		Output prices		Real output		Real output	
Activities	S	H	S	H	S	H	S	H
Agriculture	0.90	0.59	0.26	0.19	−0.29	0.01	−0.72	−0.47
Light ind	0.67	0.58	−0.22	−0.08	−0.32	−0.02	−0.72	−0.47
Heavy ind	0.43	0.30	−0.24	−0.13	−0.78	−0.45	−1.07	−0.69
Construction	0.92	0.58	0.30	0.20	−0.10	−0.04	−0.56	−0.35
Services	1.40	0.75	0.68	0.36	1.02	0.35	−0.20	−0.12

Table 4.8. Results of the Simulations for 1990 (price and quantity variables in percentage deviation)

	CGE model						CGE-SAM	
	VA prices		Output prices		Real output		Real output	
Activities	S	H	S	H	S	H	S	H
Agriculture	0.84	0.57	0.18	0.15	−0.36	0.01	−0.82	−0.54
Light ind	0.58	0.52	−0.33	−0.14	−0.44	−0.06	−0.85	−0.43
Heavy ind	0.47	0.34	−0.29	−0.16	−0.83	−0.45	−1.17	−0.74
Construction	0.89	0.57	0.28	0.19	−0.01	−0.05	−0.53	−0.34
Services	1.24	0.67	0.65	0.35	0.83	0.26	−0.40	−0.24

5.2. The Variant S: Increase in Government Demand for Services

The SAM model. In Hungary the increase in government spending on services equal to 1% of the total government income elevates the production value of services by approximately the same percentage for both years under study: 1.22% and 1.23% respectively, which is significantly higher than the increase that was found for Poland. This can be explained by the larger government sector in Hungary. Because the injection is equal to 1% of the government budget, this implies that the impulse will be a higher percentage of benchmark production than in Poland. As a result, the average rise in production value (0.56 in 1988 and 0.62 in 1990) is also higher than in Poland. As in the Polish simulations construction shows the second largest output growth. Heavy industry shows the smallest increase in output, namely 0.29% in 1988 and 0.34% in 1990, which does not differ much from the increase that was found for Polish heavy industry. So, in Hungary the injection leads to a larger sectoral dispersion than in Poland.

The rise in factor remunerations is higher (0.63% in 1988 and 0.71% in 1990) than the increase in average production value, which can be attributed to the high value-added intensity of services. Labour income rises slightly more than capital income, which corresponds with the results that were found for Poland.

The change in average household income is lower than the change of factor income for the same reason mentioned in the previous section. Because of the small share of endogenous components in the income of the lower deciles the impulse leads to a more unequal distribution of income. Contrary to the Polish simulations, in which the distribution of income has become less equal over time, the distribution of income was fairly stable over time in the Hungarian simulations.

The CGE model. In Hungary the macro adjustment to external shocks goes along the same lines as in Poland. The increase in government spending leads to a decline in the government budget surplus and results in a cutback of net debt amortisation by the government, which reduces the demand for foreign currency so that the forint appreciates. The decrease in the exchange rate amounts to − 2.29% in 1988 and to − 2.69% in 1990. The resulting decrease in exports makes the expansion of government (in the services experiment) and private consumption (in the transfer experiment) possible.

Contrary to the Polish situation, there is no boost in investment expenditure in Hungary. The reason for this is the high exogenous inflow of foreign capital. The fall in the exchange rate reduces the domestic value of these foreign savings, and this offsets the increase in domestic savings resulting from increased incomes. The outcome is a small decline in investment expenditure.

On the sectoral level, construction is least affected by the shift towards the service sector, because its strong linkages with investment have a stabilising effect on its output, while direct injections to services have also a favourable impact on its output level. The latter fact is due to the high construction intensity of services. The output of construction declines in real terms by − 0.10% in 1988 and by − 0.01% in 1990, while in nominal terms its output increases by 0.20% and 0.24%, respectively. Agriculture and light industry undergo a considerable decline in real output: − 0.29% and − 0.32%, respectively in 1988 (− 0.36% and − 0.44% in 1990); however, for light industry, nominal output has decreased even more, because the output price also has decreased. Heavy industry suffers the most because of its strong dependence on declining exports. The decline in real output amounts to − 0.78 in 1988 (− 0.83% in 1990), which is much larger than in the Polish simulations. The increase in the service sector (1.02% in 1988 and 0.83% in 1990) is much larger than in the Polish simulations. Thus in the CGE experiments the sectoral dispersion also is larger for Hungary than for Poland.

The growth in labour income exceeds the growth in capital income by 0.16 percentage point in 1988 and 0.1 percentage point in 1990. This difference is caused by the decline of output of the capital-intensive industrial sectors.

Average household income increases by 0.73% in 1988 and by 0.67% in 1990. Also, for CGE simulations the distribution of income becomes more unequal.

5.3. Variant H: Additional Government Transfer to 1st Decile Household Group

The SAM model. The additional transfer rises the income of the poorest household group by 13.36% in 1988 and 13.95% in 1990. Again, this is much larger than the increase that was found in the Polish simulations. Also, the average increase in household income, which amounts to 0.91% in 1988 and 0.99% in 1990, is larger than in Poland.

The average increase in consumption is higher than the increase in average household income (0.95% in 1988 and 1.05% in 1990), because the poorest household has a propensity to consume that is above the average. The consumption of foodstuffs, not shown in the table, increases most; its growth is 1.11% in 1988 and 1.23% in 1990. The large increase in foodstuff consumption has a favourable impact on the performance of agriculture. Among the activities, agriculture shows the largest expansion of production, while two other activities with strong linkages with consumption, services and light industry are only slightly behind. Construction experiences only a moderate increase in its output, because the growth in investment stays behind the growth in consumption. Again heavy industry is the worst performing sector resulting from its strong reliance on (fixed exports). In general, the export-oriented industrial sectors have to suffer the most from the constancy or fall in export demand (due to appreciation of domestic currency). On the other hand they are the most import-intensive sectors; so cheaper imports slightly compensate them for the loss of revenue. Loss of their revenue is partly due to the decrease in their output prices (by 0.1%-0.3%).

The CGE model. The additional transfer increases the income of the lowest decile by 13.47% in 1988 and 14.0% in 1990. Average household income increases by 1.05% in 1988 (1990: 1.07%). Average consumption increases by 1.09% in 1988 (1990: 1.12%); foodstuffs benefit most. On the sectoral level, output of agriculture is positively influenced by the increase in consumption and negatively by the fall in exports and the fall in output of light industry, to which it has strong forward linkages. Both effects outweigh each other, and ultimately there is hardly any change in output. Heavy industry suffers the most; real output declines by 0.45%, both in 1988 and 1990. The decline is caused by the decrease in export earnings. In nominal terms the decline is reinforced by a fall in the output price. For the same reason real output of light industry falls slightly. The service sector benefits most from the increase in transfers to the poorest household; its real output rises by 0.35% in 1988 and by 0.26% in 1990. Services are strongly linked to consumption, while they are not affected by the constant or falling export demand. Constant government consumption of services in case of injections to the poorest households can be viewed as a stabilising factor in CGE models (because total output is fixed), but in SAM multiplier models it pulls back the growth of its output.

Though in the individual sectors labour and capital income change at the same rate due to the assumptions of the model, the expansion of the service sector, which has a small bias in favour of labour combined with the worse performance of the capital-intensive industrial sectors, has the effect that labour incomes grow slightly more than capital income. Average factor income or GDP grows by 0.57% in 1988 and 0.55% in 1990.

Without additional government transfers to households, the income of households lags behind labour income because the non-labour components of household income are either constant (in the case of transfer income) or grows slower than labour income (in the case of capital income). Because the lower deciles receive a high percentage of their income from the government (the poorest decile receives almost half of its income from the government), increasing labour income generates income mainly for the richest deciles.

5.4. Flexible Versus Fixed Prices: A Comparison

The differences in real output levels between the flexible-price regime and the fixed-price regime are shown in tables 12.6 and 12.8. It can be seen that in real terms all activities perform worse under a flexible-price regime. The largest difference can be found for heavy industry; the change of real output is between 0.69 and 1.17 percentage point, depending on type of experiment and year, lower under the flexible-price regime, which can be attributed to the decrease in export earnings. A shift in the price regime affects agriculture and light industry to almost the same degree; under the flexible-price regime their performance is 0.43 to 0.85 percentage point worse. Contrary to the Polish simulations, construction also is performing worse; the change in its output level is 0.35 to 0.56 percentage point below the change achieved under the fixed-price regime. Services show the smallest differences between the two price regimes; real output is only 0.12 to 0.40 percentage point lower under the flexible-price regime. It is the only sector that shows a better performance in nominal terms.

Although under the flexible-price regime resources constrain output and the general price level is fixed at base level, household income and expenditure grow even more than in the fixed-price simulations. This is mainly due to the lowered exchange rate, which makes imports cheaper. The distribution of income is more unequal, because the higher level of household income is entirely the result of an increase in factor income (because transfer income is fixed in real terms), which has a bias towards the higher deciles. The difference in income changes between the two price regimes has reduced over time. In 1988 the increase in household income was in the services experiment 0.24 percentage point lower and in the transfer experiment 0.14 percentage point lower under the fixed-price regime; in 1990 this was only 0.13 and 0.08 percentage point, respectively.

6. Concluding Remarks

The results reported above illustrate the differences in the simulated behaviour of the economy under centrally planned and market regimes. Based on the arguments given above, we interpret the results of the SAM model as describing stylised centrally planned economy and we treat the results of the CGE model as reflecting ideal market mechanisms. However, the application of SAM and CGE models to a specific country is not meant to replicate a centrally planned and a free market economy, respectively, for that country. It should be mentioned that what we generate in either the SAM or the CGE model are *potentials*. In the SAM model the impact multipliers are potentials because the *ex post* realisation of any multiplier effect in any country cannot be accurately predicted by any model. It should be remarked here, too, that the alternative allocation of quantities and relative prices are also a potential; this is so because even in the most free market economies, there are deviations between the assumptions of a CGE model and the real situation. And what we study then is a comparison among potentials representing opposite poles.

In the centrally planned economy simulation case, each type of exogenous shock leads to smooth adjustments of other magnitudes. Increasing government demand for services is met by, in a sense, costless growth of output of services and all backward-linked activities. The costless adjustments mean here that the central planner is able to enlarge the production capacities of the sectors according to their needs through investment and employment policy. Thus no bottlenecks emerge. Higher output generates higher incomes of factors and then higher incomes of factor owners (institutions). Those incomes are spent on consumption and are saved/invested. Consumption and investment expenditures amplify the production effect of the initial injection. Prices are assumed not to change, which is consistent with no constraints on production capacities in the SAM model. The same mechanisms are at work in the second simulation when an additional government transfer to the lowest decile household group has been injected into economy. Higher incomes induce larger consumption and investment expenditures that are met by increasing output. As before, it is assumed that there are no rigidities hampering the adjustment of supply to the growing demand. Thus, prices do not change.

We have a quite different situation in the case of free market economy simulations. The economy adjusts to exogenous shocks by both quantity and price movements. However, because the economy is in market-clearing equilibrium in the benchmark period, total endowments of labour and capital are used at full capacity already. This implies that there is no opportunity for a general increase in production and income. Price changes can only generate a redistribution of income and production over the different actors in the economy. In this process the exchange rate plays an important role. Because the increase in the government budget deficit elicits an additional inflow of foreign capital, the exchange rate decreases and thus changes the terms of trade in favour of the home country.

The apparent effect of fixed factor supplies in the flexible price experiments is that government injections lead to levels of production that are lower than the levels that are realised in a fixed-price context. In Hungary the export-oriented activities, such as agriculture as well as light and heavy industry, are performing much worse than under a fixed-price regime. Similar results are found for Poland. These results can be attributed to the large exchange-rate changes, which lead to a deterioration of the competitive position of domestic exporters.

While in Hungary under the flexible-price regime the production level of construction and services also lies below the level realised under a fixed-price regime, in Poland this is not always the case. Depending on the year and the type of government injection, the production level in construction and services can be higher in the flexible-price situation. This somewhat surprising effect is caused by the relatively strong linkage of these activities to investment and consumption and by the high levels of the categories of demand due to high institutional income levels.

This brings us to another interesting outcome, namely that the impact of government injections on household income is larger in a flexible-price economy than in a fixed-price economy. This is found in all experiments, both for Hungary and Poland. The reason for this is that in the flexible-price economy the impact of the increase in domestic prices resulting from the impossibility to increase domestic output is outweighed by the impact of the decrease in foreign prices resulting from the appreciation of the domestic currency.

Of course, both Poland and Hungary have recently reoriented themselves appreciably towards a market economy. The representation of these centrally planned economies by means of a fixed-price regime as in the SAM model is now losing relevance. Furthermore, an instantaneous shift of regimes from planning to market will bring with it changes in technology, returns and so forth, which are not fully reflected in the specification of a CGE model based on current data. The CGE parameters are derived under the assumption that in the benchmark period the economy is a market economy that is in equilibrium. However, if the assumptions of the benchmark period do not hold, as is the case for an economy in transition, this means that parameters are misspecified. Consequently, the effects of simulated government measures, which depend on the model parameters, may not be interpreted as quantitative indicators of effects that will materialise when the economy has reached the stage of a free market economy.

Under these circumstances, what is obtained under the SAM and CGE specifications should be seen to represent the functioning of the economy under different rules of the game, and as such gives an insight into old and new mechanisms by which exogenous injections realise their quantity and price impacts.

Chapter 5

SAM Analysis for the Netherlands

1. Introduction

It can be restated for convenience that the idea of a social accounting matrix (SAM) goes back to Quesney's work on Tableau Economique in 1758. Hicks used the term social accounting in 1942. In the framework of revisions of the system of national accounts statistics, initiated by United Nations, Stone concretised the SAM framework in 1947. Several associates of Stone, working in the context of developing countries, and led by Pyatt, presented a first comprehensive publication on the SAM, for Sri Lanka, cf. Pyatt and Roe (1977), Since then, there are now SAMs for about 40 developing countries, but only for a couple of industrial countries, cf. Cohen (1986).

The case for the construction and use of social accounting matrices in the context of the developing world is based on several arguments. First, it is a convenient way of systematising related data from diversified sources on production, income and expenditure, and therefore, it is an efficient tool for directing attention to data gaps, ignored interactions, significant linkages, etc.; and there are significant data gaps in the development context. Second, the SAM can be seen as a modular analytical framework with different blocks of SAM representing the different modular components. The availability of a SAM facilitates, therefore, the solid construction and calibration of economy-wide models. Third, the structure of the economy and the changes that occur in it are made more transparent in a SAM framework. Fourth, the transactions in the SAM can be conceived to represent the functioning of the economy in the short run, and therefore, the SAM can be utilised for consistency checks and commodity balances and for an analysis of multiplier properties of an economy over time. Especially in the context of developing countries, the SAM has demonstrated its ability to analyse the underlying growth and equity properties of these economies.

The case for constructing and using SAMs for industrial countries is based more or less on the same arguments as for developing countries. There are more arguments, though. The trade-off between growth and distribution, coupled with a growing share of the population that is converted to non-earners, are major issues of concern in industrial economies. These issues raise questions as to how state policies can be effectively used to minimise the trade-off. The SAM framework is suited for the treatment of these issues and questions.

We go along the task of applying the SAM for industrial economies in the following way. In section 2 the conceptual framework of the SAM is briefly introduced and tabulated for the Netherlands. In section 3 the SAM is considered as if it is a set of equations which models the Dutch economy in a consistent but static way. The matrix is then put to an analysis of multipliers, thereby permitting the investigation of the structural properties of the Dutch economy. In section 4 the multipliers are decomposed in various effects and analysed. In section 5 additional remarks are made on the elaboration of the SAM in connection with a micro to macro accounting and modelling system for the Netherlands.

2. Structure and Construction of the SAM

In the circular flow of the national economy it was noted that in the lower bound, *households* supply labour and capital to *firms* who are organisers of *production activities (i.e.* sectors); households are also paid back for the use of their labour and capital factors. In the upper bound, households spend their incomes on products that are delivered by the firms/activities. In the centre are a government and the social insurance system, which are involved in transfers to and from households and firms/activities. Furthermore, there are the economic relations between the country and the rest of the world.

It was also remarked that the SAM is nothing more or less than the transformation of the circular flow into a matrix of transactions between the various agents, such a matrix is in table 5.1. In the rows of such a matrix we find: (1) the products account, (2) and (3) the factors account, consisting of labour income and other income from profit, interest, etc., (4) to (8) the institutions current account for respectively households, firms, government, and social insurance, as well as one aggregate institutional capital account, (9) the activities account, and (10) the rest of the world account. The columns are ordered similarly. Transactions between these actors take place at the filled cells and in correspondence with the circular flow. A particular row gives receipts of the actor while column-wise we read the expenditure of the actor. For example, row 9 is equivalent to the sum total of the input-output table, giving from left to right receipts of the production activities from final consumption, final investment, intermediate deliveries and exports to rest of world. Column 10 gives the expenditure of rest of world - or receipts for the Netherlands - in the form of income from abroad, and, respectively, negative foreign capital income, household transfers, government transfers and social insurance transfers; a positive foreign capital inflow in the 8th row, of 2370 mln. guilders, which is exceptional for 1978; and positive export and re-export balances in the 9th and 10th rows of 126002 and 6901 mln. guilders, respectively.

Table 5.1. The Social Accounting Matrix of the Netherlands, 1978
(in billion guilders)

	Receipts	Expenditures									Total
		1	2	3	4	5	6	7	8	9	10	
1	products				179.2		50.7	1.9				231.8
2	wages								0.3	172.5	0.1	172.9
3	profits									68.3	-0.4	67.8
4	households		133.4	47.7			13.8	58.3			-0.7	256.5
6	government	13.2		1.6	38.7	8.3			5.2	10.5	-0.6	76.8
7	social scrty		37.5	0.8	13.9		8.6				-0.4	60.5
8	capital				24.7	9.3	1.7	0.2		26.7	2.4	65.1
9	production	186.7							46.9	153.3	126.0	512.9
0	Rest world	31.9							12.8	81.6	6.9	133.2
	Total	231.8	172.9	67.8	256.5	17.8	76.8	60.5	65.1	512.9	133.2	1595.2

Table 5.2. The Social Accounting Matrix of the Netherlands, 1978

	1	2	3	4	5	6	7	8	9	10	11	12	13	14	15	16
1. Food										1846	2536	2994	3546	3799	3803	4230
2. Rent										3028	3561	3933	4232	4674	5288	5332
3. Cloth.										679	909	1104	1343	1371	1630	1751
4. Health										881	1279	1637	1868	2081	2209	2440
5. Edc/trnsprt										1879	2219	2893	3459	4443	4908	5667
6. Other										67	53	127	131	149	272	236
7. Pub utilities																
8. Wages																
9. Profits																
10. 1e decile								1912	611							
11. 2e decile								2345	1063							
12. 3e decile								6931	2617							
13. 4e decile								9429	3405							
14. 5e decile								11641	3941							
15. 6e decile								13074	4717							
16. 7e decile								15981	5418							
17. 8e decile								18275	6142							
18. 9e decile								22042	7438							
19. 10e decile								34737	12305							
20. Firms									17800							
21. Government	1063	4714	875	2514	3755	233			1590	460	979	1669	2015	2475	3108	4029
22. Social insur.								37490	790	187	406	937	1187	1405	1530	1700
23. Capital										-177	1579	997	844	244	979	2249
24. Agriculture	2080															
25. Mining						10										
26. Lght industr	16816	1935	1703	924	7389	236										
27. Heavy indus		1494			1201	406										
28. Public util.		6512														
29. Construction		1018														
30. Trade etc.	16230	6621	4480	1528	11053											
31. Transport					4157											
32. Banking etc.		16234		2411	1575	600										
33. Service		801	242	15908	10071	457	52610									
34. Rest world	2015	12931	8494	-1275	9211	549										
Total	38204	52260	15794	22010	48412	2491	52610	173857	67837	8850	13521	16291	18625	20641	23727	27634

Table 5.2 (Continued)

	17	18	19	20	21	22	23	24	25	26	27	28	29	30	31	32	33	34	Total
1	4888	4808	5754																38204
2	6291	7038	8882																52259
3	2037	2156	2815																15795
4	2670	2974	3972																22011
5	6472	7435	9038																48413
6	272	372	813																2492
7					50700	1910													52610
8							310	2178	153	19424	20397	2304	15162	24419	13197	14704	60528	1080	173856
9								7858	255	16187	3578	2152	4624	1434	3404	8767	7095	-430	67838
10					2577	3819												-68	8851
11					2170	8009												-68	13519
12					1452	5359												-68	16291
13					1249	4609												-68	18624
14					1093	4033												-68	20640
15					1280	4725												-68	23728
16					1343	4955												-68	27629
17					1592	5877												-68	31818
18					2061	7606												-68	39079
19					1983	7318												-68	56275
20																			17800
21	5065	7022	11857	8300			5162	276	16	2967	-50	43	54	4484	-1691	2267	2182	405	77838
22	1874	2093	2530		8660													-340	60449
23	2249	5181	10613	9500	1679	230		1460	70	4960	2550	2010	850	2780	3940	4520	3531	2370	65123
24							584	928		15058				171	4		181	5516	24522
25							203	23		67	222		59				57	230	871
26							1369	7556	47	19743	2293	5753	2461	3602	962	706	3164	55275	131934
27							6901	254	30	2268	8190	422	5508	695	748	362	2004	33014	63497
28							658	627	39	1512	1011	354	259	964	304	264	1428	27	13959
29							28725	333	8	894	1049	138	8392	367	285	1671	2248	1887	47015
30							3579	1047	32	3847	1975	137	2010	2003	1089	356	1336	11094	68417
31							347	143	19	1054	551	42	517	6929	958	1098	1485	10683	27983
32							4543	394	16	2303	1857	96	738	2001	747	3175	1313	1807	39810
33							-92	250	13	970	521	97	149	373	328	635	5055	6469	94857
34							12834	1195	173	40680	19353	411	6232	5281	3708	1285	3250	6901	133228
Total	31818	39079	56274	17800	77839	60450	65123	24522	871	131934	63497	13959	47015	68417	27983	39810	94857	135308	

Note: Totals of each row and column are the same except for rounding. Totals of row and column 34 are slightly different due to residual errors and omissions.

Table 5.1 giving, thus, the aggregate SAM for the Netherlands in 1978 is exclusively constructed from the definite and published estimates of the national accounts for 1978, as found in the publication of the Dutch Central Bureau of Statistics, CBS (1982). The SAM has been disaggregated further into 7 products, 2 factors, 10 household groups classified by income deciles, firms, government, social insurance, an aggregate capital account, 10 production activities and rest of world account, together resulting in a matrix of 34 rows by 34 columns, as found in table 5.2.

The required data for disaggregating the SAM of table 5.1 into that of table 5.2 include: (a) the household budget survey as in CBS (1978. 1) for breaking up the household account into the ten income groups, specifying their incomes by source and expenditures by type of product, (b) the input-output table for disaggregating the production activities as in CBS (1978.2), and (c) an initial converter table for transforming a products classification into a sectoral classification.

The household budget survey provides distribution structures of receipts and expenditures by household groups. These are multiplied by the number of households and applied to the aggregate household account in table 5.1, to give the greater details of table 5.2.

Regarding the data in the input-output table these are converted to the standard industrial classification using CBS codes. The absolute values thus obtained fit directly within the disaggregated SAM.

The initial converter matrix between products and sectors referred to above was constructed in a preliminary way from the codes of the household budget survey, the input-output and the industrial classification, and later subjected to several adjustments to assure consistency of the grand totals of its rows and columns. The adjustments are obtained by applying the RAS method.

The recordings in the SAM reflect the fact that the household budget surveys do not consider income transfer between household groups, which is a limitation. It was also necessary to assume, for lack of data, that all household groups receive transfers from government and social insurance in the same proportion.

3. The SAM as a Static Model: Aggregate Multipliers

In the input-output analysis an endogenous vector of sectoral production, q, can be predicted from a matrix of input-output coefficients, L, and a vector of exogenous final demand, f, as in eq. (1).

$$q = Lq + f = (I-L)^{-1} f = M_1 f \tag{1}$$

where M_1 is the Leontief multiplier or, as we shall call them later in section 4, the transfer effects.

The SAM can be used similarly with the obvious difference that the SAM contains more variables and relationships. To transform the social accounting matrix into an economy-wide model along the above lines requires performing several steps.

First, the accounts of the SAM need to be subdivided into endogenous and exogenous and regrouped accordingly so that the exogenous accounts would fall to the right and bottom of the endogenous accounts.

The choice regarding subdivision into exogenous and endogenous variables can lead to lengthy discussions on alternative closure rules. Instead, we shall follow here an established convention, which coincides with the step-wise closure of demand models and assumes, initially, government and rest of world as exogenous. Because social insurance is predominantly under state control we take this account as exogenous as well. As a result, the endogenous accounts would count four categories:

1. Products, rows and columns 1 to 7,
2. Factor incomes, rows and columns 8 and 9,
3. Institutions of households and firms, rows and columns 10 to 20; and capital, row/column 22',
4. Sectoral activities, rows and columns 24 to 33.

These endogenous accounts form a 31 * 31 submatrix within the regrouped SAM, containing all the flows from exogenous accounts to endogenous accounts.

The outgoings of other accounts constitute a 31 * 3 submatrix to the right which contains flows of sectoral export and income transfers from the rest of the world, government and social insurance. These are exogenous outgoings and can be summed into one exogenous vector.

To the bottom of the endogenous accounts is a submatrix that contains the outgoings of the endogenous accounts into the other accounts, *i.e.*

imports, taxes, and levies. These residual balances need not be treated further here.

Of course, there can be reasons for transforming some of the exogenous into endogenous variables in a step-wise fashion. For example, social insurance can be endogenised. This will be a logical step if the transactions and control in this account would occur mainly in the private market.

Secondly, the flows in the endogenous accounts need to be expressed as average propensities of their corresponding column totals. Thus each flow in the 31 * 31 matrix is divided by its respective column total to give the matrix of average propensities, denoted by A.

Table 5.3. SAM in the Form of $A_y + x = y$

Expenditures / Receipts Endogenous	Endogenous accounts y				Exogenous account x	Totals
	1.Wants	2.Factors	3.Institutions	4.Activities	Government, capital and rest of the world	
1. Wants			A_{13}		x_1	y_1
2. Factors				A_{24}	x_2	y_2
3. Institutions		A_{32}	A_{33}		x_3	y_3
4. Activities	A_{41}			A_{44}	x_4	y_4
Exogenous	Residual		balances			
Totals	y_1	y_2	y_3	y_4		

As a result of the above manipulations the SAM takes the form of table 5.3. The row totals of the endogenous accounts, i.e. the endogenous variables, are represented by the y vector; the exogenous variables are represented by the x vector. Note that the A matrix, which relates the y and x vectors to each other, appears in a partitioned form to facilitate a decomposition of the multipliers later in section 4.

The vector of endogenous variables y can now be solved from eq. (2)

$$y = Ay + x = (I-A)^{-1} x = M_a x \qquad (2)$$

where M_a is the aggregate multiplier matrix.

M_a is a matrix of 31*31. For reasons of space we shall select only a few parts of this matrix for comment. For instance, a distinction can be made between two types of exogenous impulses: demand injections into the activities account, x4, and transfer injections to the institutions account x_3. The impact of either injection can be traced on four types of variables: (1) expenditure by product, (2) earnings by factor, (3) income by household, and (4) output by activity, so that one can speak of expenditure multipliers, earning multipliers, income multipliers and output multipliers, as is shown in table 5.4. We shall ignore multiplier effects on the capital account, as these are indirectly processed in the output and income multipliers.

Table 5.4. Selected Multipliers for Further Analysis

Endogenous accounts y	Product accounts 1	Factor accounts 2	Exogenous impulse x = transfers to households (accounts 3, results in table 4.5)	Endogenous impulse x=injections to sectors (accounts 4, results in table 4.7)
product accounts 1	ns	ns	$M_{a,13}$	$M_{a,14}$
Factor accounts 2	ns	ns	$M_{a,23}$	$M_{a,24}$
income by households, accounts 3	ns	ns	$M_{a,33}$	$M_{a,34}$
Output by sectors, accounts 4	ns	ns	$M_{a,43}$	$M_{a,44}$

ns = not selected

The results can be studied now. Table 5.5 gives the multiplier effects of demand injections in a few selected activities on variables of expenditure $M_{a,14}$, earnings $M_{a,24}$, income $M_{a,34}$, and Output $M_{a,44}$. The selected sectors for the purpose of presentation are those of agriculture, industry, trade and other services, respectively. Later we shall deal with transfer injections.

The results of table 5.5 are obtained from the inversion of the SAM as explained in eq. (2). The results show that a demand injection in selected sectors, of say, one million guilders has a multiplier effect which ranges between 2.21 and 1.8 1, averaging about 1.95 million guilders.

Table 5.5. The Effects of Demand Impulses to Sectoral Activities: Aggregate Multiplier M_a for the Netherlands, 1978

Endogenous	24. Agriculture	27. Heavy Industry	30. Trade	33. Services
1 Food	0.096	0.082	0.108	0.128
2 Rent	0.131	0.112	0.147	0.174
3 Clothing/footwear	0.041	0.035	0.046	0.054
4 Health	0.057	0.048	0.064	0.075
5 Education transport	0.126	0.108	0.142	0.168
6 Private services	0.007	0.006	0.008	0.009
7 Public services	0.000	0.000	0.000	0.000
Total	0.458	0.390	0.515	0.608
8 Labour earnings	0.397	0.579	0.653	0.949
9 Profits etc	0.509	0.168	0.345	0.208
Total	0.907	0.747	0.997	1.158
10 First decile	0.007	0.005	0.007	0.007
11 Second decile	0.013	0.010	0.014	0.016
12 Third decile	0.036	0.030	0.039	0.046
13 Fourth decile	0.047	0.040	0.053	0.062
14 Fifth decile	0.056	0.049	0.064	0.076
15 Sixth decile	0.065	0.055	0.073	0.086
16 Seventh decile	0.077	0.067	0.088	0.104
17 Eighth decile	0.088	0.076	0.100	0.119
18 Ninth decile	0.107	0.092	0.121	0.144
19 Tenth decile	0.172	0.147	0.194	0.229
20 Firms	0.134	0.044	0.090	0.055
Total	0.803	0.616	0.844	0.944
24 Agriculture	1.110	0.025	0.035	0.036
25 Mining	0.002	0.004	0.000	0.001
26 Light Industry	0.540	0.171	0.220	0.219
27 Heavy Industry	0.047	1.172	0.042	0.058
28 Public Utilities	0.059	0.041	0.044	0.049
29 Construction	0.037	0.037	0.025	0.049
30 Trade	0.178	0.139	1.167	0.172
31 Transport	0.046	0.041	0.143	0.058
32 Banking	0.098	0.098	0.114	0.108
33 Services	0.095	0.079	0.098	1.163
Total	2.212	1.808	1.888	1.914

The averages for the multiplier effects on earnings, income and expenditure are 0.95, 0.81, and 0.49, respectively.

The sectoral injections have differentiated results, however. While a unit injection in agriculture generates higher output multipliers than other sectors, injections in trade or in services overrate that of agriculture regarding earnings, income and expenditure multipliers. Industrial expansion is more uniform in its effects: industry has lowest multiplier effects on the output, earnings, income and expenditure accounts.

It is also significant to study how multiplier effects on a specific account, *i.e.* the output multiplier $M_{a,44'}$ distribute themselves on the constituents of that account, *i.e.* the individual sectors in the accounts denoted by 4. RDM gives such a Relative Distributive Measure, and it can be formulated to give sector on sector effects, $RDM_{44'}$, and sector on households effects $RDM_{34'}$, both of which are displayed in table 5.6.[1]

---

[1] The formula for sector on sector effects can be written as

$$RDM_{44'} = \frac{M_{a,44'} - d_{44'}}{\sum_4 M_{a,44'} - 1} \bigg/ \frac{Output_{4,0}}{\sum_4 Output_{4,0}}$$

where the individual multiplier effect of injections in accounts denoted by 4' on 4, $M_{a,44}$, is divided by the column sum of multipliers of accounts denoted by 4 after deducting the initial injection. Here $d_{44'}$ stands for the Kronecker symbol that equals 1 if 4=4' and 0 in other cases. The result is divided by the actual output share of sector in accounts 4 in year 0, *i.e.* the SAM of 1978. For values of $RDM_{44'} > 1$, < 1, and $= 1$, there are positive, negative and neutral redistributive effects. For instance, of $RDM=1$ means that sectoral injections would reproduce exactly the sectoral distribution pattern of the base year.

Similarly, a relative distributive measure for the multiplier effects of sectoral injections on institutional income $RDM_{34'}$ can be calculated as in eq. (4)

$$RDM_{34'} = \frac{M_{a,34'}}{\sum_3 M_{a,34'}} \bigg/ \frac{income_{3,0}}{\sum_3 income_{3,0}}$$

Values of $RDM_{34'} = 1$ mean that sectoral injections would reproduce exactly the become distribution pattern of the base year. A positive value for income group i would mean an increase in its income share relative to the base year, a negative value would mean a deterioration.

Table 5.6. Demand Impulse $RDM_{34'}$ and $RDM_{44'}$

	Distribution shares of income multiplier by institution and sector, excluding initial impulse				Initial Shares in SAM origin	RDM = columns 1,2,3,4 divided by column 5, respectively			
	Agrclt	Hvy Ind	Trade	Srvcs		Agrclt	Hvy Ind	Trade	Srvcs
1 decile	0.83	0.74	0.78	0.73	3.23	0.26	0.23	0.24	0.23
2 decile	1.67	1.70	1.69	1.71	4.93	0.34	0.35	0.34	0.35
3 decile	4.43	4.82	4.68	4.88	5.94	0,75	0.81	0.79	0.82
4 decile	5.89	6.50	6.27	6.59	6.79	0.87	0.96	0.92	0.97
5 decile	7.02	7.92	7.58	8.05	7.53	0.93	1.05	1.01	1.07
6 decile	8.16	9.01	8.69	9.14	8.65	0.94	1.04	1.00	1.06
7 decile	9.65	10.88	10.41	11.05	10.07	0.96	1.08	1.03	1.10
8 decile	10.98	12.42	11.88	12.62	11.60	0.95	1.07	1.02	1.09
9 decile	13.27	14.99	14.34	15.24	14.25	0.93	1.05	1.01	1.07
10 decile	21.46	23.85	22.96	24.20	20.52	1.05	1.16	1.12	1.18
Firms	16.65	7.16	10.72	5.79	6.49	2.57	1.10	1.65	0.89
Agriculture	9.04	3.15	3.99	3.93	4.78	1.89	0.66	0.83	0.82
Mining	0.13	0.54	0.05	0.13	0.17	0.78	3.15	0.27	0.74
Light indstry	44.60	21.16	24.73	23.93	25.72	1.73	0.82	0.96	0.93
Heavy indstry	3.87	21.29	4.68	6.39	12.38	0.31	1.72	0.38	0.52
Public Utilities	4.83	5.06	4.95	5.35	2.72	1.77	1.86	1.82	1.97
Construction	3.06	4.61	2.85	5.39	9.17	0.33	0.50	0.31	0.59
Trade	14.68	17.23	18.85	18.85	13.34	1.10	1.29	1.41	1.41
Transport	3.83	5.07	16.07	6.37	5.46	0.70	0.93	2.95	1.17
Banking	8.08	12.08	12.83	11.87	7.76	1.04	1.56	1.65	1.53
Services	7.87	9.80	11.00	17.79	18.50	0.43	0.53	0.59	0.96

Note: $RDM_{34'}$ = 1.0, all other nine deciles have an effect lower than 1.0.

Taking first the effect of sectoral injections on sectoral distribution of output it is noted that for all sectoral injections there is a highly positive growth bias towards the sector of utilities, the value of $RDM_{44'}$ being between 1.77 and 1.97. In contrast, the results show a negative growth bias for the sector of construction. The results also show significant reallocation effects such as those of RDM of industry on mining, reaching 3.15, and RDM of trade on transport, reaching 2.95. These redistribution effects are understandable in view of the concentrated backward and forward linkages between industry and mining, and between trade and transport, respectively.

Considering the effects of sectoral injections on income distribution, $RDM_{34'}$ the results show injections in agriculture to be extremely regressive in their income effects. The households representing lower income deciles experience RDM below unity, the richest decile is unaffected, while most benefits go to firms with an RDM of 2.57. The tendency for regressive income effects is also apparent for other sectoral injections but in a less pronounced manner: the income is below unity for deciles 1 to 4 and above unity for deciles 5 to 10.

Table 5.7 treats another type of multiplier: the effects of transfer injections to household groups. The table shows such multipliers for the selected cases of transfer injections to the first, fourth, seventh and tenth income decile household group. The effects of a unit transfer leads to an increment in output averaging about 1.0; this can be compared to the case of demand injections where the average was about 2.0. However, it is transfer injections that lead to higher income and expenditure multipliers, and not demand injections. Table 5.7 shows, furthermore, that transfer injections to lower deciles have higher multiplier effects on all accounts and, therefore, more national growth and income, than the case of transfer injections to upper deciles.

To study the redistribution effect of transfer injections to alternative deciles on the sectoral compositions of output and on the distribution of income, we need another set of defined $RDMs$.[2] These are quantified in table 5.8. Alternative transfers influence the distribution of output on sectors in the same way (a growth bias towards S131 sectors 4, 6 and 8, $RDM_{43'} > 1.7$). Similarly, the distribution of income is affected in the same way (an income bias against deciles 1 to 4).

---

[2] The formulas of RDM for household income transfers:

$$RDM_{33''} = \frac{\left(M_{a,33''} - d_{33''}\right)}{\left(\sum_3 M_{a,33''} - 1\right)} / \frac{Income_{3,0}}{\sum_3 Income_{3,0}}$$

$$RDM_{43''} = \frac{M_{a,43''}}{\sum_4 M_{a,43''}} / \frac{Output_{4,0}}{\sum_4 Output_{4,}}$$

Table 5.7. Transfer Impulses: Aggregate Multiplier M_a, the Netherlands 1978

Endogenous	1 decile	4 decile	7 decile	10 decile
Food	0.280	0.251	0.208	0.145
Rent	0.440	0.309	0.267	0.216
Clothing, footwear	0.107	0.097	0.086	0.068
Health	0.142	0.136	0.120	0.096
Education, transport	0.306	0.265	0.277	0.216
Private services	0.013	0.011	0.012	0.017
Public services	0.000	0.000	0.000	0.000
Total	1.287	1.069	0.971	0.758
F8 Labour earnings	0.445	0.376	0.343	0.268
F9 Profits etc.	0.213	0.177	0.158	0.122
Total	0.657	0.553	0.502	0.390
1 decile	1.004	0.004	0.003	0.003
2 decile	0.009	0.008	0.007	0.006
3 decile	0.026	0.022	0.020	0.015
4 decile	0.035	1.029	0.027	0.021
5 decile	0.042	0.036	0.032	0.025
6 decile	0.048	0.041	0.037	0.029
7 decile	0.058	0.049	1.044	0.035
8 decile	0.066	0.056	0.051	0.039
9 decile	0.080	0.067	0.061	0.048
10 decile	0.128	0.108	0.098	1.076
Firms	0.056	0.046	0.042	0.032
Total	1.553	1.465	1.422	1.328
Agriculture	0.057	0.049	0.043	0.032
Mining	0.001	0.001	0.000	0.000
Light industry	0.336	0.288	0.256	0.191
Heavy industry	0.053	0.043	0.040	0.033
Public utilities	0.073	0.054	0.047	0.037
Construction	0.035	0.028	0.025	0.020
Trade	0.318	0.271	0.243	0.183
Transport	0.074	0.063	0.060	0.046
Banking	0.205	0.155	0.137	0.111
Services	0.197	0.179	0.169	0.134
Total	1.348	1.129	1.020	0.789

Table 5.8. Transfer Impulses: $RDM_{33'}$ and $RDM_{43'}$

	Distribution shares of income multiplier by institution and sector, excluding initial impulse				Initial Shares in SAM	RDM = columns 1, 2, 3, 4 divided by column 5, respectively			
	1 decile	4 decile	7 decile	10 decile	Original	1 decile	4 decile	7 decile	10 decile
1 decile	0.77	0.77	0.77	0.77	3.23	0.24	0.24	0.24	0.24
2 decile	1.69	1.69	1.69	1.69	4.93	0.34	0.34	0.34	0.34
3 decile	4.7	4.71	4.71	4.72	5.94	0.79	0.79	0.79	0.79
4 decile	6.31	6.32	6.33	6.33	6.79	0.93	0.93	0.93	0.93
5 decile	7.64	7.65	7.67	7.67	7.53	1.02	1.02	1.02	1.02
6 decile	8.75	8.76	8.77	8.78	8.65	1.01	1.01	1.01	1.01
7 decile	10.5	10.51	10.53	10.54	10.07	1.04	1.04	1.04	1.05
8 decile	11.97	11.99	12.01	12.02	11.6	1.03	1.03	1.04	1.04
9 decile	14.46	14.48	14.5	14.52	14.25	1.01	1.02	1.02	1.02
10 decile	12.12	23.15	23.17	23.2	20.52	1.13	1.13	1.13	1.13
Firms	10.09	9.97	9.85	9.76	6.49	1.55	1.54	1.52	1.5
Agriculture	4.22	4.38	4.22	4.01	4.78	0.88	0.92	0.88	0.84
Mining	0.05	0.05	0.05	0.05	0.17	0.27	0.28	0.28	0.31
Light ind	24.93	25.5	25.08	24.28	25.72	0.97	0.99	0.97	0.94
Heavy ind	3.93	3.78	3.89	4.13	12.38	0.32	0.31	0.31	0.33
Utilities	5.39	4.74	4.6	4.73	2.72	1.98	1.74	1.69	1.74
Construction	2.61	2.45	2.43	2.49	9.17	0.29	0.27	0.26	0.27
Trade	3.57	24	23.86	23.25	13.34	1.77	1.8	1.79	1.74
Transport	5.48	5.56	5.88	5.86	5.46	1	1.02	1.08	1.07
Banking	5.19	13.68	13.46	14.13	7.76	1.96	1.76	1.73	1.82
Services	14.63	15.86	16.53	17.05	18.5	0.79	0.86	0.89	0.92

Although an initial transfer to a certain decile increases initially this decile's income absolutely and relatively, the effect tends to vanish when the circular flow of the SAM is completed (from income to expenditure, to production, to earnings and income and back again and again). The inherent distributive properties of the system are shown to be generally regressive.

That, nevertheless, the actual income distribution in the Netherlands shows more equality than the SAM multipliers demonstrate is due to the positive effect of annually repeated initial injections to the poorest income deciles.

4. Decomposed Multipliers

The decomposition of the aggregate multipliers into meaningful effects will be the focus of this section. Recalling eq. (2), the aggregate multiplier matrix M_a in this equation can be decomposed into three multiplier matrices M_1, M_2, M_3, as in eq. (3) (see Appendix for derivation of the decomposition).

$$y = Ay + x = (I-A)^{-1}x = M_a x = M_3 M_2 M_3 x \tag{3}$$

In terms of the SAM, M_1, which is known as the transfer multiplier, captures intra effects resulting from transfers which happen between one variable and other variables belonging to the same endogenous account (*i.e.* effects of an impulse in a production activity on other production activities, or in other words, the Leontief multipliers). The open-loop effects M_2 capture the effects of one endogenous account on other endogenous accounts (*i.e.* from production to factor income to household income). The closed-loop effects M_3 ensure that an effect from a specific account is subjected to circular flows through all endogenous accounts (i.e. from household income to product consumption to production activities to factor income, and then to household income, and so on again and again through all four types of endogenous accounts). The transfer, closed-loop and open-loop effects are also known as intergroup, intragroup and cross-effects.

The understanding of the terms direct and indirect effects in the traditional output-input context may cause confusion in the SAM context. The following can be stated on terminology: tile transfer effects are the Leontief effects and they include both the direct and indirect effects in the limited sense and scope of the activities accounts. Similarly, the open-loop effects can be interpreted to include direct and indirect effects. However, the closed loop effects are exclusively indirect effects, but then in the broader sense of the whole SAM framework. The formal derivation of the decomposed multipliers is found in the Appendix.

We shall limit the presentation here to the decomposed impacts of exogenous demand injections in activities on activities, $M_{a,44}$, and comment briefly on the decomposition of other impacts.

The decomposition of $M_{a,44}$ in terms of the three effects is shown in eq. (4).

$$M_{a,44} = M_{3,44} * M_{2,44} * M_{1,44} \quad (4)$$
aggregate = closed *open *transfer

Since $M_{2,44}$ does not engage other accounts than its own account 4, the open loop effects are not applicable here; $M_{2,44}$ being an identity matrix as shown in the Appendix. The aggregate multiplier falls thus into the transfer effects (which are the Leontief multipliers), $M_{1,44}$ and the closed-loop effects, $M_{3,44}$.

Table 4.9 shows the average for $M_{a,44}$ to be 1.956. This is broken down into a transfer effect $M_{1,44}$ (Leontief effect) of 1.467, and a closed loop effect $M_{3,44}$ of 0.489, the open loop effect $M_{2,44}$ being non-existent here. The effects are derived from an additive formula which gives

$$M_a = I + (M_1 - I) + (M_2 - I)M_1 + (M_3 - I)M_2M_1 \quad (5)$$
= initial + transfer + open loop + closed loop

Table 5.9. Sectoral Injections: Decomposition of SAM Output Multipliers into Transfer and Closed Loop Effects (derived from the additive decomposition formula[d])

Key sectors	SAM multipliers, M_a		Transfer effects, M_1		closed loop effects	
	(a)	Rank	(b)	Rank	(c)	Rank
Agriculture	2.212	1	1.732	2	0.480	6
Mining	1.792	10	1.348	6	0.444	7
Light Industry	1.925	4	1.570	4	0.355	10
Heavy Industry	1.808	9	1.399	5	0.409	9
Public Utilities	2.208	3	1.786	1	0.422	8
Construction	2.163	2	1.648	3	0.515	5
Trade	1.888	6	1.348	7	0.540	3
Transport	1.812	8	1.273	10	0.539	4
Banking	1.833	7	1.292	8	0.541	2
Services	1.914	5	1.277	9	0.637	1
Average	1.956		1.467		0.489	

(a) = sum of multipliers
(b) = sum of multipliers $M_{a,44}$, known as the transfer effect or Leontief multiplier
(c) = (a)-(b), noting that the open loop effects are not applicable in this case

These results show transfer effects within the production activities to account for 75% of the overall economy-wide linkages. The closed-loop effects account for the remaining 25%. The closed loop effects stand for carrying the generated production increase through factor incomes, household incomes, product consumption and back to production activities in the form of final demand, and so on again and again. The results are evidence of the fact that the SAM includes significantly more linkages than the input-output matrix.

The same table shows sectors ranked according to the Leontief total column multipliers in the order of public utilities 1.79, agriculture 1.73, construction 1.65, lowest being transport 1.27. The contribution to production activity and their ranking are significantly different in the SAM total column multipliers: agriculture 2.21, construction 2.16, public utilities 2.21, the lowest being mining 1.79. Growth policy implications regarding activity demand would have been misleading in a structural analysis based on the Leontief framework as compared to a SAM framework. However, the results should not be interpreted to mean that if the country, for instance, would have expanded in the past relatively more in agriculture than in public utilities, it would have necessarily achieved a higher overall growth; for the multipliers have to be complemented by the exogenous expansion potential both domestically and in the rest of the world - denoted by x - for agriculture *versus* public utilities. Besides, both the SAM and the input-output emphasise the demand side of the economy and do not consider limits on the supply side sufficiently. Finally, it is important to note the shift in position of the sector of other services from the ninth in the input-output to the fifth in the SAM framework. Significant closed loop effects are tied to this sector.

As is well known, labour use and capital use per unit of additional production can be multiplied by the contribution to production activities to give the employment and investment effects. It is obvious that, given the above, the impacts of demand for alternative activities on the marginal use of labour and capital would be less meaningful when these impacts are derived from the partial framework of Leontief's transfer effects than when they are derived from a more general framework which incorporates SAM's aggregate effects.

The impact of exogenous institutional income transfers to institutions on institutional income can be decomposed along the same lines, as in eq. (6).

$$M_{a,33} = M_{3,33} * M_{2,33} * M_{1,33} \tag{6}$$
$$\text{Aggregate} = \text{closed} * \text{open} * \text{transfer}$$

The decomposition in eq. (6) is even simpler than in eq. (4). The transfer effect is absent for lack of data on transfers among household groups (see last paragraph of section 2), and the open-loop effect is not relevant in this context; as a result, the closed-loop effect is equal to the aggregate multiplier, which was discussed in the previous section.

The closed loop effects are behind the phenomenon that income redistribution injections, after rotating through the circular flow of the SAM, have a tendency to vanish and reproduce the initial situation. The expenditure patterns of the different household groups tend to benefit sectors, earnings and the households incomes themselves in very much the same ways.

It is now relevant and easier to consider the decomposition of the two other remaining multiplier effects: sectoral demand injections on household incomes, eq. (7), and household income transfer injections on sectoral production, eq. (8).

$$M_{a,34} = M_{3,33} * M_{2,34} * M_{1,44} \tag{7}$$

$$M_{a,43} = M_{4,44} * M_{2,43} * M_{1,33} \tag{8}$$

since the only two new effects not yet encountered are those of the open-loop, $M_{2,34}$ which links income effects to output effects, and $M_{2,43}$ which does the opposite.

In eq. (7) a production injection creates $M_{1,44}$ transfer effects (i.e. Leontief multiplier), carries these through $M_{2,34}$ open-loop effects, thereby creating household incomes, after which these household incomes are engaged in a circular flow through the whole system and back to incomes - i.e. the closed-loop effect of $M_{3,33}$.

In eq. (8), given that $M_{1,33}$ is not applicable, the transfer injections will be passed directly to sectoral activities through $M_{2,43}$ and from thereon subjected to a circular flow through $M_{3,44}$.

5. Concluding Remarks

It has been demonstrated that the SAM forms an appropriate framework for integrating various statistical sources and for studying the static properties of the economy and the decomposition of its multiplier effects.

There are various ways in which this analysis can be expanded. In the first place, the static nature of the SAM can be remedied by reproducing SAMs for later years. Because the household budget surveys for the Netherlands are available for 1978, 1981, 1984, and so on every three years, the SAM can be readily estimated up to the current year. In the next chapters we draw on applications of the SAM for later years. Secondly, although we report here on a 34 x 34 matrix, the available data would allow constructing a much more disaggregated SAM for the Netherlands except for a few missing data on transfer incomes, and the desirability of incorporating a socio-economic classification of household groups. Thirdly, there is a long list of possible refinements in particular as regards the factor accounts and the Dutch data suggest that it is feasible to incorporate many of them.

Regarding the SAM multipliers these have been determined under a specific set of exogenous variables and it will be instructive to apply the step-wise endogenisation of these exogenous variables referred to earlier. In this respect, the endogenisation of the transactions of social insurance can produce more progressive income multipliers than the results show so far. The sensitivity of the multipliers presented here is not unique and alternative decomposition can be investigated.

The classification and configuration of the SAM can be modified, when the data permits that, so as to fit for the study and appraisal of policy issues that are regularly encountered in an industrial economy. For instance, as will be done in the following chapters, it is feasible to modify the SAM framework to analyse regional imbalances and their effect on the growth and distribution of the whole economy; this is done in chapter 6. Urban dynamics that is mostly studied as an exclusively spatial phenomenon can be fruitfully examined in a circular flow model of the whole economy; this is done in chapter 7. The ageing problem in industrial economies and its economic consequences for expenditure, earnings and production patterns is another major issue that can be successfully examined in SAM frameworks, as will be shown in chapter 8.

Finally, if the SAM is to be used as a modular analytical framework complementary to its roles as a data system and a diagnostic tool - albeit static - the relationships among variables at a more micro level have to be specified in other manners than the fixed price form followed here. In this way the SAM can fulfil an important role in linking micro to macro models of economic systems. It is relevant to refer here to an ambitious study that applies a model that links the micro decision-making to the macro results and data in a SAM framework for the Netherlands, cf. Van Tongeren (1997).

Chapter 6

Inter-Temporal Analysis of Regional Multipliers

1. Introduction

The economics of regional differences in the Netherlands are regularly studied from different perspectives and within different analytical frameworks. Recent studies focus on respectively the regional growth and distribution of firms, and households, their interactions, and impact on the regional labour markets, and the evaluation and formulation of regional public policy. Although the Netherlands falls in 12 provinces, most analysis aggregates the provinces in the four regions of North, East, West and South. Most studies agree that the West, which is economically the most developed region, has been growing in recent years at lesser rates than the East and South, and that the North lags behind and is not in a position to catch up with the rest.

Kemper and Pellenbarg (1991, 1993) studied the spatial dynamics of firms in the Netherlands. They concluded that in spite of a greater mobility of firms in the West, yet on balance there was a movement of firms towards the East and the South. Meester (1994) discussed location preferences of firms in the Netherlands giving ground to expectations that economic activity in the West tends to decrease and the attraction of the East and the South as regions for the establishment of new firms tends to increase. As a result, a reduction of regional differences takes place.

On patterns of households, studies by Priemus et al., (1995) treating regional housing preferences come to the conclusion that when potential movers act according to their preferences (environmental quality, social contacts, costs etc.) then the northern, eastern and southern regions tend to grow at the expense of the West. At the same time, the studies point to a reduction in the regional differences of population growth in recent years, leading to a regional deconcentration of population. Government policy on the housing market, i.e. location of new building, is seen to be significant in the moving decisions of households. According to Priemus et al., congestion in the West has been leading to negative migration balances of households, resulting in the so-called "half-way zone"-Utrecht, Gelderland, Noord-Brabant- growing quicker than the West."

The regional structure and development of labour supply during the eighties and early nineties have been analysed in several studies. Although there is a tendency towards a lesser degree of regional differentiation regarding labour market characteristics, regional differences in labour market participation (age/sex) are substantial, cf. Laan (1991).

Regarding regional public policy the northern part of the country remains to be the main problem area. In the early eighties regional public policy distinguished between a dispersal policy (elimination of regional differences in income and unemployment based on arguments of equity) and a development policy (optimisation of the joint contributions of all regions to the gross national product based on arguments of efficiency). In the late eighties a new regional policy memorandum was released which postulated a shift from equity and solidarity to efficiency. Regions are urged now to utilise their possibilities and become responsible for their own economy. Attention is also shifting to specific sectors, cf. Delft (1995).

The studies mentioned above approach the problem of regional development using primarily frameworks that lay emphasis on the spatial settlement of business and households in the regional context. These studies pay less attention to the economy-wide linkages which couple activities, households and public policy to each other in the different regions. The objective of this chapter is to attack this shortcoming by modelling the economy-wide circular flow as a general equilibrium framework. This will allow treating economy-wide linkage effects and explore growth and distribution tendencies of changing regional patterns over an intermediate period of time. The actual regional configuration at any one time is considered to be the result of an interaction between internally structuring forces and externally intervening forces.

To that purpose, a social accounting matrix for the Netherlands, which distinguishes between the four regions, is inverted to give multiplier effects. Multipliers of the SAM are analysed to show the impact of various injections on the growth and distribution in the four regions in two different periods, namely 1981 and 1985.

The questions addressed are how can internal structuring forces and external intervening forces working together in the economy-wide circular flow, explain patterns of regional development? And when and where are the external intervening forces more significant than the internal structuring forces? The hypothesis that we pose is that while the external forces are statistically more significant than the internal forces in shaping regional development, the combination of the two forces is different for different regions.

The chapter falls into the six following sections. We first introduce the SAM as a framework of analysis in sections 2 and 3. Changing trends in regional multipliers are examined between 1981 and 1985 in section 4. The results of decomposition of changes in multipliers are discussed in section 5. Concluding remarks are added in section 6.

2. The SAM for Four Regions and Two Periods

We constructed SAMs with regional specifications for 1981 and 1985. The SAMs are disaggregated into 7 products, 2 factors, 8 institutional accounts consisting of four regional household groups of East, South, West and North, firms, government, social insurance, an aggregate capital account, 10 production activities, and the rest of the world. This results in a matrix of 28 rows by 28 columns.

It may be objected that the SAMs of 1981 and 1985 are not strictly comparable in real terms, since they are expressed in current process of their respective years. It is noted however that between 1981 and 1985 the Paasche price index values increased for the gross domestic product, for the consumption and for the investment expenditure, respectively with 3.6%, 3.9% and 2.8% per year. The price values by sector showed more variation. Given the narrow range within which prices of various categories moved between 1981 and 1985, a comparative analysis of the level of multipliers may not be handicapped if it is in current prices. In so far as the main concern of the analysis is a comparison of the growth and distribution patterns of the multiplier effects between two periods, it is legitimate and practical to treat each period in terms of its own set of prices.

3. The Analytical Framework of SAM Models and Multipliers

Assuming proportional relationships for the cells in terms of their column totals a SAM coefficient matrix is obtained which can be written as a model of the economy with the exogenous part on the right hand side and the endogenous part on the left hand side.

The exogenous variables in such a model are those of government expenditure and social insurance, that happens to be dominated by government transfers, and the rest of the world. The endogenous variables include production, income, consumption, and investment, among others.

The model considers the column totals of government expenditure and insurance transfers and rest of the world as exogenous variables x, appearing on right side of the equality side. d The columns of output by activity, product by activity, and disposition by factors, households, capital and firms are endogenous variables y, appearing on left side of the equality side. Furthermore, proportional relationships are assumed between individual cells and column totals, brought together in a coefficient matrix to be denoted by A. The system can be described in matrix form by $y - Ay = x$, solving gives

$$y = (I - A)^{-1} x = M_a x \tag{1}$$

where M_a is the aggregate multiplier matrix.

For reasons of space we shall select only a few parts of this matrix for comment. For instance, a distinction can be made between two origins of exogenous impulses: regional transfers to household groups, x_3, and sector injections, irrespective of whether they come forth from domestic or foreign demand sources, x_4. The impact of each impulse can be traced on four types of endogenous variables: expenditure by product, y_1; earnings by factor, y_2, income by regional households, y_3, and output by sector, y_4. One can thus speak of expenditure multipliers, earning multipliers, income multipliers and output multipliers. We are interested in the latter two. We shall thus limit our analysis to multipliers of regional transfers on output and income, and to the multipliers of sector injections on output and income. As a result, the analysis will be concerned with the four multiplier groups $M_{a,44'}$, $M_{a,34'}$ referring to sectoral injections in accounts group 4, and $M_{a,43'}$, $M_{a,33'}$ referring to regional transfers in accounts group 3, as described below.

Endogenous accounts y	Types of exogenous impulses x	
	Transfers to regional household accounts 3	Injections to sectoral accounts 4
3. income of regional household accounts 3	$M_{a,33'}$	$M_{a,34'}$
4. output by sectoral accounts 4	$M_{a,43'}$	$M_{a,44'}$

Besides studying the multipliers of regional transfers or sectoral injections, it is significant to study also the relative distribution of the multiplier effects on the various segments of the economy since this distribution pattern determines the future structure of the economy. A relative distributive measure of the effects of regional transfers on regional incomes is denoted by RDM_{33}'. Similarly, there is RDM_{43}' giving the effects of regional transfers on sectoral output[1]. Both concepts were discussed in the previous chapter. It is recalled that RDM is the quotient of the percentage distribution of the predicted individual multiplier effects on households (sectors) to the actual share of income of households (output of sectors) in the total household income (total sectoral output), and reflects therefore the long term income (output) growth bias of the economy. For values of $RDM < 1, > 1$ and $= 1$, there are positive, negative and neutral redistribution effects. Results will be reviewed in table 6.1.

In correspondence with the above, two types of RDM for sectoral demand injections can also be formulated, giving RDM_{44}', and RDM_{34}'. Results will be reviewed in table 6.2.[1]

Before examining the results it requires noting that the input-output and SAM models share together two common limiting features that should be given due consideration in interpreting results. First, that both models are basically demand representations of the economy, and second, by assuming fixed coefficients they display a static picture of the economy.

The first problem is that multiplier effects from these models do not consider the supply side. It is assumed that supply adjusts to demand, i.e. that there are no capacity restrictions that will obstruct the realisation of the potential multiplier effect. Accordingly, the role of investment in these models is confined to that of enhancing the purchase of capital goods, and not of adding to the productive capacity. Whether the potential multiplier effects of impulses will be realised in increased quantities in full or for a part disappear in incised relative prices depends on the elasticity of supply. If the size of the impulse is relatively small, which is usually the case, these multipliers can still be seen to represent realisable quantity effects with little leakage into price effects. It was suggested in a previous chapter that one could check whether the capacity limits would be violated or not. To repeat, the supply side can be simply modelled as a relationship between the investment rate and economic growth via an incremental capital output ratio κ, as in $K/Y = \kappa \ (\Delta Y/Y)$. From the SAM we obtain multiplier effects for K and Y. If division of the multiplier effects of K by those of Y gives values equal to or above K/Y for the base period then this implies that the SAM solves for sufficient investment to meet the projected

---

[1] See tables 6.1 and 6.2. (p. 115 and p. 117)

capacity increase. It is noted that multiplier results show that this condition is fulfilled for both years. In principle, similar checks can be applied to trace whether the base period equilibrium in the balance of payments and the government budget are reproduced by multiplier effects.

The second problem is that of assuming average fixed values for coefficients representing the propensities to consume and to use intermediate deliveries in the production process. This is a shortcoming. Compared to averages, working with marginal coefficients is better since dynamic effects are given due consideration. Moreover, fixed coefficients do not allow for substitution effects since the SAM qualified framework takes relative prices as given and assumes quantity adjustment. However, estimates of marginal coefficients may not be stable. We prefer to remedy the problem of fixed average coefficients in our context by repeating the SAM analysis for two periods. The differences in the obtained results over the two periods reflect the effects of changing average coefficients, which would include both the income and substitution effects.

4. Changes in Multipliers over Time

Tables 6.1 and 6.2 give for 1981 multipliers of the SAM and the *RDM* for regional transfers and sectoral injections, respectively. It is interesting to note from table 6.1 that irrespective of where the regional transfer takes place the income multiplier effect is about the same, namely 1.46 or 1.45. The percentage distribution of this effect on the four regions is exactly the same irrespective of where the transfer takes place.

There is a built-in general bias in regional transfers with a slight advantage to the west (*RDM = 1.01*) and a disadvantage to the north (*RDM = 0.95*). Regarding output multipliers, these amount to about 1.34 and their percentage distribution over the sectors vary slightly depending on the specific regional transfer i.e. agriculture, mining and light industry have highest shares in the south, trade and transport in the west and heavy industry in the east.

Table 6.1 gives selected multipliers of sectoral injections for 1981. These show an average income multiplier of 0.77, with an output multiplier of 2.27.

Table 6.1. Selected Multiplier Effects of Regional Transfers, $M_{a,33'}$ and $M_{a,43'}$, the Netherlands, 1981

	average for all transfers (1)	North (2)	East (3)	West (4)	South (5)	Actual (6)	RDM average (1)/(6)
Income multiplier $M_{a,33'}$	1.458	1.45	1.46	1.46	1.46		
% share							
North	11.13	11.13	11.13	11.13	11.13	11.69	.95
East	19.96	19.96	19.96	19.96	19.96	19.99	1.00
West	43.54	43.54	43.54	43.54	43.54	42.98	1.01
South	25.37	25.37	25.37	25.37	25.37	25.34	1.00
Total	100.0	100.00	100.00	100.00	100.00	100.00	
Output multiplier $M_{a,43'}$	1.34	1.33	1.34	1.34	1.35		
% share							
Agriculture	3.23	3.16	3.20	3.26	3.30	4.81	.67
Mining	2.81	2.82	2.78	2.75	2.91	4.40	.64
Light industry	17.53	17.17	17.37	17.59	17.99	24.44	.72
Heavy industry	6.19	6.37	6.36	6.20	5.82	11.65	.53
Public utilities	5.42	5.44	5.33	5.26	5.64	3.40	1.59
Construction	13.26	13.94	13.95	13.23	11.92	8.03	1.65
Trade	19.20	18.97	19.03	19.47	19.32	12.11	1.59
Transport	5.15	5.10	5.10	5.26	5.13	5.63	.91
Banking	13.88	14.00	13.68	13.57	14.26	7.77	1.79
Services	13.34	13.02	13.19	13.44	13.71	17.76	.75
Total	100.00	100.00	100.00	100.00	100.00	100.00	

Note to table 6.1. The formulas of RDM for regional transfers are below. See also footnotes 3 and 4 in chapter 5.

$$RDM_{33'} = \frac{M_{a,33'} - d_{33'}}{\sum_3 M_{a,33'} - 1} \bigg/ \frac{Income_{3,0}}{\sum_3 Income_{3,0}}$$

$$RDM_{43'} = \frac{M_{a,43'}}{\sum_4 M_{a,43'}} \bigg/ \frac{Output_{3,0}}{\sum_4 Output_{4,0}}$$

The *RDM* bias for the west and against the north is also noted here. An additional important piece of information is shown in the last column: there is a sectoral growth bias towards construction, public utilities, banking, mining and trade, all with *RDM* > *1,0* and a decline bias for services, agriculture, light and heavy industry.

Tables 6.1 and 6.2 for 1981 can now be compared with table 5.3 for 1985. It is noted that in 1981 a regional transfer of 1.0 million guilders (mg) has lead to an average income multiplier amounting to 1.458 mg and an output multiplier of 1.340 mg. In contrast, in 1985 a regional transfer of 1 mg will generate, on average, an income multiplier of 1.448 mg, which is less than 1% the value in 1981. The average output multiplier is 1.310, which is about 2% less than in 1981. Over the five-year period there is in fact only a slight deterioration of both multipliers, but is the relative change of the income effects distributed on the regional household groups and of the output effects on sectors of the same magnitude? For this purpose we shall compare the *RDM* indicators for 1985 with those of 1981.

Taking first the relative distribution of the income multiplier, we note an increase of the values of *RDM* for households in the north and in the south by 6.3% and 3.0%, respectively, accompanied with a reduction of *RDM* for households in the west and in the east by 3.0% and 1.0%, respectively. Given the fact that the north and south are economically less advanced than the west and east of the Netherlands, the obtained results show that the period of 1981-85 was characterised by tendencies in the economy towards correcting this regional imbalance. This can be explained by the fact that the shares of north and south in the actual income distribution during the period decreased, while those of east and west increased.

Taking next the relative distribution of the output multiplier on sectors of production in consideration, we see that there is much similarity between 1985 and 1981. In the Netherlands there is a growth bias towards four sectors: banking, construction, public utilities and trade, with values of RDM_{43}' in 1985 above 1.5. Except for trade, the other three sectors show in 1985 higher rates of its *RDM* than in 1981. The increases are modest and vary between 2.8% for banking and 4.4% for public utilities. The other sectors have a decline basis.

Table 6.2. Selected Multiplier Effects of Sectoral Injections, $M_{a,34'}$ and $M_{a,44'}$, the Netherlands, 1981

	average for all injections (1)	light industry (2)	heavy industry (3)	trade (4)	services (5)	actual (6)	RDM average (1)/(6)
Income multiplier $M_{a,34'}$	0.772	0.42	0.59	0.83	0.95		
% share							
North	11.16	11.14	11.11	11.14	11.10	11.69	0.95
East	19.93	19.96	19.99	19.95	20.00	19.99	1.00
West	43.58	43.54	43.49	43.55	43.48	42.98	1.01
South	25.33	25.37	25.41	25.36	25.43	25.34	1
Total	100	100	100	100	100	100	
Output multiplier $M_{a,44'}$	2.273	2.08	2.03	2.24	2.24		
% share							
Agriculture	4.16	15.24	2.37	3.03	3.03	4.81	0.86
Mining	6.35	4.88	0.93	2.87	3.12	4.40	1.44
Light industry	18.49	27.50	4.36	17.33	16.86	24.44	0.76
Heavy industry	9.24	6.30	9.05	6.93	8.00	11.65	0.59
Public utilities	5.07	4.77	5.81	5.55	6.04	3.40	1.49
Construction	16.51	10.73	4.00	14.01	15.48	8.03	2.06
Trade	14.46	12.2	4.99	15.82	15.82	12.11	1.19
Transport	5.63	3.66	4.67	12.76	5.53	5.63	1.00
Banking	11.32	8.63	12.39	12.62	12.19	7.77	1.46
Services	8.78	6.10	8.42	9.08	13.93	17.76	0.49
Total	100	100	100	100	100	100	

Note to table 6.2. The formulas of RDM for sectoral injections are below. see also footnotes 3 and 4 in chapter 5.

$$RDM_{44'} = \frac{M_{a,44'} - d_{44'}}{\sum_4 M_{a,44'} - 1} \bigg/ \frac{Output_{4,0}}{\sum_4 Output_{4,0}}$$

$$RDM_{34'} = \frac{M_{a,34'}}{\sum_3 M_{a,34'}} \bigg/ \frac{income_{3,0}}{\sum_3 income_{3,0}}$$

In 1985 heavy industry and agriculture are mostly disfavoured with values of *RDM* of 0.55 and 0.62; compared to 1981 there is a deterioration of 7.5% for agriculture and a small increase of 3.8% for heavy industry. In 1985, light industry and mining are also experiencing low *RDM* values of

0.68 and 0.75, but compared to 1981 for the first there is a reduction of 5.6% of its *RDM*, while for the latter there is a rise of 17.2%.

For a discussion of changes over time of multiplier effects of sectoral injections tables 6.3 and 6.4 can be compared. The latter table reports in columns 4 and 5 the average of all sectoral injections. The results also show slightly lower multiplier effects on income and output for 1985 as compared to 1981.

The tendencies that held over the five years for the distribution of income multiplier effects on regional household groups from sectoral injections are on the average similar to those described above for institutional transfers. The distribution of the output multiplier effects on sectors of production shows differences. In both years light industry and services are the most disfavoured sectors with *RDM* values in 1985 of 0.68 and 0.51 respectively. Agriculture and heavy industry are also characterised by a negative production bias, whereby the following qualification should be made: the position of heavy industry is improving over the considered period *(ΔRDM = 5.1%)*, while that of agriculture is getting worse *(ΔRDM = -10.5%)*. In 1985 the results show construction to have the highest positive growth bias followed by mining, public utilities and banking. The *RDM* values of public utilities and banking are in 1985 more or less the same as in 1981, but construction and mining are experiencing a gain, namely an increase in *RDM* values of 9.7% and 12.5%.

Summarising the effects of sectoral injections as compared to regional transfers, we can conclude that the income effects of both show the same growth pattern, but that the sectoral growth bias is somewhat different. In both cases banking, construction and public utilities are leading sectors, but the output effects of sectoral injections show revitalised growth prospects for mining in contrast to a weakening of the growth position of trade.

In the results for 1985 we did not consider the multiplier effects of household transfers to each region separately but we analysed, instead, the regional average. This is because the separate regional multipliers do not vary much in this effect from the case for 1981.[2]

---

[2] There is in fact only one exception, namely the smaller output effect of a regional transfer to household groups in the southern region on the construction sector is significantly lower than the average value for all regions.

Table 6.3. Selected Multiplier Effects of Regional Transfers, $M_{a,33'}$ and $M_{a,43'}$, and Sectoral Injections, $M_{a,34'}$ and $M_{a,44'}$, the Netherlands, 1985

	Actual	Average of all regional transfers		Average of all sectoral injections	
		Multiplier	RDM	Multiplier	RDM
Income multiplier		$M_{a,33'}$		$M_{a,34'}$	
Level		1.448		0.769	
Percentage distribution					
North	9.72	9.81	1.01	9.84	1.01
East	20.96	20.83	0.99	20.97	1.00
West	44.43	43.74	0.98	43.72	0.98
South	24.89	25.62	1.03	25.47	1.02
Total	100	100		100	
Output mutiplier		$M_{a,43'}$		$M_{a,44'}$	
Level		1.310		2.269	
Percentage distribution					
1. Agriculture	4.73	2.94	0.62	3.66	1.77
2. Mining	5.09	3.83	0.75	8.25	1.62
3. Light industry	24.71	16.84	0.68	16.84	0.68
4. Heavy industry	12.16	6.66	0.55	10.07	0.83
5. Public utilities	3.53	5.86	1.66	5.27	1.49
6. Construction	6.77	11.59	1.71	15.29	2.26
7. Trade	12.32	18.49	1.50	14.21	1.15
8. Transport	5.51	5.04	0.91	5.43	0.98
9. Banking	8.38	15.42	1.84	12.35	1.47
10. Services	16.79	13.32	0.79	8.63	0.51
Total	100	100		100	

5. Effect of Shifts in Multipliers of Past Performance

An analysis of SAM multipliers of the Netherlands for the period between 1978 and 1981, see previous chapter, showed diminishing multiplier effects over time for all the sectors (except for public utilities and banking). We see here once again in the later period between 1981 and 1985 diminishing multiplier effects over time for most of the sectors and regions. Exceptions are mining, heavy industry, public utilities, banking and households in the eastern part of the Netherlands with growing multiplier effects.

The diminishing multiplier effects coincide with increasing economic growth in the Netherlands between, 1978 and 1981, which was further accelerated between 1981 and 1985. The diminishing multiplier effects over time can be interpreted as a weakening of the endogenous circular flow mechanisms in the economy, i.e. the internal mechanisms, as the growth of the economy accelerates. This is in contrast to an increased dependence on the exogenous variables in influencing the course of the economy, i.e. the external mechanisms. The exogenous variables, it is recalled, are those of the government sector, social security, and the rest of the world. The hypothesis of a weakening of - internal - multiplier effects and an increased dependence of the economy on - external - exogenous variables with the occurrence of accumulated growth will be treated in this section.

The two SAMs for 1981 and 1985 allow a decomposition of the performance of the economy over time into the part that is due to changes in SAM multipliers and the part due to changes in exogenous variables.

Keeping in mind that we have solved the vector of endogenous variables y from the following eq. (8):

$$y = Ay + x = (I - A)^{-1} x = M_a x \qquad (8)$$

where M_s is the aggregate multiplier matrix and x is the vector of exogenous variables. Rewriting this equation for the two periods of 1981 and 1985 and subtracting gives the change in the endogenous variables, Δy, yields eq. (9).

$$\begin{aligned}
\Delta y &= y_{85} - y_{81} \\
&= M_{a.85} x_{85} - M_{a.81} x_{81} \\
&= M_{a.85} x_{85} - M_{a.85} x_{81} + M_{a.85} x_{81} - M_{a.81} x_{81} \\
&= M_{a.85} \Delta x + \Delta M_a x_{81}
\end{aligned} \qquad (9)$$

The change in endogenous variable Δy is decomposable into a change in exogenous variables (at constant SAM multipliers) and a change in SAM multipliers (at constant exogenous variables), as in end eq. (9).

Table 6.4 explains the changes in overall and sectoral output and in overall income and its distribution across the different household groups distributed by region in terms of the two terms in eq. (9). Results show that total income and total output respectively increased with 17.8% and 18.8%.

Table 6.4. An Explanation of Changes in Regional Income and Sector Output between 1981 and 1985 in terms of Changes in Exogenous Variables and SAM Multipliers, the Netherlands

	Changes in millions of current Dutch guilders						Percentages		
	Over-all	Due to multiplier	Due to Exogenous	Of which government	Of which social scrty	Of which rest world	Overall	Multiplier	Exogenous
	(1)	(2)	(3)	(4)	(5)	(6)	(7)	(8)	(9)
Regional income									
North	- 756	- 3068	2312	872	11316	2756	- 2.10	- 8.51	6.41
East	14521	1243	13728	3775	3635	5869	23.55	2.02	21.54
West	28874	- 688	29562	8422	8924	12216	21.78	- 0.52	22.30
South	12288	- 79	12367	3610	1633	7124	15.72	- 0.10	15.83
Total	54927	- 2593	57520	16680	12876	27964	17.81	- 0.84	18.65
Sectoral output									
Agriculture	5233	- 2270	7502	452	371	6681	6.64	- 7.22	23.86
Mining	10769	3960	6809	571	541	5697	37.44	13.77	23.67
Lght industry	32075	- 6575	38649	2463	2263	33923	20.09	- 4.12	24.21
Hvy industry	18270	2219	16051	149	1823	14078	24.01	2.92	21.09
Pblc util.	5191	854	4337	901	802	2634	23.36	3.84	19.52
Cnstrction	54	- 5077	5131	-429	3749	1811	0.10	- 9.68	9.78
Trade	6480	- 2570	19050	2401	2674	1975	20.83	- 3.25	24.07
Transport	6007	- 779	6786	735	733	5319	16.33	- 2.12	18.44
Banking	14315	4512	9803	2013	2246	5544	28.21	8.89	19.32
Services	14292	- 839	5131	6727	2001	6402	12.32	- 0.72	13.04
Total	122685	- 564	129250	15982	17204	96064	18.78	- 1.00	19.78

Note: (7) = (1)/value of variable in 1981. (8) = ((2)/(1)) X (7). (9) =((3)/(1)) X (7)

This is basically due to the exogenous change of 18.7% for total income and of 19.8% for total output, together with a minor decrease in the percentage change of the multiplier 0.8%, and 1.0%, respectively.

We can see from this table that during 1981-85 the income prospects of household groups living in the eastern part of the Netherlands were the best. Namely the growth rate of income in the eastern region amounted to 23.6% of 19.8% for total output, together with a minor decrease in the percentage change of the multiplier 0.8%, and 1.0%, respectively; as compared to a national average of 17.8%.

There is also a positive change in the multiplier effect over time of 2.0% as compared to negative changes in the multiplier effects for the other regions. There is also a positive change in the exogenous effect of 22% in favour of the east, as compared to a national average of 19%. In consequence, both the endogenous and exogenous forces have worked in favour of the eastern region during the period considered. In the northern part of the Netherlands economic activity is relatively low and so it is not surprising that together with a high degree of unemployment households in this region are in an unfavourable position. Total income decreased in 1981-85 by 2.1% that is due to deterioration in the multiplier value of 8.5% and to a modest increase of the exogenous stimulus of 6.4%. In the 1980s the Dutch government has tried to improve the income position of the northern region by enhancing the attractiveness of this area by giving settlement premiums to industries. Apparently this policy did not have the expected success. The endogenous circular flow located in the north of the economy works against northern growth; besides, the exogenous contribution to northern growth, at 6%, is less than that for national growth, at 19%.

Table 6.4 allows also for a decomposition of the exogenous stimulus by source of the government, social security and rest of the world. What are the consequences of the exogenous stimuli by source on regional growth in the period 1981/85? In the first place, all three exogenous impulses are particularly beneficial for households in the eastern/western and southern part of the Netherlands in the order of rest of the world, government and social security (in absolute amounts and in percentages). Further, it has been already mentioned that the change in exogenous stimulus of 6.4% for households in the north is quite modest and that counts for all three changes. Compared to other regions the region is much more dependent on foreign impulse. Government stimulus had some effect but the stimulus of social security lead to a deterioration of income of northern households (due to a lower average value of social security for 1985 in the budget survey).

What are the consequences of the exogenous stimuli on the economic activities? Realised growth of mining (37%) and banking (28%) are remarkably high as compared to low figures of services (12%) and construction (almost zero growth). The endogenous circular flow has favoured mining and banking as reflected in positive multiplier changes for mining (13.8%) and banking (8.9%). Also public utilities (3.8%) and heavy industry (2.9%) have benefited. For agriculture and construction we note the highest negative multiplier changes of -7.2% and -9.7%, respectively. The exogenous changes are positive for all sectors and have varied between 9.8% for construction and 24.2% for light industry. Table 6.4 shows once again that the stimulus to growth differ across sectors, with growth generally more dependent on exogenous than endogenous mechanisms.

With respect to exogenous stimulus by source the results indicate the relative importance of government stimulus for services and light industry, of social security for construction and trade, and the external world for light and heavy industry and trade. Roughly speaking these findings are in agreement with results for the period over 1978-81 reported upon in the previous chapter.[3]

Of course, the decomposition results in this chapter have ignored the effects of changing relative prices over time. Converting input-output matrices to constant prices of one basic year, not to mention the more difficult task of converting extended social accounting matrices, is a shortcoming that has been hardly resolved in the literature. What one can do to qualify the results, as will be shown in the next chapter, is that eqs. (9) and (10) be alternatively reformulated to give a decomposition of performance starting from a different base (year), for instance taking 1985 as base instead of 1981. This was done. It is comforting to note that the obtained results under the 1985 base do not differ in any significant ways from those where 1981 is the base, as reported here; implying that in the case at hand correction for relative changes in prices did not matter.

6. Concluding Remarks

In this chapter we compared the results obtained from two SAMs for the Netherlands, 1981 and 1985, in which we introduced households classified by four regions (north, east, west and south). It has been demonstrated that the SAM forms an appropriate framework for integrating various statistical

---

[3] One important exception is that the role of public utilities in 1978-81, as the sector with the highest growth potential and built-in endogenous growth has been taken over by mining in 1981-85. Banking maintains a stable second place.

sources and for studying the changes in structural properties of the economy over a medium period of time, and for the decomposition of such multiplier effects. For both SAMs a multiplier analysis was carried out to illustrate the effects of regional income transfers to households and of sectoral injections on the regional income distribution and output growth. The analysis was extended to a decomposition of regional income and growth patterns between 1981 and 1985. It was shown empirically for the country and periods concerned that the externally intervening forces gain in strength as compared to the internally structuring forces in determining the income growth of the four regions and the output growth of production sectors. It was shown further that growth and distribution mechanisms favoured the eastern region, while the northern region experienced negative growth bias in terms of both internal and external influencing forces.

Taking into account the working of the circular flow, the economic model employed here suggests that these regional tendencies go simultaneously with enhanced growth for the sectors of mining, banking and public utilities at the cost of light industry, construction and services. It needs emphasising that as the multiplier effects are assumed to be fully realised in quantity terms and without leakage into price increases, the SAM results are most meaningful in the short to medium periods in an economy in which inflationary tendencies are modest.

Chapter 7

Urban Dynamics and the Circular Flow in Industrial Economies

1. Introduction

In seeking a simplified way of looking at trends and changes in urban development, urban dynamics is usually described as a four stage cyclus: (1) Industrialisation occurs with major growth for the manufacturing sector, (2) the service sector and transport facilities grow, (3) increased appreciation for quality of life and the rise of what can be called an environmental sector, and (4) rise of the information sector. The cyclus is marked by spatial concentration at first, followed by a deconcentration later. The predictions of this urban dynamics model are accordingly described as structurally determined. The actual urban configuration at any one time is considered to be the result of an interaction between internally structuring forces and externally intervening forces.

Analysts isolate and study the underlying interactions and changes in different analytical frameworks ranging from the partial and more specific to the more general. Furthermore, while many frameworks emphasise the spatial dimension, others emphasise the sectoral. Our objectives are to present an analytical framework which focuses on the economy-wide circular flow and sectoral interactions, and demonstrate its usefulness for understanding recent changes in the urban development of the small and developed economy of the Netherlands.

Urbanisation studies for the Netherlands by Berg and Meer (1988) suggest that the Dutch urban system is in stage (3) of the cyclus. This stage is marked by spatial deconcentration, which means a shift of people and jobs from cores (central towns) to rings (surrounding suburban municipalities). Some features of this stage are a rapid rise in energy prices and a contraction of average family size, while public transport, town renovation and spatial planning are given more weight in government policy. The Dutch urban system saw a deconcentration of population that peaked in the early 1970s and has since then declined. There has been also a movement towards stage (4), in which we see a more balanced development of central towns and suburban areas (revitalisation or re-urbanisation policy), a widespread computerisation of society, increased attention to small-scale industry and a structural increase of leisure time.

More specifically, during the 1960s and early 1970s, a period with considerable economic growth, there was a strong emphasis in the Netherlands on suburbanisation, which led to the decline of cores and even of entire agglomerations. The introduction of growth towns in ring areas was important for the increasing population in the suburban municipalities. A change in the downward trend was observed at the end of the 1970s, which coincided, with the gloomy economic prospects of towering unemployment figures and weak (negative) economic growth. In the course of the 1980s, which are years of cautious recovery of the Dutch economy, there were once again tendencies towards a slight increase in deconcentration.

Policy studies by Berg (1987) show that in these years there was a change in the growth towns policy towards a different market-oriented policy aimed at consolidating the foundations of the competitive position of the agglomeration for which one would try to attract high-grade companies, high-income groups and tourists. The town is looked upon as an enterprise to be managed efficiently and whose continuity must be safeguarded. Evidence on the success of growth towns policy is mixed. In some instances, cities are not deconcentrating, in other instances city deconcentration is occurring.

The studies mentioned above approach the problem of urban dynamics and reach their conclusions using primarily frameworks that lay emphasis on the spatial settlement of households and business in different urbanisation levels. However, these studies pay no attention to the economy-wide linkages that couple activities and households at different levels of urbanisation. This is a disadvantage that we shall attempt to remedy by modelling the economy-wide circular flow as a general equilibrium framework. This will allow treating economy-wide linkage effects and explore growth and distributionary tendencies of changing urbanisation patterns over an intermediate period of time.

We shall attempt to give answers to several questions that were raised also in the previous chapter, though in a different context. For example, how can internal structuring forces and external intervening forces, working together in the economy-wide circular flow, explain the pattern of urban dynamics that occurred during the 1980s in the Netherlands? When and where were the external intervening forces more significant than the internal structuring forces? And what are the future prospects of both forces? Can it be concluded here as well that while the external forces are statistically more significant than the internal forces in shaping urban dynamics, the combination of the two forces is different for different urbanisation levels?

To that purpose we construct and analyse a social accounting matrix (SAM) of the Netherlands for two-periods. This SAM will distinguish between household groups classified by six urbanisation levels. For applications of SAM to comparative statistics, regional and interregional analysis see also Adelman, Taylor and Vogel (1988), and Round (1989).

The chapter focuses on the conversion of the SAM into a circular flow model. After introducing the construction and structure of the SAM, multipliers of the SAM circular flow model are analysed to show the impact of various injections on the growth of the six urbanisation levels in two different years namely 1981 and 1985. Finally, a decomposition of urban growth performance in terms of internal and external forces is done over the four years.

2. Structure and Construction of a SAM for the Netherlands

There are several options for the disaggregation of the SAM depending on available data and the purpose of the analysis, cf. Cohen and Tuyl (1991). The SAM in this chapter is classified into four sets of accounts: (1) products, falling into seven categories (2) factors, distinguishing between labour and capital (3) institutions, falling further into six household groups who receive and spend incomes. They are classified according to their residence by various degrees of urbanisation, which are denoted by the index h. The available statistics make the following classification feasible:

- rural municipalities (rm); with more than 20% of the labour force active in agriculture.
- urbanised rural municipalities (urm); with less than 20% of the labour force active in agriculture.
- dormitory towns (dt); with at least 30% non-residents.
- small towns (st); with 10.000 - 30.000 inhabitants.
- medium-sized towns (mst); with 50.000 - 100.000 inhabitants.
- large towns (lt); with more than 100.000 inhabitants, i.e. cities.

Table 7.1. The Social Accounting Matrix of the Netherlands 1981, (in mln. guilders)

	1	2	3	4	5	6	7	8	9	10	11	12	13	14	15
Products															
1. Food										2453	8373	4613	3314	7578	11539
2. Rent										3421	12309	6785	5032	10533	14840
3. Clothing										1004	3421	1998	1751	3132	4464
4. Health										2080	6192	3674	2645	6112	9527
5. Educ/trnsprt										3739	12161	8116	5333	12490	19061
6. Other										1344	3916	1572	1649	3344	3715
7. Public utility															
Factors															
8. Earnings															
9. Profits															
Institutions															
10. Rural mun								11646	4220						
11. Urb rl mun								35584	12672						
12. Dorm twns								23129	8502						
13. Small twns								14307	5159						
14. Mdm twns								29696	11496						
15. Large twns								40718	15770						
16. Firms								17960							
17. Government	1481	3347	1842	303	6636	1815			5010	2631	9272	6685	3891	9473	12198
18. Social insur								46560	940	1423	4438	2609	1859	3696	5555
19. Capital										1962	4170	3502	2167	6950	12730
Activities															
20. Agriculture	1792	12			832										
21. Mining	4				7										
22. Light indust	14942	4309	6234	1486	4845	507									
23. Heavy indus		820	25	104	1779	227									
24. PubUtilities		10117													
25. Construction		1217													
26. Trade	9659	5614	3757	2428	21842	1275									
27. Transport					5307										
28. Banking		21184	67		5123	1230									
29. Services		2272		21254	5424	5321	62750								
30. Rest World	9993	4029	3846	4655	9105	5165									
Total	37870	52920	15770	30230	60900	15540	62750	201640	81728	20057	64252	39554	27641	63308	93629

Key. 10. Rural municipalities. 11. Urbanised rural municipalities. 12. Dormitory towns. 13. Small towns. 14. Medium sized towns. 15. Large towns

Table 7.1 (Continued)

	16	17	18	19	20	21	22	23	24	25	26	27	28	29	30
Products															
1. Food															
2. Rent															
3. Clothing															
4. Health															
5. Educ/tmsprt															
6. Other															
7. Public utility		60100	2650												
Factors															
8. Earnings					2577	576	21456	23026	2612	16300	28591	15792	18899	71701	110
9. Profits					9583	24014	899	2441	2223	5487	15086	3655	10794	8616	-1070
Institutions															
10. Rural mun		948	3308												-65
11. Urb rl mun		3611	12601												-216
12. Dorm twns		1791	6250												-118
13. Small twns		1842	6430												-97
14. Mdm twns		4976	17366												-226
15. Large twns		8352	29145												-356
16. Firms															
17. Government	11100			5811	427	43	3234	-496	51	79	4596	-2132	2427	2824	-1378
18. Social insur		9850													-590
19. Capital	6860	-300	-1410		1970	930	5870	3350	2720	1190	3570	5090	6350	4577	-7756
Activities															
20. Agriculture				130	921	0	19133	0	0	0	189	7	0	238	8188
21. Mining				87	20	134	3639	710	9315	129	0	0	0	54	14665
22. Light indust				-1062	10047	53	22130	2241	1103	2533	4169	1388	965	4005	48634
23. Heavy indus				6256	287	243	2517	9413	527	5659	806	864	407	2403	43766
24. PubUtilities				810	1016	101	2638	1650	448	375	1533	544	439	2459	89
25. Construction				31849	349	105	835	1094	150	9581	364	327	2038	2818	1742
26. Trade				3544	1300	96	4953	2416	274	2169	2352	1291	444	1638	14079
27. Transport				467	176	253	1095	679	49	583	8288	1360	1377	1804	15353
28. Banking.				4452	532	124	2950	2509	113	781	2457	996	3823	1965	2436
29. Services				-287	319	17	1247	723	135	198	487	463	831	5880	8978
30. Rest World				12431	1918	2075	67076	26349	2499	7405	6644	7146	1948	5030	14928
Total	17960	91170	76340	64488	31442	28764	159672	76105	22219	52469	79132	36791	50743	116012	192241

Key. 10. Rural municipalities. 11. Urbanised rural municipalities. 12. Dormitory towns. 13. Small towns. 14. Medium sized towns. 15. Large towns

Table 7.2. The Social Accounting Matrix of the Netherlands 1985,
(in million guilders)

	1	2	3	4	5	6	7	8	9	10	11	12	13	14	15
1. Food										4596	9513	6124	4263	7317	10957
2. Rent										6208	13805	10332	6388	11209	16838
3. Clothing										1695	4132	2500	1813	2776	4094
4. Health										3599	7148	5280	3719	6126	9108
5. Educ,transport										6537	14327	10501	7858	12202	19005
6. Other										1564	3379	2756	1880	4338	3833
7. Public utility															
8. Earnings															
9. Profits															
10. Rural mun								18650	9193						
11. Urb rl mun								37193	16624						
12. Dorm twns								29186	13265						
13. Small twns								19293	10117						
14. Mdm twns								27423	15537						
15. Large twns								34347	19985						
16. Firms									33610						
17. Government	1979	4109	2141	403	8258	2234			2670	3695	7529	8296	4671	7111	11118
18. Social insur								50750	750	3989	7978	5361	3750	5832	8330
19. Capital										4872	4990	6417	4777	6374	10557
20. Agriculture	2053	11			955										
21. Mining	4				9										
22. Light industry	17144	4383	6818	1860	5366	603									
23. Heavy industr		699	24	98	1835	182									
24. PubUtilities		13455													
25. Construction		1232													
26. Trade	9542	5441	3589	3342	24374	1762									
27. Transport					6445										
28. Banking		28711	86		6295	1492									
29. Services		2263		22064	5837	9052	67670								
30. Rest World	12047	4475	4352	7212	11056	2424									
Total	42770	64780	17101	34980	70430	17750	67670	216842	121952	36755	72801	57567	29119	63285	93840

Key. 10. Rural municipalities. 11. Urbanised rural municipalities. 12. Dormitory towns. 13. Small towns. 14. Medium sized towns. 15. Large towns

Table 7.2 (Continued)

	16	17	18	19	20	21	22	23	24	25	26	27	28	29	30
1. Food															
2. Rent															
3. Clothing															
4. Health															
5. Educ,transport															
6. Other															
7. Public utility		64550	3120												
8. Earnings				3081	814	23300	24350	2662	14808	31231	17526	22350	76640		80
9. Profits				10911	33157	7457	7007	2687	4997	20899	5184	19092	9961		600
10. Rural mun		2527	6533												-149
11. Urb rl mun		5378	13903												-297
12. Dorm twns		4274	11049												-208
13. Small twns		2750	7108												-149
14. Mdm twns		5740	14838												-253
15. Large twns		11140	28799												-431
16. Firms															
17.Government	13060			6288	679	51	2346	269	62	49	698	-2917	1254	3574	-959
18. Social insrnc		2720													-730
19.Capital	20550	-5250	3380		2470	1350	6980	4060	3140	1410	4190	6490	7490	5287	-16790
20. Agriculture				-136	974		21779				203	12		259	10565
21. Mining				134	22	285	5280	740	15040	84				121	17814
22. Light industry				1445	10786	46	23952	2503	364	2185	4817	901	1044	4465	103065
23. Heavy industry				10053	351	276	3156	11968	704	5800	805	784	426	2931	54283
24. Public utilities				827	1503	120	2748	1781	435	381	1885	646	560	3052	17
25. Construction				30706	459	97	1026	1135	147	10131	326	278	2208	3273	1505
26. Trade etc.				5342	1632	126	6598	2803	129	2448	2792	1672	564	1981	21474
27. Transport etc.				461	202	256	1289	776	52	538	9552	1576	1669	2095	17887
28. Banking etc.				4890	670	143	4039	3369	136	943	3432	1201	4731	2447	2471
29. Service				-944	369	26	1801	1001	172	227	672	700	1169	7034	11189
30. Rest world				23678	2567	2786	79996	33151	1680	8522	8610	8745	2499	7184	24522
Total	33610	93830	88730	82744	36676	39533	191747	94375	27410	52523	95612	42798	65056	130304	245508

Key. 10. Rural municipalities. 11. Urbanised rural municipalities. 12. Dormitory towns.13. Small towns. 14. Medium sized towns. 15. Large towns

In addition to these there are the other institutional accounts belonging to firms, government, social insurance, and an aggregate capital account.

Finally, there is a fourth subset of accounts representing activities. This consists of 10 sectors of production activities, denoted by the index s, and the rest of the world. The result is a matrix of 30 rows by 30 columns, as seen in table 7.1.

The data required for the disaggregation include: (a) the household budget survey produced by the Dutch Central Bureau of Statistics in CBS/DBO 1981), in order to break up the household account into the 6 urbanisation groups, specifying their incomes by source and expenditures by type of product (the entries in the SAM reflect the fact that the household budget surveys do not consider income transfer between household groups, which is a limitation); (b) the input-output table, in order to disaggregate the production activities; and (c) an initial converter table, to transform a classification by products into a classification by sector. The same SAM has been constructed for 1985 at current prices of 1985, to give table 7.2.

In the following we want to sketch only a few characteristics of the changes which the household groups underwent during the period 1981/85. One interesting phenomenon is with regard to the variance and change in the average household size over the different urbanisation levels. In 1981 the size varied from 3.5 for households in the rural municipalities to 2.3 for households in the large towns. During the period 1981/85 we see for each urbanisation level a slight decrease of theaverage household size. The decrease in the household size is a general trend in the Netherlands and is predicted to continue partly due to ageing and partly to a preference by the young for the one-person household.

Several steps are required in converting the SAM into a model. First, a sub-division of the 30 x 30 SAM between endogenous, y, and exogenous, x, variables is required. We shall assume for a country like the Netherlands the columns of government expenditure, social insurance and rest of the world as exogenous. Why these three columns? Government behaviour cannot be explained in terms of demand and supply or utilisation and availability in the same sense as earnings and expenditure of households are explained economically, even though it is not denied that there are analytical advances in endogenising government behaviour.

Transfers under the social security system in the Netherlands are legally determined. They were considered in the 1970s to be a given constant. The height and coverage of social security payments have since then become controversial. Social security payments are very much the result of political pressures than economic motivations.

Finally, for a small open-economy country like the Netherlands, it is most realistic to consider the demand pattern of the rest of the world as exogenous.

By separating the influence of these three externally intervening forces from the rest of the economy, those are government expenditure, social security and exports; it becomes feasible to study the rest of the economy consisting of factors, households, firms and sectors, as an internally functioning economic structure. In a sense, the externally intervening forces are the impulses that drive the economy, while the internally functioning economic structure - via factor earnings, consumption and investment of households, and intersectoral relations of firms - give shape to the outcome.

As a result of the above exogenous assignments, variables belonging to the remaining 27 accounts are endogenous, x. These consist of variables of the seven product accounts, those of the two factor accounts, those of the current institutions account pertaining to six household types distinguished by urbanisation level, then those of the firms, the capital institution account and finally the ten sectoral activities.

After dividing the flows in the endogenous matrix are divided by their respective totals, columnwise, to give the matrix of average propensities, A, this can be inverted to give the SAM multiplier matrix M_a:

$$y = Ay + x = (I - A)^{-1} x = M_a x \tag{1}$$

This particular sub-division into exogenous and endogenous variables will allow the study of the multiplier effects of (a) exogenous institutional transfers to households by urbanisation level, and (b) exogenous sectoral injections. We shall be interested in tracing the effects of both exogenous impulses on the incomes of households located by urbanisation level, h, as well as the output effects on sectoral activities, s. Therefore, the portions of M_a in which we are primarily interested are denoted by $M_{a,hh'}$ and $M_{a,sh'}$ standing for the effects of income transfers to households h' on income of households h, and output by sector s; and $M_{a,hs'}$ and $M_{a,ss'}$ for the effects of demand injections in sector s' on incomes of households h and output by sector s, respectively.

3. Multiplier Effects

Besides the size of the multipliers it is interesting to know how the *predicted* income multiplier effect will be distributed on the households by residence, and how the *predicted* output multiplier effect will be distributed on the sectors of Production, these as compared to the actual distribution of income on households and actual distribution of output on sectors, respectively. We use for such a measure the Relative Distributive Measure (RDM), as defined in previous chapters. It is the quotient of the percentage distribution of the predicted individual multiplier effects on households (sectors) to the actual share of income of households (output of sectors) in the total household income (total sectoral output), and reflects therefore the long term income (output) growth bias of the economy. For values of RDM < 1, > 1 and = 1, there are positive, negative and neutral redistributive effects. For example, a predicted multiplier share of 27% and an actual share of 30% as far as household income of large towns is concerned gives a RDM of 0.87, which is an indication of a negative growth bias, as will be shown in table 6.4. In the next section we shall discuss to which direction the income and output growth patterns of institutional transfers and sectoral injections are biased in the Netherlands.

Table 6.3 gives average values of SAM multipliers for 1981 of institutional transfers and their relative distribution on households and sectors, $M_{a,hh'}$ and $M_{a,sh'}$, and similarly those of sectoral injections under $M_{a,hs'}$ and $M_{a,ss'}$.

It is interesting to note from table 7.3, second column, that irrespective of the urbanisation level to which institutional transfers take place, the generated income multiplier effect of one unit of transfer is about 1.45 units. Results, not taken in the table, cf. [9] show very little variance; namely between a low value of 1.44 in case of an injection to dormitory towns and a high value of 1.47 in case of an injection to large towns, cities.

The percentage distribution of the generated income multiplier effect shows cities to benefit most, 26%, and rural municipalities least 7%. Results, not taken in the table, show also that almost the same pattern of distribution of benefits on the six urbanisations is repeated irrespective of the urbanisation level to which the initial transfer is directed.

Table 7.3 shows in the fourth column a sectoral injection of 1.0 to generate an average income multiplier of 0.77, which is distributed on the urbanisation levels along the same above mentioned pattern.

Table 7.3. Average multiplier effects of institutional transfers, $M_{a,hh'}$ and $M_{a,sh'}$, and sectoral injections, $M_{a,hs'}$ and $M_{a,ss'}$, the Netherlands, 1981

	Actual	Average of all institutional transfers		Average of all sectoral injections	
		Multiplier	RDM	Multiplier	RDM
	(1)	(2)	(3) =(2)/(1)	(4)	(5) =(4)/(1)
Average income multiplier level		$M_{a,hh'}$ 1.457		$M_{a,hs'}$ 0.771	
% share					
Rural municipalities	6.50	7.45	1.15	7.43	1.14
Urban. rural mun.	20.83	22.65	1.09	22.57	1.08
Dormitory towns	12.82	14.85	1.16	14.84	1.16
Small towns	8.96	9.14	1.02	9.12	1.02
Medium towns	20.53	19.36	0.94	19.41	0.95
Large towns	30.36	26.54	0.87	26.62	0.88
Total	100.00	100.00		100.00	
Average output multiplier level		$M_{a,sh'}$ 1.333		$M_{a,ss'}$ 2.271	
% share					
Agriculture	4.81	3.25	0.68	4.16	0.86
Mining	4.40	2.82	0.64	6.36	1.44
Light industry	24.44	17.68	0.72	18.51	0.76
Heavy industry	11.65	6.08	0.52	9.22	0.79
Public utilities	3.40	5.43	1.60	5.08	1.49
Construction	8.03	12.84	1.60	16.44	2.05
Trade	12.11	19.30	1.59	14.46	1.19
Transport	5.63	5.17	0.92	5.63	1.00
Banking	7.77	13.90	1.79	11.34	1.46
Services	17.76	13.52	0.76	8.79	0.50
Total	100.00	100.00		100.00	

The table gives in the first column the actual distributions of household income by urbanisation level and output by sector. It is then possible to compute RDM, which is the division of the predicted share by the actual share. The results show that rural municipalities and dormitory towns are experiencing the highest growth bias with values of RDM of 1.15 and 1.16, respectively. Large towns are mostly disfavoured (RDM = 0.87). The results support the hypothesis of a built-in decline bias for large towns in favour of outskirts. More or less the same tendencies are obtained for multipliers and RDM relating to sectoral injections.

The lower part of the table gives results on output multipliers and their distribution on sectors. Results show a sectoral growth bias favourable to construction, public utilities, banking, mining and trade, all with RDM > 1.0 and an unfavourable bias for services, light and heavy industry. This would indicate a confirmation of the hypothesis that urban development in the Netherlands which has already passed cyclus stages 1 and 2, is during the eighties in stage 3 and approaching stage 4, which is consistent with [3].

The availability of the SAMs for 1981 and 1985 permits an investigation of how the above multiplier effects have changed, admittedly though, over a relatively short period of time. The analysis may be limited by the fact that both SAMs are in current prices. The extent of this limitation cannot be fully determined yet. In this respect It is comforting to know that between 1981 and 1985 the annual increases of the Paasche price indices for the categories of consumption, investment and the GDP were 3.9%, 2.8% and 3.6%, respectively which are low and reasonably close to each other.

Table 7.4 gives the SAM multipliers for 1985. It can be restated that in 1981 an institutional transfer of 1 million guilders (mg) has lead to an average income multiplier amounting to 1.457 mg and an output multiplier of 1.333 mg In contrast, in 1985 an institutional transfer of 1 m.g. would generate, on average, an income multiplier of 1.445 mg, which is 0.8% less than in 1981 and an output multiplier of 1.282, which is 3.8% less than in 1981.

Over the four years there has been in fact only a slight deterioration of both multipliers, but did the relative distribution of the income effects on the households and of the output effects on the sectors remain the same? For this purpose we shall compare the RDM indicators for 1985 with those of 1981.

Taking first the relative distribution of the income multiplier we note an increase of the values of RDM for households in small towns (from 1.02 to 1.09) and in middle sized towns (from 0.95 to 0.99); accompanied with a reduction of RDM for households in the other urbanisation's, particularly in the rural municipalities, dormitory towns and large towns, experiencing reductions of about 4%, 8%, and 4% respectively. The obtained results show that the period of 1981-85 was characterised by convergence tendencies in income growth bias of the various urbanisation levels, especially the decline bias for large towns appears to have been intensified, RDM declining from 0.88 to 0.84.

Taking next the relative distribution of the output multiplier on sectors of production, we see here that there is much similarity between 1985 and 1981. In the Netherlands there is a growth bias towards four sectors: banking, construction, public utilities and trade, with values of RDM in 1985 above 1.50. Except for trade, the other three sectors show in 1985 higher rates of its RDM than in 1981. The increases vary between 2.8% for banking and 6.9% for construction. The other sectors have a decline basis. In 1985 the urbanisation sectors of heavy industry and agriculture are mostly disfavoured with values of RDM of 0.55 and 0.62, (in 1981 these were 0.52 and 0.68). In 1985, light industry and mining are also experiencing low RDM values of 0.68 and 0.75, (in 1981 these were 0.72 and 0.64).

The noted growth and decline bias in the contexts of household incomes at urbanisation levels and sectoral output feed each other. Large towns with an income decline bias (RDM = 0.85) have relatively more of such sectors as light industry and services with RDM's of 0.68 and 0.51, respectively. The demands for these sectors are likewise more dependent on the prosperity of the large towns than other urbanisation levels.

It requires noting that the Keynesian, Leontief and SAM models share together the common feature that they are basically demand representations of the economy. The multiplier effects from these models do not consider the supply side. It is assumed that supply adjusts to demand i.e. there are no capacity restrictions that will obstruct the realisation of the potential multiplier effect. Accordingly, the role of investment in these models is confined to that of enhancing the purchase of capital goods, and not that of adding to the productive capacity. Whether the potential multiplier effects of impulses will be realised in increased quantities in full or in part depends on the elasticity of supply. If the size of the impulse is relatively small, which is usually the case, these multipliers can still be seen to represent realisable quantity effects with little leakage into price inflationary effects.

Table 7.4. Average multiplier effects of institutional transfers, $M_{a,hh'}$ and $M_{a,sh'}$, and sectoral injections, $M_{a,hs'}$ and $M_{a,ss'}$, the Netherlands, 1985

	Actual	Average of all institutional transfers		Average of all sectoral injections	
		Multiplier	RDM	Multiplier	RDM
	(1)	(2)	(3)=(2)/(1)	(4)	(5)=(4)/(1)
Average income multiplier level		$M_{a,hh'}$ 1.445		$M_{a,hs'}$ 0.780	
% share					
Rural municipalities	10.12	11.10	1.10	11.07	1.09
Urban. rural mun.	20.04	21.43	1.07	21.24	1.06
Dormitory towns	5.84	16.91	1.07	16.77	1.06
Small towns	10.77	11.73	1.09	11.75	1.09
Medium towns	17.42	17.15	0.98	17.27	0.99
Large towns	25.83	21.69	0.84	21.89	0.85
Total	100.00	100.00		100.00	
Average output multiplier level		$M_{a,sh'}$ 1.282		$M_{a,ss'}$ 2.269	
% share					
Agriculture	4.73	2.95	0.62	3.66	0.78
Mining	5.09	3.83	0.75	8.25	1.62
Light industry	24.71	16.85	0.68	16.85	0.68
Heavy industry	12.16	6.65	0.55	10.07	0.83
Public utilities	3.53	5.86	1.66	5.27	1.49
Construction	6.77	11.55	1.71	15.29	2.26
Trade	12.32	18.54	1.50	14.21	1.15
Transport	5.51	5.06	0.92	5.43	0.98
Banking	8.39	15.42	1.84	12.35	1.47
Services	16.79	13.30	0.79	8.63	0.51
Total	100.00	100.00		100.00	

4. Decomposition of Past Performance

SAM multipliers of the Netherlands for the periods 1978 and 1981 reported in [5], showed diminishing effects over time for all the sectors (except for public utilities and banking). We see once again in a later period between 1981 and 1985 diminishing multiplier effects over time for most of the sectors. Exceptions are mining, heavy industry, public utilities and banking. The situation for households is less clear because only three out of six urbanisation types show negative multiplier effects, namely household groups in the urbanised rural municipalities, middle sized towns and large towns.

The diminishing income and output multiplier effects between 1981 and 1985 can be interpreted as a weakening of the endogenous circular flow mechanisms in the economy.

Since the Netherlands has experienced some economic growth between 1978 and 1981 and still a greater economic growth between 1981 and 1985, there must have been during these years a strengthening of the positive exogenous effects so as to overcompensate for the weakened endogenous effects and produce the realised economic growth. This implies that there has been an increased dependence on the exogenous variables in influencing the course of the economy. The exogenous variables, it is recalled, are those of the government sector, social security, and the rest of the world. The hypothesis of a weakening of the internally structuring forces - the endogenous multiplier effects - and an increased dependence of the economy on externally intervening forces - exogenous effects - will be treated here.

The availability of the two SAMs for 1981 and 1985 allows a decomposition of the performance of the economy in the medium term into the part that is due to changes in SAM multipliers and the part due to changes in exogenous variables. This can be done along the same lines of the previous chapter.

Keeping in mind that we have solved the vector of endogenous variables y from eq. (2) where M_a is the aggregate multiplier matrix and x is the vector of exogenous variables.

$$y = Ay + x = (I - A)^{-1} x = M_a x \qquad (2)$$

Rewriting this equation for the two periods of 1981 and 1985 and subtracting 1981 from 1985 gives the change in the endogenous variables, Δy, and yielding eq. (3).

$$\begin{aligned}\Delta y &= y_{85} - y_{81} \\ &= M_{a,85} \, x_{85} - M_{a,81} \, x_{81}\end{aligned} \qquad (3)$$

Changes in the endogenous sector can be explained in terms of two effects: a change in the multiplier matrix and a change in the exogenous vector. The assumption of a zero value for one effect allows for measurement of the other effect. This is done by adding, subtracting and simplifying terms to give equation (4):

$$\Delta y = M_{a,85} x_{85} - M_{a,81} x_{81}$$
$$= M_{a,85} x_{85} - M_{a,85} x_{81} + M_{a,85} x_{81} - M_{a,81} x_{81}$$
$$= M_{a,85}\Delta x \quad + \quad \Delta M_a x_{81} \tag{4}$$

As a result, the change in an endogenous variable is decomposed into a change in exogenous variables at constant SAM multipliers, this being the first term inn eq. (4); and a change in SAM multipliers at constant exogenous variables, this being the second term in eq. (4).

Table 6.5 applies the above factorisation to the SAMs of 1981 and 1985 in an effort to explain the changes in overall and sectoral output and in overall income and its distribution across the different household groups distributed by urbanisation level. Results show that total income and total Output respectively increased with 17.8% and 18.8%. This is basically due to the exogenous change of 18.7% for total income and of 19.8% for total output, together with a minor decrease in the percentage change of the multiplier 0.8% resp. 1.0%.

We can see from table 7.5 that during 1981-85 the income performance of household groups living in the rural municipalities of the Netherlands was the best in spite of the previously observed unfavourable relative income distribution bias. Income growth of this urbanisation level amounted to 83.2% as compared to a national average of 17.8%. This is the result of a positive change in the Multiplier effect over time of 37.4% and an even higher positive change in the exogenous effect of 45.9% as compared to the national averages of -0.8% and 18.6% respectively. It can be asserted that both the endogenous and exogenous forces have worked in favour of the households in rural municipalities during the period considered.

Households in urbanised rural municipalities, middle sized towns and large towns experienced least favourable performance. Total income of middle sized towns decreased in 1981-85 by 0.03% that is due to a deterioration of the multiplier component of -8.2% and to an increase of the exogenous stimulus of 8.2%. Total income of households in large towns hardly changed in 1981-1985, a nominal growth of 0.23%, which is due to a deterioration of the multiplier component of -11.7% and an increase in the exogenous stimulus of 11.9%. Total income of households in urbanised rural municipalities increased by 13% consisting of a decline in the multiplier effect of -5% and a rise in the exogenous effect of households in urbanised rural municipalities increased by 13%, consisting of a decline in the multiplier effect of -5% and a rise in the exogenous effect of 18%.

Table 7.5. An Explanation of Changes in Urbanisation Income and Sectoral Output between 1981 and 1985 in terms of Changes in Exogenous Variables and SAM Multipliers, the Netherlands

	Changes in millions of current Dutch guilders						Percentages		
	over-all	Due to multi-plier	Due to exoge-nous	of which gvrnt	social security	rest of world	Over-all	Multi-plier	Exog-enous
	(1)	(2)	(3)	(4)	(5)	(6)	(7)	(8)	(9)
Urbanization income									
Rrl mun.	16695	7493	9202	2289	3857	3056	83.24	37.36	45.88
Urb Rrl Mnc	8550	-3065	11615	3148	2525	5942	13.31	-4.77	18.08
DrmTown	18011	4009	14002	3571	5763	4667	45.54	10.14	35.40
Small Town	11477	5196	6281	1655	1345	3281	41.52	18.80	22.72
Mdm Town	-22	-5189	5167	1849	-1554	4873	-0.03	-8.20	8.17
LargeTown	213	-10964	11178	4157	885	6135	0.23	-11.71	11.94
Total	54924	-2521	57444	16688	12821	27955	17.81	-0.82	18.62
Sectoral output									
Agriculture	5233	-2265	7498	451	367	6680	16.64	-7.20	23.85
Mining	10769	3962	6806	571	539	5696	37.44	13.77	23.66
Lght Indstry	32075	-6556	38631	2459	2250	33922	20.09	-4.11	24.19
Hvy Indstry	18270	2208	16062	154	1833	14075	24.01	2.90	21.10
Public Utlts	5191	859	4331	901	798	2632	23.36	3.86	19.49
Construction	54	-5122	5178	-416	3788	1805	0.10	-9.76	9.87
Trade	16480	-2503	18984	2389	2624	13970	20.83	-3.16	23.99
Transport	6007	-753	6760	730	714	5317	16.33	2.05	18.37
Banking	14315	4540	9773	2009	2225	5539	28.21	8.95	19.26
Services	14292	-774	15065	6714	1950	6401	12.32	-0.67	12.99
Total	122685	-6404	129088	15962	17088	96038	18.78	-0.98	19.76

Note: (7)= (1)/value of variable in 1981. (8)= ((2)/(1)) X (7). (9)= ((3)/(1)) X (7)

Summarising, we see that the endogenous multiplier effects work against the urbanised rural municipalities, middle-sized towns, and large towns, in that they show negative multiplier effects of -4.8, -8.2 and -11.7%, respectively. Furthermore, the contributions of the exogenous effects to overall growth at 18.1, 8.2 and 11.9 %, respectively, are also less than that for a national growth at 18.6%.

Table 7.5 also allows for a decomposition of the exogenous stimulus by source: namely, the government, social security and the rest of the world. What, then, are the consequences of the exogenous stimuli by source on urban growth in the period 1981/1985? In the first place, in absolute amounts, the exogenous stimuli of the *government* are particularly beneficial for households in large towns, dormitory towns and urbanised rural municipalities, who are clearly associated with public employment and related jobs. The exogenous stimuli of *social security* are found to favour dormitory towns, rural municipalities and urbanised rural municipalities, where, presumably, old-age pensioners live, while the exogenous stimuli of the *rest of the world* favour large towns, urbanised rural municipalities and middle-sized towns.

Realised growth of mining (37%) and banking (28%) are remarkably high as compared to low figures of services (12%) and construction (almost zero growth). The endogenous multiplier effects have favoured mining and banking as reflected in positive multiplier changes for mining (13.77%) and banking (8.95%). Further, public utilities (3.86%) and heavy industry (2.90%) have benefited. For agriculture and construction we note the highest negative multiplier changes of -7.20 and -9.76%, respectively. The exogenous changes are positive for all sectors and have varied between 9.87% for construction and 24.19% for light industry. Table 7.5 shows once again that the stimulus to growth differs across sectors, with growth generally more dependent on exogenous than endogenous mechanisms.

With respect to exogenous stimulus by source the results indicate the relative importance of government stimulus for services and light industry, of social security for construction and trade, and the external world for light and heavy industry and trade.

It must be kept in mind, however, that eq. (4) can alternatively be reformulated to give a decomposition of performance starting from a different base (year), as in eqn (5):

$$\Delta y = \Delta M_a x_{85} + M_{a,81} \Delta x \qquad (5)$$

A more general formula would be that of eq. (6).

$$\Delta y = \Delta M_a x_{81} + M_{a,81} \Delta x + \Delta M_a \Delta x \qquad (6)$$

However, the results obtained from application of eq. (5) do not vary much from those of eq (4) and, hence, to save space, are not reported here. The similarity of results in using eq (4) and (5) offers some evidence that selection of a base year, 1981 or 1985, for decomposition of past performance does not significantly influence the obtained results. Consequently, one can speculate that the results in this section may not have been much different if the SAMs were expressed in constant prices.

5. Concluding Remarks

From our work we suggest that insight can be gained by analysing growth patterns of urbanised levels within an economy-wide framework that gives justice to circular flow. In this paper, results on urban performance were obtained from two social accounting matrices (SAMs) for The Netherlands, one for 1981 and one for 1985.

Admittedly, this short period cannot succeed in distinguishing long trends, but when our results are taken together with similar results obtained for the period 1978-81 in a comparable context as was done in the previous chapter, they do indicate some very likely trends in the medium term.

In our SAMs, we introduced households classified by degree of urbanisation (rural municipalities, urbanised rural municipalities dormitory towns, small towns, medium-sized towns and large towns). The SAM is demonstrated to form an appropriate framework for integrating various statistical sources on regional development, and for studying the structural properties of the economy and intervening external forces in determining growth and distribution. It was shown empirically for the country and period concerned that the externally intervening forces gain in strength as compared to the internally structuring forces in determining the income growth of urbanisation levels and the output growth of production sectors. It was shown further that large towns and the services sector are experiencing negative growth bias in terms of both internal and external influencing forces.

Taking into account the working of the circular flow, the economic model employed here suggests that a deconcentration of cities towards towns, rural municipalities, dormitory towns and small towns goes simultaneously with enhanced growth for the sectors of mining, banking and public utilities at the cost of light industry, construction and services.

Chapter 8

Growth and Equity Effects of Demographic Change in Industrial Economies

1. Introduction

Demographic change is forecast to bring more differentiated forms of household composition in industrial countries. Although the need to explore the economic consequences of a changing demography has been felt by many economists such explorations still find themselves at an early stage. Most research in this area is concerned with formulating the problem rather than producing solid results on the economy-wide impact of demographic differentiation.

This chapter is written along the above lines and is meant to explore one line of research that has been proved efficient in the past. Using comparative statics it is possible to demonstrate the functioning of the economy under the present economic demographic situation and under a future simulated situation featuring a more differentiated demographic structure with a greater number of smaller households. The analytical framework chosen is that of general equilibrium that is made operational in the form of a social accounting matrix.

Several studies have attempted to trace the impact of changes in the demographic composition of the future population on specific variables of the economy. One elaborate study for the Netherlands is by Alessie and Kapteyn (1986); they estimate, test and apply for the year 2010 a (multi-period) expected utility maximisation model of the joint determination of savings and of consumer expenditures on seven different goods. By introducing demographic factors (size of the household and age of the head of the household) and with emphasis on the estimation of within period preferences consistent with inter-temporal two-stage budgeting under uncertainty they develop a method for estimating the lifecycle model.

Another study is for Austria by Chaloupek, Lamel and Richter (1988). They analyse the economic and social consequences of the change in population structure in the coming decennia. In quantifying the increased ageing process of the population they used two scenarios formulated for each of the four key variables (fertility, mortality, participation rate, number of persons per household). The important and relevant element in this study is the quantification of the effects of a changed age structure on employment, imports, final demand and total production for the year 2000. An input-output model for Austria provides the link between final demand and production levels by industry, and demand for primary factors of production, estimates of total output and value-added per sector, and demand for imports (by groups of commodities) are derived from it. About one-third of final demand represented by private and public consumption (health services, education and social services) was assumed to be directly affected by ageing. Richter et al. conclude that ageing will lead, generally speaking, to a lower level of economic activity, to a lower demand for imports and for labour and to some structural change in the pattern of industrial production.

An important study that raises many questions on the economic effects of population ageing is by Jackson (1987). In a Keynesian model allowing unemployment the outcomes of population ageing are more complex than the full capacity view. First, output is constrained by aggregate expenditure rather than by the size of the labour force. Second, there is uncertainty about the impact of ageing on both expenditure and productivity. An ageing population stimulates expenditure through transfer payments or reduced savings; but the impact on investment expenditure is likely to be contractionary. As regards productivity an older workforce is (perhaps) less productive, but slowing population growth and higher capital/labour ratios can be seen as raising productivity. Third, population ageing occurs at the same time as many structural changes. Even population growth may be partly endogenous, the overall position being highly intricate and the assumption of *ceteris paribus* absent in reality. Thus it is unclear whether population ageing has truly general consequences or whether its influence is specific to prevailing economic and social circumstances.

Typical of the Alessie and Kapteyn study is the loose-ended calculation of income and expenditure effects of the demographic changes. The calculations are not ploughed back in the economy. The study made by Richter et al. for Austria goes a step further than that by Alessie and Kapteyn by incorporating these effects within an input-output framework for the economy, while Jackson encounters other effects under conditions of factor unemployment and constrained demand. However, none of the three studies considers fully other mechanisms typical of the circular flow in a mature economy, such as effects from production to factor income to household income or effects from household income to product consumption to production activities to factor income. In this context the social accounting matrix framework provides a more comprehensive coverage of economic relationships.

Section 2 of this chapter will elaborate on a social accounting matrix of the Netherlands for 1981 that is suited for the dealing with the issue posed. Section 3 will reconstruct the SAM so as to correspond with a forecast of a more differentiated demographic structure for 2010. Section 4 will compare the basic figures in both SAMs. Section 5 contains the main thrust of the analysis: this section reports on a multiplier analysis of allocations and transfers in the two SAMs with the objective of throwing light on the changing properties of the economy under a changing demographic structure. The final section gives concluding remarks on limitations and adds suggestions for future research.

2. The Social Accounting Matrix for the Netherlands 1981

The SAM is an authentic reproduction of the circular flow, as depicted in figure 1 of Chapter 1, into a matrix form as in table 8.1. In the rows of such a matrix we find the products account, the factors account consisting of labour income and other income from profit and interest, the current account for households, firms, government and social insurance respectively, as well as one aggregate institutional capital account, and finally the activities account and rest of the world account. The columns are ordered similarly.

Transactions between these actors take place at the filled cells and in correspondence with the circular flow. A particular row gives the receipts of the actor while column-wise we read the expenditure of the actor. For example, in table 8.1 that displays the SAM for the Netherlands in 1981, row 9 is equivalent to the sum total of the input-output table, giving from left to right receipts of the production activities from final consumption, final investment, intermediate deliveries and exports to rest of the world. Column 10 gives the expenditure of rest of world, or receipts for the Netherlands, in the form of income from abroad (110), negative foreign capital income (-1070), household transfers (-1078), government transfers (-1378), social insurance transfers (-590), a negative foreign capital inflow (-7756); and positive export and re-export balances in the ninth and tenth rows of 189075 and 14928 million guilders, respectively. Table 8.1 is exclusively constructed from the definite and published estimates of the national accounts of the Netherlands for 1981. The SAM has been disaggregated further into seven products, two factors, six household groups classified by size (1, 2, 3, 4, 5, 6 and more persons), firms, government, social insurance, an aggregate capital account, ten production activities and ROW, together resulting in a matrix of 30 rows by 30 columns, as found in table 8.2.

The required data for disaggregating the SAM of table 8.1 into that of table 8.2 include:

(i) the household budget survey (known as DBO) and housing needs survey (known as WBO) for breaking up the household account into the six household size groups, specifying their incomes by source and expenditures by items CBS/DBO (1981) and CBS/WBO (1983);
(ii) the input-output table for disaggregating production activities as published by CBS;
(iii) an initial converter table for transforming a product classification into a sectoral classification

Table 8.1. The social accounting matrix of the Netherlands, 1981 (in billion guilders)

	1	2	3	4	5	6	7	8	9	10	Total
1 Products				213.2		60.1	2.7				276.0
2 Wages									201.5	.1	201.6
3 Profits									82.8	-1.1	81.7
4 Households		155.1	57.8			21.5	75.1			-1.1	308.0
5 Firms			18.0								18.0
6 Government		15.4	5.0	44.2	11.1			5.8	11.1	-1.4	91.2
7 Social insur		46.6	.9	19.6		9.9				-.6	76.3
8 Capital				31.5	6.9	-.3	-1.4		35.6	-7.8	64.5
9 Activity	223.8							46.2	206.9	189.1	666.0
10 Rest world	36.8							12.4	128.1	14.9	192.2
Total	276.0	201.6	81.7	308.4	18.0	91.1	76.3	64.5	666.0	192.2	1976.0

The reconciliation of household account statistics with national account statistics is done in three steps.

(i) first, call the average value of expenditure or income item i, per household size group h, as given in CBS/DBO (1981), W_{ih}, and the number of households by household size groups as given in WBO 1981, N_h. Multiplying and summing gives $\Sigma_h W_{ih} N_h$,

(ii) second, calculate an adjustment factor $α_I$ as the ratio of $\Sigma_h W_{ih}\, N_h$ to the corresponding value in the observed SAM of 1981, which value we call V_i for each item i.

(iii) third, the values of $W_{ih}\, N_h$ are divided by the adjustment factor $α_i$. In general, the values of $α_i$ were slightly above or below unity with two exceptions. First, profits due to households where the budget surveys give figures significantly higher than those from the national accounts, Accordingly, the budget survey data were scaled down to the national accounts. Second, government transfers where the budget surveys give significantly lower figures than national accounts. Here the budget survey data were rescaled upwards. As a result of these steps the observed subtotals of the rows and columns of the SAM 1981 are reproduced under a specification of households by size. The data in the input output table is converted to the standard industrial classification using CBS codes. The absolute values thus obtained fit directly within the disaggregated SAM. With the availability of data of final consumption expenditure of households by type of use and by origin (class of industry) it is possible to make a more reliable converter matrix between products and sectors for SAMs from 1980.

Table 8.2. The Disaggregated Social Accounting Matrix of the Netherlands, 1981 (in million guilders)

	1	2	3	4	5	6	7	8	9	10	11	12	13	14	15
1.Food										5204	12435	7322	11494	4940	3013
2.Rent										10009	20600	10867	16586	6280	3364
3.Clothing										1951	4630	3031	4582	1943	1377
4.Health										3439	8221	4842	6736	2880	1583
5.Education										7012	16056	8589	12981	5734	3102
6.Other services										193	495	524	790		263
7..Public Utilities															
8.Earnings															
9..Profits															
10.1 person hh								10893	5307						
11.2 person hh								17686	15767						
12.3 person hh								27302	9687						
13.4 person hh								49198	16561						
14.5 person hh								19879	6624						
15.6+ person hh								10123	3871						
16. Firm									17960						
17.Government	1199	6021	821	3110	4028	245			5010	4509	13415	6521	12651	4770	2284
18.Sosial insurance									940	1674	4908	3653	5753	2313	1279
19.Capital										4815	10924	4875	6463	3162	1241
20.Agriculture	1792	12			832										
21.Mining	4														
22.Light industry	15018	4385	6310	1562	4921	126									
23.Heavy industry		863	68	147	1821	57									
24.Public Utilities		10117													
25.Construction		1217													
26.Trade	9320	5762	3744	3534	21848	367									
27.Transport					5307										
28.Banking		21492	374		5430	306									
29.Services		6267		21255	5424	1326	62750								
30.Rest world	17075	11569	6197	-1907	3855										
Total	44408	67706	17514	22701	53474	2427	62750	201640	81728	38806	91684	50224	78036	32284	17406

Key: hh= household

Table 8.2 (Continued)

	16	17	18	19	20	21	22	23	24	25	26	27	28	29	30
1.Food															
2.Rent															
3.Clothing															
4.Health															
5.Education															
6.Other services															
7.Public Utilities		60100	2650												
8.Earnings					2577	576	21456	23026	2612	16300	28591	15792	18899	71701	110
9.Profits					9583	24014	899	2441	2223	5487	15086	3655	23458	-4048	-1070
10.1 person hh		5088	17755												-237
11.2 person hh		8587	29968												-324
12.3 person hh		2984	10413												-162
13.4 person hh		2785	9718												-226
14.5 person hh		1307	4560												-86
15.6+ person hh		769	2686												-43
16. Firm															
17.Government	11100			5811	427	43	1234	-496	51	79	4596	2132	2427	2824	-1378
18.Sosial insurance		9850													76340
19.Capital	6860	-300	-1410		1970	930	5870	3350	2720	1190	3570	5090	6350	4577	-7756
20.Agriculture				130	921		19131				189	7		238	8188
21.Mining				87	20	134	3639	710	9315	129				54	14665
22.Light indust				-1062	10047	53	22130	2341	1103	2533	4169	1388	965	4005	79777
23.Heavyidust				6 256	287	243	2 517	9413	527	5639	806	864	407	2403	43768
24.Public Util				810	1016	101	2638	1650	448	375	1533	544	439	2459	89
25.Construction				31 849	349	105	835	1094	150	9581	364	327	2038	2818	1742
26.Trade				3544	1300	96	4953	2416	274	2169	2352	1291	444	1638	14079
27.Transport				467	176	253	1095	679	49	583	8288	1360	1377	1804	15353
28.Banking				4452	532	124	2950	2509	113	781	2457	996	3823	14629	2436
29.Service				-287	319	17	1247	723	135	198	487	463	831	5880	8978
30.Rest world				12431	1918	2075	67076	26349	2499	7405	6 644		7146	1948	5030	14928
Total	117960	91170	76340	64 491	31442	28764	159672	76105	22219	52469	79132	36791	63406	116012	192241

Key: hh= household

3. SAM Reconstructed on the Basis of a Prospective Demographic Structure

To analyse the impact of a changing demographic structure on the economy we construct a hypothetical social accounting matrix that reflects a prospective demographic structure. The SAM for 1981 has been constructed on the basis of the demographic structure as found in the housing needs survey, CBS/WBO (1981), because there is no demographic survey of the Netherlands. The number of households by household size following CBS/WBO (1981) is found in table 8.3, first row.

Projections of the future composition of households by size groups for the Netherlands are scarce. One very plausible projection is that of a trend scenario for 2010 based on the official population forecasts of the CBS and on simulations by Nelissen and Vossen (1988) that gives the number of households distributed by size (see table 8.3, second row). Traditional demographic forecasts are mostly limited to applying the events of birth, marriage, divorce and migration to models determining household composition by means of the inappropriate headship rate method.

NEDYMAS (NEtherlands DYnamic Micro-Analysis Simulation model of Nelissen and Vossen (1988) is a micro-simulation model giving household forecasts for the Netherlands for the year 2010. This solves the consistency problems arising from traditional methods. The NEDYMAS model can be described as a dynamic cross section simulation model: every year the characteristics of all micro-units are adjusted or simulated. The population is represented by individual micro-data. All persons in the micro-simulation model are followed over time and individuals are grouped to obtain families and households by means of Monte Carlo simulation techniques. The model enables household structures at any given moment to be generated. The trend scenario is the result of applying a set of demographic trend projections carried out by the Dutch Central Bureau of Statistics, based on a conventional cohort component model. Within a simply conceptualised lifecycle, divided into five subsequent modules, 22 household formation and dissolution processes describe the transitions between five main household types (parental home, one-person households, marital family households, non-marital family households and one-parent households). In addition demographic key variables of fertility, mortality and migration are integrated and modelled to complete the household system. The results of the trend scenario must be considered as preliminary only, mainly because of the highly aggregated hypotheses used both in structuring the scenario and in applying the household theory.

Nevertheless it must be noted that the proportion of one-and two-person households will increase from 52%, in CBS/WBO (1981), to 77% in trend 2010 and we consequently see a decrease in the mean household size from 2.53 in 1981 to 1.96 in 2010. This persistent tendency towards individualisation is one of the most prominent societal features of this century.

Summarising the trend scenario the following may be stated. There is in particular a relative increase in one-person households. This increase is mainly concentrated in certain age groups. First, there are young people between 15 and 20 years, who will leave their parental homes at an earlier age. Second, there are middle-aged people between 50 and 65 years who will show a higher divorce rate and a lower remarrying rate. Third, there are very old people between 80 and 90 years whose numbers will increase through the process of ageing (and lowering of the mortality rate). As a result the growth of the number of households between 1981 and 2010 is greater than the growth of the population. This naturally has major consequences for the number of dwellings needed. The individualisation and the diversification of household types must bring about a shift in demand from traditional to smaller dwellings. Another trend arising from the growing number of one-person household (singles) is an increase in the labour supply and a consequent increase in the need for durables like refrigerators, radio and TV sets, other electrical household appliances etc. Furthermore, a change in patterns of eating and food habits in general may lead to an increase in consumption of convenience goods and ready made meals, to mention only a few effects.

We may now turn to the construction of a hypothetical SAM based on the trend projection of the demographic composition as shown in table 8.3. The reconstruction of the SAM is done in several steps.

(i) The transactions of households are calculated in conformity with the procedure explained above. Wi, is the average value of item i of expenditure or income by household group It as reported in the household budget surveys. T_h is the trend projection of the number of households by size (table 8.3).

(ii) The product $W_{ih} T_h$ is summed over h and divided by the relevant adjustment factor a_i as explained earlier. In this way the deviation between budget estimates and national accounts which held for 1981 is also applied to the reconstructed SAM. For each item i we find a new SAM value.[1]

---

[1] It is remembered that $a_i < 1.0$ for the profit income received by households since the national accounts sources give lower figures than budget surveys. This implies an allocation in both SAMs of the profit income among household groups which is more in line with their

(iii) There is no reason to assume that the share of value-added in the production of a sector is different under different demographic compositions. We assume, therefore, that the share of labour earnings and profits per sector in the total production value of that sector remains the same as in 1981. The same applies for the share of imports and exports per sector in the total production value of that sector and for the share of domestic investment in the overall value of production. So in practice new values of labour earnings and profits by sector will be associated with new production values by sector and new imports by sector and new column totals of the submatrix of intermediate deliveries. Thus a first consequence of a different demographic structure is a rescheduling of factor incomes, value-added, production, imports and intermediate goods by using sector.

(iv) Adjustments the other way round is caused by the change in the consumption expenditure of households due to the changed demographic components. The simulated changes in the consumption expenditure of the households pass through the conversion between the products and the production activities to give new values of final demand per sector, and after deduction from gross output, lead to new row totals of the submatrix of intermediate deliveries. This is the second major effect of the different demographic structure laid down in the SAM for 2010.

(v) We applied the RAS method to the new *column* totals, in (iii), and row totals, in (iv), of the submatrix of intermediate deliveries in order to get a consistent input-output table which fits the reconstructed SAM.

Table 8.3. The Number of Households and their Distribution by Size for CBS/WBO (1981) and for the Trend Scenario 2010

Source	Year	Households in 000's	Percentage of households with					
			1 person	2 person	3 person	4 person	5 person	>6 person
WBO	1981	5111	22	30	15	21	8	4
Trend	2010	7842	44	33	11	8	3	1

Source: Nelissen and Vossen (1988)

---

numbers than with their numbers multiplied by the average values per household, as found in the budget survey. As a result, the reconstructed SAM, with a forecast low number of households with more persons, ends up with relatively low amounts of profits received by these households.

Table 8.4. Postulated Social Accounting Matrix of the Netherlands for 2010 (in billion guilders)

	1	2	3	4	5	6	7	8	9	10	Total
Products				278.9		60.1	2.7				341.6
Wages									218.3	.1	218.4
Profits									121.6	-1.1	120.5
Households		171.8	96.6			36.1	126.1			-1.5	429.2
Firms			18.0								18.0
Government	15.4		5.0	54.8	11.1			5.8	11.1	2.6	106
Social insur		46.6	.9	22.7		9.9				47.3	127.4
Capital				72.8	6.9	-.3	-1.4		44.0	-42.2	79.7
Activities	278.8							61.4	220.7	219.1	780.1
Rest World	47.4							12.4	164.5	14.9	239.9
Total	341.6	218.4	120.5	429.2	18.0	105.8	127.4	79.7	780.1	239.2	2459.8

The result of applying the above five steps are table 8.4 (aggregated) and table 8.5 (disaggregated) which stand for a reconstructed SAM based on an alternative demographic structure with consequences for altered income and expenditure and the impact of both on balanced delivery of inputs and outputs. Other relationships in the SAM are unaffected by the changing demographic structure.

Table 8.5. The Postulated Disaggregated Social Accounting Matrix of the Netherlands, 2010 (in million guilders)

	1	2	3	4	5	6	7	8	9	10	11	12	13	14	15
1.Food										15970	20986	8238	6718	2842	1 157
2.Rent										30715	34767	12227	9695	3611	1 290
3.Clothing										5987	7814	3411	2679	1 117	528
4.Health										10555	13874	5447	3937	1657	607
5.Education										21 519	27099	9663	7 589	1299	1 190
6.Other services										592	837	590	462	151	63
7.Public Utilities															
8.Earnings															
9.Profits															
10.1 person hh								33427	38870						
11.2 person hh								63605	43710						
12.3 person hh								30719	7636						
13.4 person hh								28756	3532						
14.5 person hh								11438	1133						
15.6+ person hh								3884	1698						
16. Firm									17960						
17.Government	1199	6021	821	3110	4028	245			5010	13816	22641	7 337	7 394	2744	877
18.Sosial insurance								46560	940	5 137	8284	4110	3363	1 131	491
19.Capital										37423	35610	2240	-2360	-852	689
20.Agriculture	2277	17			1118										
21.Mining	5				9										
22.Light industry	19086	6177	7872	2090	6612	142									
23.Heavy idustry		1216	85	197	2447	64									
24.Public Utilities		14252													
25.Construction		1715													
26.Trade	11845	8117	4671	4728	29355	412									
27.Transport					7131										
28.Banking		30276	467		7297	344									
29.Service		8828		28436	7288	1488	62750								
30.Rest world	21499	15688	7620	-2484	5074										
Total	55911	92307	21536	36077	70359	2695	62750	218389	120509	141734	171912	53263	39477	15902	6892

Key: hh= household

Growth and Equity Effects of Demographic Change

Table 8.5 (Continued)

	16	17	18	19	20	21	22	23	24	25	26	27	28	29	30
1.Food															
2.Rent															
3.Clothing															
4.Health															
5.Education															
6.Other services															
7.Public Utilities		60100	2650												
8.Earnings					2791	624	23239	24940	2829	17655	30967	17104	20470	77660	110
9.Profits					14071	35262	1320	3584	3264	8057	22152	5367	34446	-5914	-1070
10.1 person hh		15613	54484												-660
11.2 person hh		14493	50579												-495
12.3 person hh		3357	11716												-165
13.4 person hh		1628	5681												-120
14.5 person hh		752	2624												-45
15.6+ person hh		295	1010												-15
16. Firm															
17.Government	11100			5811	427	43	3234	-496	51	79	4596	-2132	2427	2824	2561
18.Sosial insurance		9850													47288
19.Capital	6860	-300	-1410		2433	1149	7251	4138	3360	1470	4410	6287	7843	5653	-42236
20.Agriculture				173	2005	0	25862				378	12		403	11354
21.Mining				116	52	376	5837	1430	12328	314				109	21402
22.Light industry				-1409	12613	72	17247	2193	709	2996	4810	1380	1269	3912	87642
23.Heavy industry				8308	365	336	1989	9341	344	6789	943	871	543	2380	49022
24.Public Utilities				1076	1443	156	2326	1826	326	502	2001	612	653	2717	112
25.Construction				42294	349	114	518	853	77	9027	335	259	2134	2192	2056
26.Trade				4708	1475	118	3488	2136	159	2318	2452	1160	527	1446	17123
27.Transport				620	217	339	840	654	31	679	9413	1331	1782	1734	17740
28.Banking				5913	781	197	2688	2870	85	1080	3314	1158	5785	16703	3158
29.Service				-381	197	11	478	348	43	115	276	226	537	2822	9517
30.Rest world				12431	4381	3180	79097	31423	4394	10841	10191	8876	3701	8369	14928
Total	17960	105788	127354	79660	43600	41977	175414	85240	28000	61922	96239	42512	82206	122979	239209

Key: hh= household

4. A Comparison between Base SAM 1981 and Reconstructed SAM 2010

A few remarks may be made on the differences between the base SAM and the reconstructed SAM making use of tables 8.1 and 8.4. The reconstructed SAM, reflecting a more differentiated demographic composition with more single-person/elder-age households and fewer traditional four-person family households, shows an overall increase in household receipts with relatively higher increases in profits, government transfers and social security receipts than wages (row 4). Although expenditure on consumption increases there is still an opportunity for higher savings (column 4). The two exceptions are the four- and five-person household groups that show negative savings.

Having the same investment level in both SAMs means that the established trends for the Netherlands, as a net transferer of capital to the rest of the world, will continue in the future (row 8). As a result there is a substantially higher leakage of multiplier effects in the future but nevertheless, as will be seen in the next section, the multipliers in the reconstructed SAM are still higher than in the base SAM due to the overall increases in incomes and expenditure. The multiplier effects could have been somewhat higher if domestic investment in 2010 was allowed to rise.

Comparing the disaggregated SAMs shows major shifts in the distribution of income on household categories. One and two person households that had a combined share of income of 42% in 1981 will carry a share of 73% in 2010.

The distribution of output by sector in 2010 shows increases of about 1% each in the share of agriculture and of mining at the cost of a 2% decrease in the share of light industry. Otherwise the reconstructed SAM shows slight shifts favouring public utilities, construction, trade and banking and disfavouring heavy industry, transport and services. The forecast sectoral pattern is mainly the result of the corresponding income and expenditure patterns of the differentiated demographic structure.

5. A Comparison of SAM Multipliers

In the input-output analysis an endogenous vector of sectoral production can be predicted from a matrix of input-output coefficients, and a vector of exogenous final demand. The SAM can be used similarly, with the obvious difference that the SAM contains more variables and relationships. To transform the social accounting matrix into an economy-wide model along the above lines requires several steps.

First, the accounts of the SAM need to be subdivided into endogenous and exogenous and regrouped accordingly so that the exogenous accounts fall to the right and bottom of the endogenous accounts. The choice regarding subdivision into exogenous variables x and endogenous variables y can lead to lengthy discussions on alternative closure rules. Instead, we shall, *initially*, assume for a country like the Netherlands that the three variables of social insurance, government and rest of the world are exogenous. As a result the remaining 27 variables are endogenous, consisting of variables of the products accounts denoted by y_1, those of the factors accounts, y_2, those of the institutions accounts pertaining to households and firms, y_3, and those of the activities accounts, y_4. The grouping of these accounts and denoting them by 1,2,3 and 4 is crucial for the further analysis.

Second, each flow in the endogenous matrix is divided by its respective column total to give the matrix of average propensities, denoted by A.

The vector of endogenous variables y can now be solved from equation (1):

$$y = Ay + x = (I - A)^{-1} x = M_a x \qquad (1)$$

where M_a is the aggregate multiplier matrix.

Such a matrix consists of 27 rows by 27 columns on the assumption that the exogenous impulses can be injected into and will affect each endogenous account. We shall limit our interest to parts of this matrix, namely the multipliers of injections into sectors s and of transfers to households h on output of sectors and income of households. As a result, the analysis will be concerned on the four multiplier groups denoted by $M_{a,ss'}$, $M_{a,hs'}$ referring to effects of injections in the sector accounts, and $M_{a,sh'}$ and $M_{a,hh'}$ referring to effects of transfers to the household accounts., as described below.

Endogenous accounts y	Types of endogenous impulses x	
	household transfers	sectoral injections
income of households h	$M_{a,hh'}$	$M_{a,hs'}$
output of sectors s	$M_{a,sh'}$	$M_{a,ss'}$

Besides studying the level of a multiplier as an indication of the short-run impact of a shock it is important to study the distribution of the multiplier effects on the constituents of the system since these indicate the long-term growth bias of the economy. A relative distributive measure of the effects of household transfers on household incomes is denoted by $RDM_{hh'}$. Similarly, there is $RDM_{sh'}$ giving the effects of household transfers on sectoral output[2]. Both concepts were discussed in previous chapters. *RDM* is the quotient of the percentage distribution of the predicted individual multiplier effects on households (sectors) to the actual share of income of households (output of sectors) in the total household income (total sectoral output), and reflects therefore the long term income (output) growth bias of the economy. For values of $RDM < 1$, > 1 and $= 1$, there are positive, negative and neutral redistributive effects.

In correspondence with the above, two types of *RDM* for sectoral demand injections can also be formulated, giving $RDM_{ss'}$ and $RDM_{hs'}$.

We shall begin with discussing the differences in multipliers between the base and the reconstructed SAM for the future. After that we take up the differences in the *RDM*. Table 8.6 shows the effects on income and output from a transfer of one million guilders (mg) to a particular household group. In the base year, income increases on the average by 1.462 mg while output increases by 1.355 mg. The increases are found to

---

[2] The formulas of RDM for household income transfers can be repeated here for convenience.

$$RDM_{hh'} = \frac{(M_{a,hh'} - d_{hh'})}{\sum_h M_{a,hh'} - 1} / \frac{Income_{h,0}}{\sum_h Income_{h,0}}$$

$$RDM_{sh'} = \frac{M_{a,sh'}}{\sum_s M_{a,sh'}} / \frac{Output_{s,0}}{\sum_s Output_{s,0}}$$

where h stands for the affected household group, and h' for the injected household group.

The individual multiplier effect of h' on h, $M_{a,hh'}$ is divided by the column sum of multipliers of h' after deducting the initial injection. Here we use $d_{hh'}$ for the Kronecker symbol that equals 1 if $h=h'$ and o in other cases. The result is then divided by the actual output share of the region in the base year for which the SAM was constructed. For values of $RDM_{hh'} > 1$, <1, and $=1$, there are positive, negative and neutral redistributive effects, respectively. Second, we have

Similarly, the two RDM formulas for sectoral demand injections are

$$RDM_{ss'} = \frac{(M_{a,ss'} - d_{ss'})}{\sum_s M_{a,ss'} - 1} / \frac{Output_{s,0}}{\sum_s Output_{s,0}}$$

$$RDM_{hs'} = \frac{M_{a,hs'}}{\sum_h M_{a,hs'}} / \frac{Income_{h,0}}{\sum_h Income_{h,0}}$$

be higher under a changed demography: 1.508 mg and 1.395 mg respectively. As was commented earlier, there is more income and more expenditure in the reconstructed SAM and as a result the multiplier effects should be higher.

There is an expected change in future effects, however. Transfers to larger household groups show higher multiplier effects in 2010 than in 1981. This is due to the following. As the share of larger households in all households is forecast to drop the income and expenditure of these groups will drop appreciably. In addition the amount of profit income which larger households receive drops at an even higher rate because ai < 1.0. As a result larger households end up with negative savings (see reconstructed SAM, table 8.5, row 19 with columns 13 and 14). Negative savings correspond to no (or negative) leakage from the system, which automatically leads to high multiplier effects. Under the future circumstances, transfers to larger families may have an edge on middle size families in stimulating higher growth of income and output.

Table 8.6. **Income and Output Multipliers of Institutional Transfers to Household Groups**

	Average of all households	Household types					
		1p	2p	3p	4p	5p	6+p
SAM base Income multiplier							
$M_{a,hh'}$	1.462	1.49	1.47	1.46	1.44	1.45	1.45
Output multiplier							
$M_{a,sh'}$	1.355	1.44	1.37	1.36	1.3	1.33	1.34
SAM reconstructed Income multiplier							
$M_{a,hh'}$	1.508	1.55	1.52	1.51	1.48	1.49	1.5
Output multiplier							
$M_{a,sh'}$	1.395	1.51	1.43	1.4	1.3	1.33	1.39

Table 8.7. Multipliers of Sectoral Injections

	Average all	Sector 20	21	22	23	24	25	26	27	28	29
SAM base											
Income multiplier $M_{a,hs'}$	0.8	0.72	0.97	0.43	0.59	0.79	0.77	0.83	0.82	0.92	0.93
Output multiplier $M_{a,ss'}$	2.3	2.56	2.07	2.08	2.03	2.58	2.42	2.24	2.22	2.25	2.37
SAM reconstructed											
Income multiplier $M_{a,hs'}$	0.8	0.78	1.13	0.45	0.62	0.89	0.68	0.96	0.85	1.00	0.96
Output multiplier $M_{a,ss'}$	2.3	2.54	2.21	2.04	2.00	2.62	2.03	2.46	2.22	2.27	2.34

Table 8.7 compares the effects of sectoral injections in 1981 and 2010. As might be expected, income and output effects are on the average higher in 2010. In addition the income content of output, $M_{a,hs'} / M_{a,ss'}$ is expected to increase under demographic change: in 1981 this share amounted on the average to 0.775/2.283 or 34% and in 2010 it is expected to be 37%.

In which direction are the income and output growth patterns biased in the Netherlands, and how would these directions be modified under demographic change? To answer these questions we calculate the values of *RDM* in tables 8.8 and 8.9.

We take first the income effects. Table 8.8 shows that 7.7% of the income effects of institutional transfers, on average, go to the one-person household group while this group is actually getting 12.6 % of household income. As a result the transfer disfavours this group and is regressive in effect. The value of *RDM* is found to be 0.61. Larger families are favoured and have values of *RDM* > *1.0*. Sectoral injections (columns 4, 5 and 6) show the same income bias.

How would the mechanisms of income distribution work under demographic change? Table 8.9 shows that the income distribution bias of the Netherlands undergoes modifications under a changed future demographic structure. Institutional transfers in the reconstructed SAM will lead, on average, to an *RDM* for the one-person household of 0.83 as compared to 0.61 in the base SAM, an increase of 21 percentage points which tends towards a more progressive income distribution.

That the actual income distribution in the Netherlands in 1981 shows more equality than the SAM multipliers for 1981 demonstrate is due to the positive effect of annually repeated initial injections by the public sector to the poorest income groups which are usually the smaller households. Under the future demographic structure examined here the need for repeated injections by the public sector to correct the distributionary bias is somewhat relaxed because of the more balanced *RDMs* in 2010. We note that the ageing of the population is not taken into account! Should ageing be incorporated the redistributionary burden that goes with a wealthier aged population and a less wealthy younger population might increase.

Take next the output effects. Table 8.8 shows relevant statistics for constructing *RDM* measures: $RDM_{,hs'}$ and $RDM_{,ss'}$. Considering the effect of sectoral injections there is, on average, a highly positive growth bias towards the five sectors of mining, utilities, construction, trade and banking, the values of $RDM_{ss'}$ being above 1-20. In contrast, the results show a negative growth bias for light and heavy industry and services, recording values below 0.79. Table 8.9 gives the growth bias under the forecast demographic change, showing a revitalised growth for heavy industry and electronics and a departure away from mining, other sectors maintaining their present bias towards growth or decline. The redistributive effect of transfer injections to alternative household groups on the sectoral compositions of output corresponds generally with what was described above. Alternative transfers influence the distribution of output on sectors in the same way (a growth bias towards mining, construction, utilities, trade and banking, and against light/heavy industry and services). The growth bias is reversed towards higher shares of heavy industry and services under SAM 2010, reflecting a reorientation of consumer expenditure associated with a differentiated demographic decomposition. Most of the other sectors show deterioration in their growth bias.

Table 8.8. SAM Base. Percentage Distribution of Multiplier Effects due to Institutional Transfers and Sectoral Injections

	Institutional transfers			Sectoral injections		
	Average	Actual	RDM	Average	Actual	RDM
% distribution of income effect on household groups						
One person	7.68	12.58	0.61	7.84	12.58	0.62
Two persons	25.2	29.73	0.85	25.43	29.73	0.86
Three persons	17.35	16.28	1.07	17.28	16.28	1.06
Four persons	30.79	25.3	1.22	30.56	25.3	1.21
Five persons	12.4	10.47	1.19	12.3	10.47	1.18
Six or more persons	6.58	5.64	1.17	6.59	5.64	1.17
% distribution of output effect on sectors						
Agriculture	3.26	4.72	0.69	4.13	4.72	0.87
Mining	2.75	4.32	0.64	6.27	4.32	1.45
Light industry	17.65	23.97	0.74	18.33	23.97	0.76
Heavy industry	5.98	11.43	0.52	9.04	11.43	0.79
Public utilities	5.27	3.34	1.58	4.97	3.34	1.49
Construction	12.61	7.88	1.60	16.01	7.88	2.03
Trade	19.21	11.88	1.62	14.31	11.88	1.20
Transport	5.09	5.52	0.92	5.50	5.52	0.99
Banking	14.89	9.52	1.56	12.76	9.52	1..34
Service	13.28	17.42	0.76	8.68	17.42	0.50

Table 8.9. SAM Reconstructed. Percentage Distribution of Multiplier Effects due to the Institutional Transfers and Sectoral Injections

	Institutional transfers			Sectoral injections		
	Average	Actual	RDM	Average	Actual	RDM
% distribution of income effect on household groups						
One person	27.45	33.02	0.83	28.97	33.02	0.88
Two persons	40.19	40.06	1	40.8	40.06	1.02
Three persons	14.04	12.41	1.13	13.31	12.41	1.07
Four persons	11.7	9.2	1.27	10.74	9.2	1.17
Five persons	4.55	3.71	1.23	4.14	3.71	1.12
Six or more persons	2.07	1.61	1.29	2.03	1.61	1.26
% distribution of output effect on sectors						
Agriculture	3.72	5.59	0.67	Apr-89	5.59	0.87
Mining	3.17	5.38	0.59	7.15	5.38	1.33
Light industry	16.64	22.49	0.74	16.44	22.49	0.73
Heavy industry	5.98	10.93	0.55	9.12	10.93	0.83
Public utilities	5.4	3.59	1.5	5.17	3.59	1.44
Construction	12.66	794	1.59	15.95	7.94	2.01
Trade etc	19.05	12.34	1.54	14.07	12.34	1.14
Transport etc	4.9	5.45	0.9	5.24	5.45	0.96
Banking etc	15.69	10.54	1.49	14.12	10.54	1.34
Service	12.79	15.76	0.81	7.87	15.76	0.5

6. Concluding Remarks

In this chapter the impact of changing demographic structures on the economy is studied by introducing households by size and by applying comparative static analysis to a general equilibrium framework. The social accounting matrix was chosen as an analytical framework to investigate the functioning of the economy under the present economic demographic situation (1981) and under a future simulated situation (2010). The latter features a more differentiated demographic structure with an increase of the share of the one- and two-person households from 0.52 in 1981 to 0.77 in 2010. Comparing the multiplier results of both SAMs, we see that there is the same income bias towards the three- and more-person households. However, in the reconstructed SAM for 2010 is a tendency towards a more progressive income distribution. Considering the output effects, the sectoral injections in both cases show a positive growth bias towards mining, public utilities, construction, trade and banking. In the simulated future situation, the growth potential of mining is worse than under the existing situation.

There are a few possible refinements that could be introduced in reconstructing a future hypothetical SAM which, at the same time, suggest the limitations of the present analysis. First, there may possibly be a better way to handle the labour earnings and the profits of the households (ic variance between the data of the household budget survey and the national accounts affects the receipts of the four- and five-person households more significantly than other groups). Second, the future composition in terms of other characteristics such as age or labour force participation can be as determinant for the economy as the size of household. These were not considered in the analysis and it may be difficult to integrate them simultaneously in the SAM framework. Third, it is desirable to construct social accounting matrices under alternative scenarios and with other classifications of household groups. Such classifications of households groups as region, status, urbanisation degree and income decile can then be included and multiplier analyses for different classifications can be mapped on to each other, as was done in the previous chapters.

Appendices

Appendix 1: Decomposition Formulas

Appendix 2: Differences between the System of National Accounts (SNA) and the Material Product System (MPS)

Appendix 3: Construction and Structure of SAMs for West and East European Countries

Appendix 4: SAMs of Six European Countries: Germany, Italy, Netherlands, Spain, Hungary, and Poland

Appendix 5: SAMs of China and Russia

Appendices

Appendix 1. Decomposition Formulas

Specifically, the SAM can be written as a partitioned coefficient matrix. The A Matrix takes the form of eq. (1).

$$A = \begin{matrix} 0 & 0 & A_{13} & 0 \\ 0 & 0 & 0 & A_{24} \\ 0 & A_{32} & A_{33} & 0 \\ A_{41} & 0 & 0 & A_{44} \end{matrix} \qquad (1)$$

A_{13} represents the intersection between wants and households and firms, A_{24} for those between factors and activities, etc. From A separate $\tilde{A}$ and invert to obtain M_1, as in eq. (2).

$$\tilde{A} = \begin{matrix} 0 & 0 & 0 & 0 \\ 0 & 0 & 0 & 0 \\ 0 & 0 & A_{33} & 0 \\ 0 & 0 & 0 & A_{44} \end{matrix}, \quad M_1 = (I-\tilde{A})^{-1} = \begin{matrix} I & 0 & 0 & 0 \\ 0 & I & 0 & 0 \\ 0 & 0 & (I-\tilde{A}_{33})^{-1} & 0 \\ 0 & 0 & 0 & (I-\tilde{A}_{44})^{-1} \end{matrix} \qquad (2)$$

It is noted that $(I-\tilde{A}_{44})^{-1}$ is nothing more than the Leontief-inverse from the simple sectoral models. It translates original exogenous impulses in final demand into sectoral output. It does not take into account the impact of the composition of endogenous final demand. $(I-\tilde{A}_{33})^{-1}$ fulfils the same role with regard to institutions. It calculates the first round effect of an exogenous increase in institutional income through the transfer mechanisms between the different institutions.

As a result of the separation in eq. (2), we have A^* in eq. (3).

$$A^* = \begin{matrix} 0 & 0 & A_{13}^* & 0 \\ 0 & 0 & 0 & A_{24}^* \\ 0 & A_{32}^* & 0 & 0 \\ A_{41}^* & 0 & 0 & 0 \end{matrix} \quad \text{where:} \quad \begin{matrix} A_{13}^* = A_{13} \\ A_{24}^* = A_{24} \\ A_{32}^* = (I-\tilde{A}_{33})^{-1} A_{32} \\ A_{41}^* = (I-\tilde{A}_{44})^{-1} A_{41} \end{matrix} \qquad (3)$$

A^* shares some of the properties of a permutation matrix: (1) It contains only one block of non-zero entries within each set of rows and each set of columns. (2) Raising such a matrix to the k-th power does not alter this property, it only shifts the position of each block. All blocks shift at the same time, so there are only four permutations showing different positions of the blocks.

Given $k = 4$ in the SAMs we deal with, one obtains M_2 and M_3 as specified in eqs. (4) and (5), respectively.

$$M_2 = \begin{bmatrix} I & A_{13}*A_{32}* & A_{13}* & A_{13}*A_{32}*A_{24}* \\ A_{24}A_{41} & I & A_{24}*A_{41}*A_{13}* & A_{24}* \\ A_{32}*A_{24}*A_{42}* & A_{32}* & I & A_{32}*A_{24}* \\ A_{41}* & A_{41}*A_{13}*A_{32}* & A_{41}*A_{13}* & I \end{bmatrix} \quad (4)$$

$$M_3 = \begin{bmatrix} (I-A_{13}*A_{32}*A_{24}*A_{41}*)^{-1} & 0 & 0 & 0 \\ 0 & (I-A_{24}*A_{41}*A_{13}*A_{32}*)^{-1} & 0 & 0 \\ 0 & 0 & (I-A_{32}*A_{24}*A_{41}*A_{13}*)^{-1} & 0 \\ 0 & 0 & 0 & (I-A_{41}*A_{13}*A_{32}*A_{24}*)^{-1} \end{bmatrix} \quad (5)$$

Appendix 2: Differences between the System of National Accounts (SNA) and the System of Balances of the National Economy or Material Products System (MPS)

To underline the differences between the SNA and MPS. it is instructive first to review briefly several conventions of the SNA. SNA can be set out in the form of a social accounting matrix representing the system of transactions between actors as a whole. A detailed, but somewhat dated comparison of the SNA and the MPS can be found in United Nations (1977). This publication includes a manual on how to get from one system to another. In part two of the publication, this conceptual framework is applied to a number of Western countries and Hungary.

For each group of domestic actors the SNA distinguishes a production account, income and outlay account. and capital finance account which, in consolidated form, are called respectively the accounts for GDP and expenditures, the account for national disposable income and the capital finance account. In addition to the accounts for domestic sectors there is a single account which covers transactions with the rest of the world and which is called the external transactions account.

In the production account, transactors are classified by sector of activity whereby the establishment is the unit of observation. Three transactors are distinguished: industries, producers of government services and producers of private non-profit services.

In the income and outlay accounts as well as the capital finance accounts, transactors are grouped into institutional types: households, firms, government. Unincorporated government enterprises belong to government and unincorporated private enterprises are included in the household sector.

The Material Product System, MPS, is presentable in the form of five basic source and use tables (referred to as balances):

1. The balance of production, consumption and accumulation of the global product, or simply the material balance.
2. The balance of production, distribution, redistribution and final utilization of the global product and the national income. or simply the financial balance.
3. Indicators of national wealth.
4. The balance of fixed capital.
5. The balance of manpower resources.

The financial balance is the most comprehensive table of the system and can best be compared with the flows in the SNA matrix. Other balances of the

MPS can also be presented in a SNA type of matrix form but with essential differences in content and structure of accounts.

In the production accounts, in MPS production of global product and national income embrace only the material branches, capital formation is net, depreciation is included in material costs and consumption comprises only goods and material services plus material inputs in the non-material sphere.

Non-material activities in MPS are not included in input-output tables and have to be estimated separately. Non-material activities include catering trade, financial institutions, real estate (in SNA owner occupied dwellings), business services, public administration and defence, sanitary services, education and research services, health services, welfare institutions etc.

There are also differences with respect to the definitions of gross output and intermediate consumption between SNA and MPS. The SNA definition of gross output and the MPS definition for global product differ, among other things regarding the catering trades, waste materials and second-hand goods. Concerning intermediate consumption, SNA and MPS differ on the following points. Expenditure by firms on cultural and sport facilities for employees are included in intermediate consumption in SNA, but charged against operating surplus and regarded as transfers to units in the non-material sphere in MPS. The facilities are often provided by separate units, which are included in the non-material sphere. Business travel expenses are treated as intermediate consumption in SNA, but as primary incomes of the population in MPS. Other differences exist for expenditures on uniforms, expenditure on fixed assets used for military purposes and losses of stocks.

In the production accounts, SNA uses three bases for valuation: at market prices, at basic values and at factor values. MPS uses only market prices, sometimes excluding turnover taxes.

In the income and outlay accounts, differences between SNA and MPS are the result of different approaches to the concept of production. In MPS, the non-material! sphere appears for the first time in the process of redistribution of income. Value added is produced by material branches only. In MPS, institutions are shown only as groups of transactors receiving transfers at the level of secondary distribution. Final consumption includes only goods and material services.

In both systems, three categories of final consumption are distinguished. Household consumption is roughly similar (except of course for the material versus non-material division), but the twofold division of non-household consumption is based on different principles. In SNA, the criterion for division is based on the institutional character of the transactors, i.e. consumption by government and consumption by private non-profit bodies. In MPS it is based on the nature and purpose of goods and services, i.e.

consumption of institutions serving the population and consumption of institutions satisfying community needs.

Concerning household consumption, in SNA, expenditures of producers of government services are treated as transfers to households (and included in household consumption) if households are free to select these services. In MPS, material expenditures are included in the final consumption of the unit that actually pays. Non-material expenditures are treated as transfer payments of these units. Exceptions to the MPS pattern are depreciation of dwellings and other material costs connected to housing services, which are allocated to the household consumption. In SNA the total amount of rents paid and imputed rents of owner-occupied dwellings are included in household consumption, while intermediate consumption, depreciation and value added are presented as inputs of an industry.

Concerning non-household consumption, serving both population and community in MPS, this roughly equals the material part of consumption of government and non-profit bodies plus the material input of those units in the non-material sphere, that in SNA are classified as industries. Part of government consumption for population is included in household consumption in SNA when the population can choose the items freely (for example in the Netherlands this is the case for medical services, but salary payments for educational services are included as government consumption).

As regards capital formation, the conceptual differences are less important, because by its very nature, capital formation covers only goods and material services.

As regards capital consumption, in MPS, in the non-material sphere, this is treated as final consumption and is not deducted in calculations of the national income. Further differences are connected to the difference between written off and sales value of scrapped assets (capital gain/loss in SNA and adjustment on depreciation in MPS), capital consumption in respect of afforestation and land improvement (not done in SNA, done in MPS), as well as the valuation (replacement cost in SNA and adjusted purchase price in MPS).

In MPS, contrary to SNA, foreign transactions by households are recorded as part of a redistribution low relating to the balance of receipts in foreign currency from tourism. Other and smaller differences relate to treatment of gold, intangible assets and gifts.

Value added in SNA and primary income the MPS, are both defined as gross output minus intermediate consumption. As mentioned before, in MPS primary incomes are only those from material activities. Other differences between the two concepts arise from the above mentioned differences in treatment of gross output and intermediate consumption. The components of value added or primary incomes can be compared in the following way for the material sectors:

SNA compensation of employees corresponds to MPS primary income of the population.

SNA operating surplus including net indirect taxes corresponds to MPS primary incomes of enterprises.

Social security and pension contributions paid by employers on behalf of their employees are included in compensation of employees in SNA and in primary income of enterprises in MPS (after which it is paid out to the social security or pension funds). If no actual payment is made, then no imputation is made in MPS.

Net incomes of unincorporated enterprises (and private farms and firms in MPS) are included in operating surplus in SNA and in primary incomes of the population in MPS.

To illustrate the relative magnitude of the differences between MPS and SNA, produced national income according to MPS and gross domestic product according to SNA are compared in the table below. The estimates are taken from Eurostat publications.

Table A.2.1: **Gross Domestic Product (GDP) and Produced National Income (NI) at Market Prices According to SNA and MPS, Poland and Hungary (1987)**

	GDP	NI	NI as % of GDP
Poland (1000 Mio. Zloty)	16940	14013	82.7
Hungary (1000 Mio. Forint)	1226	1000	81.6

Source: Eurostat (1991)

Appendix 3: Construction and Structure of SAMS for West and East European Countries

1. Descriptions of SAM Constructions

The SAM of *Germany* for 1984 was constructed under supervision of the author, using the methodology of the SAM for the Netherlands. For the aggregated version two sources were used: the National Accounts from German Statistical Office GSO (1989), and the Input-Output tables from CSO (1970-86).

The National Accounts have been used to give the primary income distribution, the secondary income distribution and the final consumption expenditure accounts, which are inserted in the rows and columns of factors, institutions and rest of world.

In the intersection of the column of wages with the row of households the compensation of employees as received by the households can be found. Other incomes consist of the difference between entrepreneurial and property income paid and received by the different institutions.

The intersection between the columns of households accounts and the rows of wants accounts is the final consumption by households, whereas the intersection between the columns of households accounts and the row of capital account gives their savings. The figures that are found in the intersection of columns of households and the rows of firms, government and social security were taken from the secondary income distribution account (direct taxes, social contributions, social benefits and other current transfers). The same source was used for the other non-zero intersections between households, firms, government and social security.

For the disaggregation of the households, the budget survey of 1983 was used, GSO (1983). This survey allowed breaking down households into 10 income decile groups, each with its specific income and outlay pattern. The Rest of the World account was used to balance the row and column totals for the ten household groups.

The data for the activities account were taken from the input-output table in producer's values 1984. The table was also used to construct the data in the row of the account for the rest of the world (imports, exports). The disaggregation of the activities account was also done with the input-output table, where 58 sectors were aggregated to 11 sectors in the base SAM, using the same classification as for the Netherlands. The sub-matrix to convert wants to activities was not available. The Dutch structure was used as an approximation.

In the column for the rest of the world account, data were used both from the national accounts and the input-output tables. The national accounts were used to calculate for foreign transactions the difference between the compensation of employees paid and received the difference between the entrepreneurial and property income paid and received and the net current transfers for the institutions. All these payments were included in the column of the rest of the world.

The SAM of *Italy* for 1984 was constructed from initial data that were used as a reference framework for simulating effects of alternative fiscal policies on personal income distribution in a computable general equilibrium model, cf. Civardi and Lenti (1990). This SAM was constructed according to the transaction values approach, which required that the following conditions are fulfilled: each account represents only one type of behaviour, each cell in the SAM corresponds to only one type of transaction and all the transactions take place at the same price. In practice this meant that accounts of institutions and production activities are separate.

Five production factors were identified: employed labour, self-employed labour, capital invested in productive activities, capital invested in housing and financial capital.

Households were classified by income deciles and divided over two accounts: one for income generation and one for expenditure on products. The corporate sector consisted of one account for the distribution of income over the production factors and from these to the institutions. The corporate sector consisted of one account for the distribution of income over the production factors and from these to the institutions. The Central Government consisted of four accounts: one for income generation, one for expenditure, one for indirect taxes and one for direct taxes. The institutions accounts are made complete by incorporating one aggregate capital account.

The production activities were classified into seven sectors: agriculture, industry, trade, transports, credit and insurance, public administration and other services, represented by two accounts: one for the value added distribution over the production factors and one for determining the value of output. Concerning the production process there were four accounts for commodities: one for domestic, one for exported, one for imported and one for composite commodities, which all had the same sectoral classification. Furthermore, the material allowed for the inclusion of a rest of the world account.

The above data made possible the reconstruction of a social accounting matrix. Although the matrix is not available in the source mentioned above, we were able to construct it from the published tables in the source. With the cross-country comparisons in mind, we adjusted the reconstructed SAM for

Italy on several points. First, the wants account was included on activity basis for the expenditure of consumer goods by the households. Second, the factors account was limited to just two factors, i.e. labour and capital. Third, the four accounts for commodities had to be aggregated to one account. Fourth, the activity by activity table was adapted for the intermediate deliveries following the industry technology assumption.

The SAM of the *Netherlands* for 1987 is constructed from published estimates of the national accounts for 1987. The disaggregation distinguished between six wants, two factors, ten household groups classified by income deciles, firms, government and social insurance, a combined capital account, ten production activities and the rest of the world account. There is already a series of SAMs for the Netherlands dating from 1978, cf. Cohen (1988).

Three main data sources were used for disaggregation of the matrix. The first is the household budget survey of the Netherlands Central Bureau of Statistics, CBS; this allowed breaking up the household account into the ten income decile groups with specifications of their income by source and expenditures by type of want. The second is the input-output table in producer prices of CBS for disaggregating the production activities. The third is an initial converter table for transforming the classification by wants into a classification by activity. From this table, available from CBS in purchaser prices, we had to separate value added tax and imports and include them in the rows of government and rest of world, respectively. The distribution of the value added tax on the wants was estimated making use of the appropriate tax rate per want. The distribution of imports over the wants was the residual.

The SAM available of *Spain* for 1980 is based on Kehoe, T., et al. (1985). We work here with a revised version of their SAM. They presented the SAM in the form of a collection of six matrices: the intermediate consumption matrix, the primary factors matrix, the conversion matrix, the final demand matrix, the agents' expenditure matrix and the households' incomes matrix. In the above-mentioned SAM a distinction has been made between commodities and activities, so that make and use matrices can be included, to allow for the distinction between indirect taxes on production and indirect taxes on consumption. Activities sell the domestic output to commodities that are further distributed into the private consumption wants categories, and on intermediate consumption, investment, and exports.

The classification of wants (and likewise their corresponding commodities) consisted of ten categories, which we reduced to six categories: food, textiles, housing, hygiene and medicine, culture and transportation, and other goods.

Factor accounts were aggregated to give those of labour and capital.

Regarding the institutions accounts, households are divided into poor and rich according to their total income (with a border value of 700.000 pesetas) in the Household Expenditure Survey of 1981-82 and are further subdivided by the age of the head of the household: less than 25 (young), from 25 to 64 (adult) and more than 64 (elderly). Together this gives six household groups. There is one aggregate account for the firms consisting of non-financial corporate and quasi-corporate enterprises, credit institutions and insurance enterprises. For the movement sector there are five accounts: one general, one for taxes on production, one for taxes on imports, one for social security contributions and one for the employer and employee contributions paid to the government. Finally, there is one combined account for capital accumulation of all institutions together.

Regarding the classification of the activities, and likewise their corresponding commodities, these consisted of 12 branches of industry in the original matrix. To facilitate the comparison with other countries we aggregated these into five groups: industry including construction, agriculture, transport, trade and services. As usual, the matrix includes an additional trade and transfers activity belonging to the rest of the world.

The resulting base SAM for Spain has been further modified by us with respect to two points; using the industry-technology assumption we have computed an activity by activity table which made it possible to delete the account for commodities; and we accumulated the consumption of non-residents in one cell-entry.

The SAM for *Hungary, 1990*, was prepared on the same basis as the SAM for Poland i.e. using the methodology of the Netherlands SAM. The construction was done in cooperation with Budapest University of Economic Sciences. The compilation took place in both Hungary and the Netherlands and made use of data obtained from a variety of sources. A second SAM for 1987 was constructed along the same lines. For details on both SAMs see Revesz and Zalai (1993).

The SAM for *Poland, 1987*, was prepared in cooperation with the Research Centre for Statistical and Economic Analysis of the Central Statistical Office in Poland. In general, it follows the classification and methodology of the SAM of the Netherlands. A preliminary version of national accounts statistics for the base year were used, next to the usual sources such as the input-output table and household budget survey. These data became available for the first time according to SNA standards in 1990. Later data were used to produce another SAM for 1990. For details on both SAMs see Cohen, Lafeber and Zienkowski (1993).

Appendices 179

2. The Structures of the Aggregate SAMs

Table A.3.1. SAM Structure for Germany 1984

	1	2	3	4	5	6	7	8	9	Total
1 Wants				11.1						11.1
2 Labour								10.5		10.6
3 Capital								4.4	0.1	4.5
4 Households		10.6	3.8			3.3			-0.1	17.5
5 Firms			0.9						-0.0	0.9
6 Government	1.0		-0.2	5.4	0.4		0.2	0.9	-0.2	7.5
7 Accumulation				1.0	0.5	0.3		2.5	-0.2	4.0
8 Activities	9.1					3.9	3.4	16.7	5.3	38.4
9 Rest of World	1.0						0.3	3.5	0.7	5.5
Total	11.1	10.6	4.5	17.5	0.9	7.5	4.0	38.4	5.5	100.0

Table A.3.2. SAM Structure for Italy 1984

	1	2	3	4	5	6	7	8	9	Total
1 Wants				11.1						11.1
2 Labour								11.0	-0.0	11.0
3 Capital								5.4	-0.4	4.9
4 Households		11.0	3.0			4.0			0.1	18.0
5 Firms			1.8			0.7			0.2	2.8
6 Government			0.1	4.7	0.5			1.4	-0.0	6.7
7 Accumulation				2.1	2.3	-1.6			0.5	3.3
8 Activities						3.7	3.3	15.8	4.0	37.9
9 Rest of World								4.4		4.4
Total	11.1	11.0	4.9	18.0	2.8	6.7	3.3	37.9	4.4	100.0

Table A.3.3. SAM Structure for the Netherlands 1987

	1	2	3	4	5	6	7	8	9	Total
1 Wants				11.7						11.7
2 Labour								10.3		10.3
3 Capital								5.0	-0.0	4.9
4 Households		8.0	4.0			5.3			-0.1	17.2
5 Firms			1.4							1.4
6 Government	1.0	2.4	-0.4	3.7	0.7	0.1	0.3	0.5	-0.1	8.1
7 Accumulation				1.7	0.7	-0.4		2.0	-0.4	3.7
8 Activities	8.7					3.1	2.4	9.9	9.0	33.2
9 Rest of World	2.1						1.0	5.4	1.0	9.5
Total	11.7	10.3	4.9	17.2	1.4	8.1	3.7	33.2	9.5	100.0

Table A.3.4. SAM Structure for Spain 1980

	1	2	3	4	5	6	7	8	9	Total
1 Wants				12.4						12.4
2 Labour								7.5		7.6
3 Capital								8.4	0.1	8.5
4 Households		7.6	5.4			2.6			0.2	15.8
5 Firms			2.7			0.1				2.9
6 Government	0.2		0.1	1.7	0.5			2.7		5.3
7 Accumulation				1.6	2.3	0.1			0.5	4.4
8 Activities	12.2					2.4	4.4	17.5	3.0	39.4
9 Rest of World			0.3	0.1				3.3		3.8
Total	12.4	7.6	8.5	15.8	2.9	5.3	4.4	39.4	3.8	100

Table A.3.5. SAM structure for Hungary 1990

	1	2	3	4	5	6	7	8	9	Total
1 Wants				9.5		2.2			0.2	11.9
2 Labour								11.5		11.5
3 Capital								3.2		3.2
4 Households		8.9	0.8			3.2				12.9
5 Firms			2.4							2.4
6 Government	1.3	2.6		2.0	1.6		0.1	1.6	-0.8	8.3
7 Accumulation				1.4	0.3	1.4		1.5	-0.2	4.4
8 Activities	10.0				0.5	1.5	3.7	17.9	6.3	39.9
9 Rest of world	0.6						0.6	4.3		5.5
Total	11.9	11.5	3.2	12.9	2.4	8.3	4.4	39.9	5.5	100.0

Table A.3.6. SAM structure for Poland 1987

	1	2	3	4	5	6	7	8	9	Total
1 Wants				9.4						9.4
2 Labour								9.0		9.0
3 Capital								8.0		8.0
4 Households		7.2	0.9			1.7			0.4	10.2
5 Firms			6.0			0.3				6.4
6 Government		1.7	1.0	0.2	2.8			0.1	0.1	5.9
7 Accumulation				0.7	3.6	-0.2		1.2	-0.0	5.3
8 Activities	9.0					3.2	4.8	20.8	3.8	41.5
9 Rest of World	0.4					0.9	0.5	2.5	0.1	4.4
Total	9.4	9.0	8.0	10.2	6.4	5.9	5.3	41.5	4.4	100

Appendix 4: SAMs of Six European Countries

Germany
Italy
The Netherlands
Spain
Hungary
Poland

SAM Germany 1984 (million marks)

	WANTS						FACTORS		HOUSEHOLD INCOME DECILES										INSTITUTIONS			ACTIVITIES						ROW	TOTAL
	1	2	3	4	5	6	7	8	9	10	11	12	13	14	15	16	17	18	19	20	21	22	23	24	25	26	27	
1 Food									9572	12852	16206	19522	22456	25987	28603	31158	35385	37094										238835
2 Housing									12782	18528	21724	25456	28694	31906	34913	38677	46467	50552										309699
3 Clothing, ftwr									2704	3924	5241	6432	7551	8884	10282	11953	15127	16963										89061
4 Medical care									1605	2189	2891	3417	4028	4528	5211	6206	8718	10035										48828
5 Recr./Trans									7463	9521	12881	15784	21036	25333	30054	34776	44930	50616										252394
6 Other goods									1715	2610	3645	4589	5701	6297	7044	7841	11377	13934										64753
7 Labour																						8292	445030	108312	56874	331982	3510	954000
8 Capital																						16394	1110796	63978	22970	179242	10550	403930
9 1st decile								3955	7035										24882								1880	37752
10 2nd decile								14319	11575										33806								-1041	58659
11 3rd decile								34264	14235										33612								2128	84239
12 4th decile								51421	16469										33672								4986	106548
13 5th decile								74123	18448										32409								7795	132775
14 6th decile								98881	21433										30563								8933	159810
15 7th decile								121872	25636										29170								9328	186006
16 8th decile								148701	34564										27495								4909	215669
17 9th decile								196803	67181										27231								-13810	277405
18 10th decile								209660	126385										26139								-37217	324967
19 Firms									81680											3960							-480	85160
20 Government	9084	18856	9825	1847	37898	10250		-20710	2950	8262	19844	28497	39178	50705	62040	73344	93796	111176	37840		19700	-1638	47313	-13	-6170	40268	-17170	676972
21 Accumulation									-1038	774	1806	2850	4130	6171	7859	11714	21605	34598	47320	23800		10733	76167	12816	22786	99478	-22340	361229
22 Agriculture	10419	12	0	0	839	0															1278	7562	45625	245	19	6502	-4250	76751
23 Industry	119921	77951	43997	3689	70573	3388															276606	20754	599306	21158	17744	134769	408595	1798451
24 Trade	73460	9571	23170	1288	32624	1364															19115	2868	68193	6839	1873	17919	18561	276845
25 Transport	0	0	0	0	38309	0															840	1889	43445	9091	13359	18764	31139	156836
26 Services	0	192843	1957	26926	60925	30077														350230	12803	2797	114419	46297	12701	294568	14307	1160650
27 Rest of World	25951	10465	10115	15077	11228	19673															30888	7100	248156	8121	14680	37357	60558	493369
Total	238835	309698	89064	48827	252396	64752	953999	403931	37753	58660	84238	106547	132774	158811	186006	215669	277405	324968	85160	676969	361230	76751	1798450	276844	156836	1160649	499371	9037593

SAM Italy 1984 (billion lires)

	WANTS					FACTORS		HOUSEHOLD INCOME DECILES										INSTITUTIONS			ACTIVITIES					ROW	TOTAL
	1	2	3	4	5	6	7	8	9	10	11	12	13	14	15	16	17	18	19	20	21	22	23	24	25	26	
1 Food								1328	1683	1983	1901	1884	2083	1423	1474	1663	2172										17594
2 Housing								8532	11268	14939	15059	15681	17920	20250	22447	25655	34347										186098
3 Clothing, ftwr								3846	4970	6371	6305	6479	7346	8035	9685	10906	14205										78148
4 Medical care								277	466	597	1245	1335	1513	1860	2235	2517	3277										15322
5 Recr./Trans								6142	7497	9065	8715	9074	10261	11771	15329	17264	22474										117592
7 Labour																					21846	152664	50025	23077	160782	-571	407823
8 Capital																					12080	46825	23981	16244	100269	-16372	183027
9 1st decile						6169	2008											15242								47	23466
10 2nd decile						16795	3585											13707								124	34211
11 3rd decile						22369	4964											15479								166	42978
12 4th decile						27486	5864											13969								206	47525
13 5th decile						33907	6230											13879								276	54292
14 6th decile						37721	7583											13857								298	59459
15 7th decile						44801	8348											13804								372	67325
16 8th decile						53893	12101											13401								443	79838
17 9th decile						65339	17437											13720								504	97000
18 10th decile						99343	43009											20726								679	163757
19 Firms	17593					0	67990											0	26775							8808	103573
20 Government						0	3908	2683	6836	9544	11681	13854	15383	16806	21086	26039	51455	19142	0		-855	47064	5731	-9459	10568	-1091	267968
21 Accumulation								658	1491	479	2619	5985	4953	7180	7582	12956	35827	84431	-60861							18410	121710
22 Agriculture	0	186099	0	0	0															1799	13661	32885	136	156	3721	4200	242657
23 Industry	0	0	78148	0	0															113491	9769	277152	13917	13073	42930	120821	669301
24 Trade	0	0	0	15322	0															5208	1922	15743	6237	1005	4642	7135	57214
25 Transport	0	0	0	0	117592																554	16183	2625	6351	3415	11777	158497
26 Services	0	0	0	0	0														136677	1198	2379	51603	13065	4657	50299	5781	265659
27 Rest of World																				14	12797	137132	4323	2320	5441		162027
Total	17593	186099	78148	15322	117592	407823	183027	23466	34211	42978	47525	54292	59459	67325	79838	97000	163757	103573	250375	121710	74153	777251	120040	57424	382067	162013	3724061

SAM The Netherlands 1987 (million guilders)

	WANTS						FACTORS		HOUSEHOLD INCOME DECILES										INSTITUTIONS			ACTIVITIES					ROW	TOTAL
	1	2	3	4	5	6	7	8	9	10	11	12	13	14	15	16	17	18	19	20	21	22	23	24	25	26	27	
1 Food									2384	2925	3311	3464	4253	4641	4930	5329	5821	6912										43970
2 Housing									3954	4852	4867	5579	6227	6748	7253	7852	8884	10833										67049
3 Clothing, ftwr									746	1029	1124	1363	1758	1772	2212	2456	2708	3632										18800
4 Medical care									1743	2347	2671	3233	3524	3917	4260	4449	5109	5917										37170
5 Recr/Trans									3128	4327	5106	6149	6610	8458	10247	11404	14590										77360
6 Other									471	956	949	1317	1493	2457	2256	2339	2239	5103										19580
7 Labour																						3283	1666	69374	157732	232055	120	464230
8 Capital																						11021	13103	26574	61346	112044	-350	223238
9 1st decile								842											10169		10169						-162	21808
10 2nd decile							790	1805											13010		13010						-162	30432
11 3rd decile							2769	2976											13534		13334						-162	35647
12 4th decile							5765	5165											11665		11665						-162	38281
13 5th decile							9948	6908											11365		11365						-162	43156
14 6th decile							13680	9029											10169		10169						-162	47464
15 7th decile							18259	10054											11814		11814						-162	53331
16 8th decile							20011	12534											10543		10543						-162	59405
17 9th decile							25947	14938											12861		12861						-162	71476
18 10th decile							30978	26092											13310		13310						-162	103258
19 Firms							50708	30800																				30800
20 Government	2242	4654	2425	456	9354	2530	53320	-9950	1324	2259	3427	4440	6076	7945	8413	10750	13866	25241	1930	6964	24924	660	3375	-2862	10023	11196	-2012	202970
21 Capital									-2111	-1273	657	1072	1850	2473	3937	3440	8585	17720	-8080		6690	2730	2270	15180	25303	45483	-8210	119716
22 Agriculture	2065	11	0	0	996	0														-589	-589	841		19644	467	20952	11177	54975
23 Industry	9	491	0	0	3327	0														-661	-661	111	1217	13510	1577	16415	19605	54940
24 Trade	16716	16401	7201	1179	4671	811														41754	41754	10608	1298	65213	26065	103184	122945	459800
25 Transport	9979	40267	4123	26836	47445	13545													70590	12398	82988	3081	868	28628	49661	82238	49627	322274
26 Services	28769	57169	11324	28015	56438	14356													70590	52902	123492	14641	3383	126995	77770	222789	203354	1091987
27 Rest of World	12959	5226	5051	8699	11567	2694														22447	22447	2277	15389	79600	24874	121140	22529	357899
Total	72739	124219	30124	65185	133798	33936	232175	111193	11639	17422	22112	26617	31791	37294	41719	48862	59616	89948	253470	135215	419485	49253	42569	441856	434818	968496	416665	4351216

SAM Spain 1980 (million pesetas)

	WANTS						FACTORS		HOUSEHOLD INCOME DECILES						INSTITUTIONS			ACTIVITIES					ROW	TOTAL
	1	2	3	4	5	6	7	8	9	10	11	12	13	14	15	16	17	18	19	20	21	22	23	
1 Food									29031	1580891	274075	29945	751618	111749										2777309
2 Housing									17185	796843	156719	17299	560765	84307										1633318
3 Clothing, ftwr									7669	420092	47425	9040	280520	34170										799116
4 Medical care									22390	1037562	87085	34655	835929	94307										2111928
5 Recr./Trans									11057	505864	55247	14921	420216	41984										1049289
6 Other goods									21010	752512	77598	28156	658995	76513										1614784
7 Labour																		273533	2647712	785942	390369	1979922	14171	6087649
8 Capital																		799053	2115909	1729375	473813	1612587	118771	6849508
9 Young poor								98318								16551							1376	120230
10 Adult poor								4684565								757459							66350	5768190
11 Old poor								29082								655480							1206	757034
12 Youn rich								87050								2881							2147	177093
13 Adult rich								1174959								424569							57117	5271402
14 Old rich								13053								272166							3657	594060
								305184								104777								
15 Firms								2191184										29802	1194481	254954	12557	708996	21101	4265644
16 Government								59583							438265								364331	3548093
17 Accumulation																	86733							
	63995	26146	1713	74680	19124	8795			9375	452572	8659	29044	799188	52614										
									2347	212249	48694	12162	886716	91749	1843112									
18 Agriculture	417499	4736	2758	5681	5944	765											115013	324690	1224267	84838	2212	21359	136669	2346431
19 Industry	1458429	267839	464222	954553	318124	132877											3085963	492990	6548596	875916	321976	813888	1534871	17270244
20 Trade & hreca	738357	7261	284903	646725	279433	1255707											71549	66979	448581	133538	44674	67461	205865	4251033
21 Transport	96157	83882	34998	198721	26197	8855											17786	32875	99811	148370	128062	284022	1526848
22 Services	2872	1243454	10523	231568	400467	207786											1929316	257782	54100	519277	267228	75497	906567	238669	6345106
23 Rest of World							622	258718							14584	15711		272409	2204309	19430	57380	110264		3050323
Total	2777309	1633318	799117	2111928	1049289	1614785	6087649	6849508	120230	5768190	757034	177093	5271402	594060	2295961	4265643	3548093	2346431	17270244	4251032	1526848	6345106	3050323	80510593

SAM Hungary 1988 (billion forints)

	WANTS						FACTORS		HOUSEHOLD INCOME DECILES										INSTITUTIONS			ACTIVITIES											ROW TOTAL
	1	2	3	4	5	6	7	8	9	10	11	12	13	14	15	16	17	18	19	20	21	22	23	24	25	26	27	28	29	30	31	32	
1 Food									21.1	25.4	27.2	28.4	31.4	33.6	36.6	40.5	45.3	56		14.1												-4	355.6
2 Housing									6.9	9.1	10.6	12.1	13.5	14.4	14.4	17.5	20.2	24.4		3.4												-1.6	144.9
3 Clothing/ftwr									3.1	4.1	4.6	5.3	5.8	6.4	7.3	7.3	7.9	12.6		1.2												-0.7	64.9
4 Medical care									0.8	1.1	1.3	1.5	1.6	1.9	2	2.2	2.5	3.7		38.7												-0.2	57.1
5 Recr./Trans									3.8	6.7	7.9	8.6	10.3	11.5	13.3	14.6	18	27	9.3	60.5												-1.4	190.1
6 Other goods									1.1	1.6	2	3.2	2.8	3.1	3.7	4.3	5.6	9.8		5.4												-0.4	42.2
7 Labour							23.5															180.6	24.5	91.2	21.1	95.9	17.4	78.8	63.7	69.7	179.6		822.5
8 Capital							33.8															8.3	25.1	-2.2	34.5	50.6	33.5	15.1	18.2	51.7	24.1		258.9
9 1st decile							40.7												1.2	17.8													43.2
10 2nd decile							46.8												2.2	20.3													57.4
11 3rd decile							53.5												27	205													274
12 4th decile							61.4												2.7	21.8													72.8
13 5th decile							71.8												3	22.1													80.3
14 6th decile							83.7												3.6	22.2													89.1
15 7th decile							100.3												4.4	21.4													99.9
16 8th decile							160.9												5.3	21.2													112.8
17 9th decile																			7.2	21.4													132.1
18 10th decile																			11.2	22.3													199.5
19 Firms								237.5																									237.5
20 Government								146.1	4.6	6.6	7.8	9	10.6	12.5	15.1	18.1	22.6	41.9	136		4.9	9	1	11.3	26.2	25.1	3.1	8.8	6.9	3.2	14.7	-59.3	567
21 Accumulation									1.8	2.8	3.8	4.8	4.3	5.8	7.4	8.3	10.1	24.1	24	100		20.5	5.8	11.6	9	15.5	13.6	2.9	19.3	4.5	30	29	358.9
22 Agriculture	67.3	2.8	0.1	0.5	1.8	0.3														1.2	23.7	127.2	2.5	164.9	8.5	18.4	3.5	16.9	4.3	21.7	18.1	90.2	533.9
23 Mining/oil ind	0	12.1	0	0.1	0.2	0														5.9	6.6	1.4	0.6	1.9	30.1	12	11.9	0.6	0.9	0.3	6.8	3.6	95
24 Light ind	133.8	13.2	29.8	1	5.5	8.8														13.6	7.7	31.9	1.6	61.5	6.6	14.9	2.3	11.8	5.3	11.9	23.1	120.5	498.4
25 Chemical ind	0.3	15.1	0.1	10	5.9	0														2	79.3	40.7	4.3	14.4	30.9	19	12.2	4.8	19.5	3.8	16.7	78.9	286.3
26 Heavy ind	0	9.4	0.1	0.6	7.4	2.1														3.4		23.5	9	7.2	5	125.4	9.3	3.2	9.3	2.9	14.2	220.1	562.3
27 Public utilities	0	15.3	0	0.1	0.1	2.1														5.7	6.5	10	5.1	11.4	13.2	25	4.1	3.2	6.8	6.9	20.7	0.2	136.4
28 Transport	0	0	0	0.1	0.2	0														6.8	140.8	7	2	4.9	3.3	7.6	2.5	3	4	4.9	25.4	11.4	227
29 Construction	0	0.1	0	0.3	35.1	0														5	6.4	14.1	3.9	15.4	7.4	26.4	3	10.3	2.6	22.9	9.9	20.5	183.3
30 Trade	55.1	11.5	8.6	8	7.3	11.1															19.1	15.3	1.1	15	6	16.8	2	10.2	2.8	2.9	13.6	23.4	229.8
31 Services	12	72.8	1.2	43.4	86.7	11.7													24.7	101.1	1.6	10.9	1	8.8	4.5	13.2	1.6	6.6	7.3	16.2	49.1	1.6	476
32 Rest of world	9.5	11.3	12.7	6.1	21.3	3															48.7	33.4	7.5	81.1	80	96.5	16.4	12.1	16	6.1	30		491.7
Total	355.4	145	64.9	57	190.3	42.2	822.5	258.9	43.2	57.4	65.2	72.9	80.3	89.2	99.8	112.8	132.2	199.5	261.8	751.5	358.9	333.8	95	498.4	286.3	562.3	136.4	227	183.3	229.6	476	491.8	7980.8

SAM Hungary 1990 (billion forints)

	WANTS						FACTORS		HOUSEHOLD INCOME DECILES										INSTITUTIONS			ACTIVITIES										ROW TOTAL
	1	2	3	4	5	6	7	8	9	10	11	12	13	14	15	16	17	18	19	20	21	22	23	24	25	26	27	28	29	30	31	32	
1 Food									30.7	35.9	38.9	41.9	44.5	47.6	50.3	55.2	58.1	67.1		16.7												11.6	498.5
2 Housing									9.4	13.3	14.4	15.3	17.6	18.6	20.7	24	26.2	39.5		29.9												4.9	233.8
3 Clothing									4.2	5.6	5.9	6.4	7	7.6	8.1	9.2	10.3	13.2														1.9	79.4
4 Medical care									1.5	2	2.4	2.5	2.9	2.9	4	2.8	3.2	4.1		68.2												0.7	96.1
5 Recr./Trans									6.9	10.3	11.9	13.5	16.1	17	18.7	20.7	29.9	48.3		123.8												4.8	321.9
6 Other goods									3.1	4	4.6	4.9	6	6.6	7.2	8.2	10.3	13.7														1.7	70.3
7 Labour																						229.7	30.8	129	32.5	133	26.9	113	98.5	115.2	349.4		1258
8 Capital																						10.6	21.3	1	43.6	54.8	40.8	9.4	23.5	122.7	17.5		345.2
9 1st decile							34.1	0.8											1.4	29.9													66.2
10 2nd decile							49.6	1.3											2.5	33.5													86.9
11 3rd decile							59	1.6											3.2	34													97.8
12 4th decile							67.2	1.7											3.6	35.6													108.1
13 5th decile							75.7	2											4.1	37.3													119.1
14 6th decile							87.6	2.3											5	36.6													131.5
15 7th decile							101.8	2.7											6	35.6													146.1
16 8th decile							119.3	3.1											7.6	35.1													165.1
17 9th decile							143.3	3.7											10.1	35.9													193
18 10th decile							237.8	6.2											16	32.8													292.8
19 Firms								319.8																									319.8
20 Government	102.7	8.3	15.3	-21.4	28.1	6.6	282.6		6.6	9.9	11.6	13.4	16	19	22.6	27.4	33.7	56	175.2	0	6	20.2	1.2	18.7	37.9	29.9	10.7	12.4	12.2	5.1	21.2	-82.3	906.8
21 Accumulation									3.8	5.9	8.1	10.2	9	12.2	15.6	17.6	21.3	50.9	32.3	155.5		21.8	9	13.1	10.2	15.6	16.1	3.3	21.9	5.8	43.1	-23.3	479
22 Agriculture	104.6	4	0.1	0.9	3.4	0.4														1.2	33.3	152.8	2.6	211.1	10.2	19	4.2	18.7	5.4	29.4	23.2	62.5	687
23 Mining & oil ind	0	11.2	0	0.2	0.2	0														7	8.4	1.6	0.6	2	33	12.4	14.2	0.5	0.9	0.4	3.8		104.4
24 Light ind	179.5	16.3	37.9	1	9	13.7														2.1	25	46.7	1.7	71.8	8.1	15.4	3	12	6	16.4	8	157	653.7
25 Chemical ind	0.6	26.2	0.2	20.8	13.5	0														2.6	13.1	47.6	4.4	15.4	36.5	19.6	15.1	5.2	23.2	4.9	31.1	3.8	373.5
26 Heavy ind	0	21.3	0.2	1.6	22.1	2.9														4.3	96.5	29.9	10	9.3	7.3	146.1	11.9	41.1	12.3	4.4	18.2	103.1	245.9	685.9
27 Public utilities	0	19	0	0.1	0.2	3.3														9.2	7.5	13.2	5.6	13.6	17.3	29.1	5	3.9	9	9.9	28.2	3.1	177.2
28 Construction	0	0	0	0.1	0.3	0														8.2	184.6	7.8	1.9	5.3	3.8	7.6	2.7	9.9	0.5	6.1	29.7	14.1	282.6
29 Transp & com.	0	0.1	0	0.4	48.4	0														3.7	9.6	19	4.5	20	9.9	30.6	4.2	12.5	4	33.7	14.2	38.7	253.5
30 Trade	83.7	16.2	12.3	13.4	13.1	19.5															29.6	29	2	27.2	28.4	3.9	17.4	12.2	5.7	6.5	26.5		398.3
31 Other services	18.1	101	1.7	72.4	158.4	20.5														52.8	128.1	16.3	1.4	14.2	6.9	18.4	2.3	9.6	12.7	28.3	74.6	5.2	744.5
32 Rest of world	9.3	10.2	11.7	6.6	25.2	3.4															63.8	40.8	7.4	102	104.1	125.4	16.2	13.7	17.7	9.5	38.1		605.1
Total	498.5	233.8	79.4	96.1	321.9	70.3	1258	345.2	66.2	86.9	97.8	108	119.1	132	146.1	165.1	193	292.8	319.8	906.8	479	687	104.4	653.7	373.5	685.9	177.2	282.6	253.5	398.3	744.5	605.1	10981.1

SAM Poland 1987 (billion zlotys)

	WANTS						FACTORS		HOUSEHOLD INCOME DECILES										INSTITUTIONS								ACTIVITIES										ROW TOTAL
	1	2	3	4	5	6	7	8	9	10	11	12	13	14	15	16	17	18	19	20	21	22	23	24	25	26	27	28	29	30	31	32	33	34	35	36	37	
1 Food									193	263	311	352	400	440	486	539	622	799																				4405
2 Housing									60	79	103	122	142	161	185	203	243	356																				1654
3 Clothing									38	54	66	77	88	99	111	132	151	204																				1021
4 Medical care									9	12	15	18	20	23	26	28	33	45																				229
5 Recr/Trans									22	36	41	56	62	77	92	111	139	247																				883
6 Other goods									18	27	32	39	46	50	60	67	86	119																				544
7 Labour																											1251	573	994	200	1287	395	781	571	644	1636	0	8332
8 Capital																											427	261	1045	449	1709	410	1026	1085	452	567	0	7431
9 1st decile							251	14																3	70												26	364
10 2nd decile							354	19																4	93												33	503
11 3rd decile							419	23																5	121												38	606
12 4th decile							491	24																6	143												42	706
13 5th decile							525	81																7	178												27	818
14 6th decile							620	91																7	168												30	916
15 7th decile							704	103																8	191												33	1039
16 8th decile							828	124																7	184												38	1181
17 9th decile							1036	152																6	163												44	1401
18 10th decile							1509	220																8	189												64	1990
19 State owned firms							0	4944																														4944
20 Private firms							0	169																														169
21 Private farms							0	215																														215
22 Banks							0	238															316															554
23 Insurance comp.							0	50																														50
24 Government							0	964											36	116	3	122	8		62													3952
25 Social security							1592	0											2368	53	212	433	42	-194	30													1592
26 Accumulation									15	20	26	28	43	49	61	78	104	185	2576					36		-21	206	-113	-9	357	-47	139	-155	5	265	-179	-191	4884
27 Agriculture	639	0	0	0	0	0																		-81		26	1003	1	1658	10	143	43	85	136	46	17	127	3923
28 Mining & oil ind	0	117	0	0	63	0																		106		274	135	171	123	138	338	374	85	27	191	77	342	2126
29 Light ind	2685	356	757	0	0	127																		-1		163	69	31	1430	92	234	70	170	107	254	600	7532
30 Chemical ind	0	32	0	88	33	0																		12		1066	111	34	253	302	202	40	96	17	41	94	335	1840
31 Heavy ind	0	204	0	0	263	102																		-7		9	520	191	291	102	2481	178	715	108	252	248	1570	8303
32 Public utilities	0	400	0	0	15	0																		-6		2759	51	99	179	78	254	267	103	61	123	268	48	3741
33 Construction	0	75	0	0	0	0																		-67		143	93	65	88	30	131	54	87	50	42	121	152	1948
34 Trade	921	239	201	23	127	194																		8		6	60	80	214	80	308	48	100	38	82	82	6	2879
35 Transport	0	12	0	0	351	0																					60	157	340	60	221	51	261	216	146	119	335	2343
36 Services	0	114	0	113	0	118																		2937			10	5	63	11	70	19	76	55	39	358	0	3988
37 Rest of world	162	104	63	4	30	2																		831		458	39	401	404	290	605	41	86	58	210	153	109	4059
Total	4407	1653	1021	228	882	543	8329	7431	364	502	607	706	816	916	1040	1179	1403	1991	4944	169	215	555	50	3951	1592	4883	3922	2127	7533	1840	8303	1947	3741	2882	2344	3991	4048	93055

SAM Poland 1990 (billion zlotys)

	WANTS						FACTORS		HOUSEHOLD INCOME DECILES										INSTITUTIONS						ACTIVITIES											ROW	TOTAL
	1	2	3	4	5	6	7	8	9	10	11	12	13	14	15	16	17	18	19	20	21	22	23	24	25	26	27	28	29	30	31	32	33	34		
1 Food									12.5	11.8	11.1	12.2	13.4	13.8	17.8	18.8	20.5																			143.9
2 Housing										3	3	3.3	3.7	4.1	4.3	6	6.4	7.9																		44.7
3 Clothing									1.5	1.7	1.8	2.1	2.1	2.6	3.7	4.2	5.2																			27.5
4 Medical care									0.7	0.6	0.6	0.7	0.7	0.8	1.1	1.2	1.4																			8.6
5 Recr/Trans									1.2	1.6	1.7	2.2	2.3	2.9	3.4	4.5	5.6	8.5																		33.9
6 Other goods									0.7	0.6	0.6	0.7	0.7	0.8	0.9	1.1	1.3	1.9																		9.3
7 Labour																									24.7	19.6	32.6	5.2	44.3	9.1	14.2	20.9	14.4	60		245
8 Capital																									6.7	12.6	48.1	16.4	82.6	13.3	26.3	55.8	14.2	29.2		305.2
9 1st decile							2.5	0.6																											0.1	21.1
10 2nd decile							8	0.9																											2.2	21.9
11 3rd decile							11.7	1.4																											1.6	22.7
12 4th decile							14	2.4																											1.6	25.2
13 5th decile							16.4	3.6																											1.1	26.8
14 6th decile							19.1	6																											3	32.1
15 7th decile							22.6	9.6																											1.5	36.9
16 8th decile							26.1	13.2																											1.4	43.1
17 9th decile							30.8	16.8																											1.4	50.5
18 10th decile							42.3	21.6																											1.8	67.1
19 State and fms							0	162.5																												162.5
20 Private firms							0	8.5																												8.5
21 Banks & ins							0.0	30.8																												30.8
22 Government							0	27.2	0.3	0.3	0.3	0.3	0.4	0.4	0.4	0.5	0.7		85.5	2.3	21.1				-2.7	-2.6	10.6	0.8	4.3	-1.7	0.7	6.8	-1.4	-6	2.5	151.4
23 Social security							51.6	0														8.6														60.2
24 Accumulation							0	0	1.3	2.3	3.7	3.7	4.9	7.3	10.6	8.4	12.4	20.9	77	6.3	9.7		11.1		4.7	1.8	2.7	1.5	5.7	2.7	1.7	0.9	4.2	6.9	-25.1	187.3
25 Agriculture	15.1	0	0	0	0	0																		-0.9	28.5	0	37.6	0.2	12	0.1	1.2	1.6	0.7		7.5	93.8
26 Mining & oil ind	0	2.1	0	0	0	3.7																		3.6	4.9	2.3	2.3	3.8	7.2	6.1	2.7	0.4	6.2	1.3		1.3	59.6
27 Light industry	79.1	3	17.5	0	0	0.6																		20.6	1.8	0.6	41.6	2.8	5.7	0.7	5	3.9	3.1	10.4		28.9	225.3
28 Chemical ind	0	0.7	0	0.1	2.4	0																		4.6	2.8	0.9	6.1	9.7	5.3	1	3.2	0.4	1.2	5.7		16.3	61.5
29 Heavy ind	0	3.2	0	13.2	0.9																		42.5	11.7	5	9.1	3.9	71.6	4.8	25.7	2.5	8.8	7.9		60.8	271.6
30 Public utility	0	7	0	0.8	0																		1.8	1.9	4.3	2.8	6.9	5.3	1	2	0.9	3.5	7.4		0.8	48.3
31 Construction	0	8.4	0	0	0																		68.7	2.6	1.1	1.8	0.7	2.6	1	2	0.8	0.9	3.6		6.5	100.7
32 Trade	38.7	2.9	6.6	0.2	5	1.3																		15.8	2.8	2	4.3	2.8	6.9	7.5	1.1	3	0.8	2.8	2.5		0	102.2
33 Transport	0	0.1	0	0	6.3	0																		1.1	1.4	3.5	8.1	1.7	5.5	0.9	8.2	3.4	3.6	20.6		3.9	68.3
34 Services	0	11.5	0	6.7	2.4	0.1																		8.7	0.6	1.3	1.9	0.5	2.1	1.3	1.9	1	1.5	12.2		0	150.8
35 Rest of World	10.9	5.8	3.5	0.3	2.4	0.1																	93.1	22.6	1.6	9.6	12.5	8.3	18.9	0.6	1.9	2.3	4.8		1.5	149.1
Total	143.8	44.7	27.6	8.4	33.8	9.4	245.1	305.1	21.2	21.9	22.8	25.2	26.8	32.3	36.8	43	50.4	67	162.5	8.6	30.8	1513	60.3	187.3	93.9	59.6	225.4	61.4	271.4	48.2	100.7	102.4	68.5	150.8	149	3097.4

Appendix 5: Social Accounting Matrices of China and Russia

SAM China 1989 (billion yuan)

	WANTS					FACTORS				INSTITUTIONS						ACTIVITIES				TOTAL
	Food	Cloth	Misc	Educ	Serv	Ur lab	Rur lab	Profits	Urb em	Urb slf	Rur f	Rur nf	Firms	Gov	Cap	Agr	Ind	Serv	Row	
	1	2	3	4	5	6	7	8	9	10	11	12	13	14	15	16	17	18	19	
1 Food									123.8	6.2	159.8	40.1								329.9
2 Clothing									31.2	1.7	25.9	7.8								66.6
3 Miscellaneous									35.9	2	52	15.6								105.5
4 Education									19.8	1.1	17	5.2								43.1
5 Services									17.1	0.5	44.6	3.4								65.6
6 Urban lab inc																14.9	113.9	129.5		258.3
7 Rural lab inc																324	43.5	11.3		378.8
8 Profits																75.4	228.9	183.7		488
9 Urban employee						237.7								4.2						241.9
10 Urban self-emp						20.6														20.6
11 Rural farm							301.1													301.1
12 Rural non-farm							77.7													77.7
13 Firms								483.1												483.1
14 Government								4.9	14.1	4		2.2	483.1			5.3	162.5	79.9		258.8
15 Capital										5.1	1.8	3.4				5.2	20	20	28.7	581.4
16 Agriculture	230.9	6.7	10.6		9.8									15.5	95.4	28.7	101.6	33.7	71.2	604.1
17 Industry	29.9	46.6	73.9	32.3	13.1									110.2	242.3	134.6	752.8	295.9	51.3	1782.9
18 Services	69.1	13.3	21	10.8	42.7									128.9	243.7	3.4	173.8	60.4	54.3	821.4
19 Rest world																12.6	185.9	7		205.5
Total	329.9	66.6	105.5	43.1	65.6	258.3	378.8	488	241.9	20.6	301.1	77.7	483.1	258.8	581.4	604.1	1782.9	821.4	205.5	7114.3

SAM Russia 1990 (billion roubles)

	WANTS				FACTORS					INSTITUTIONS								ACTIVITIES				TOTAL
	Food	Alc	N food	Servcs	Wage	SoS	W col	In P F	Oth In	<200	<300	<350	<400	>400	Firms	Gvmnt	Capit	Agric	M & Ind	Svcs	RoW	
	1	2	3	4	5	6	7	8	9	10	11	12	13	14	15	16	17	18	19	20	21	
1 Food										33.8	30.1	34.2	32.8	105.2				29.7	152.1	273.7		236.1
2 Alcohol										2.6	2.5	3	3	11.9				1.4	48.3	88		23
3 Non-food										19.5	23.9	32.1	33.3	111.7				13.4	1.3	1.4		220.5
4 Services										5	5.8	7.4	7.3	36.1				53		2.9		
																		32.4	230.2	226.2		488.8
5 Wages in enterprises					26.3		2.7	0.9	3.5													517.1
6 Soc. Sec. in enterpr.					38		2	4	3.6													150.3
7 Wages in collect. farm					53.4		2.4	5.7	4.5													16.1
8 Income from priv. farm					57		2.5	6.5	4.2													55.9
9 Other income					280.8		6.5	38.8	19.5													488.8
10 Hh.< 250 Rbl. p. m.									3.5						2.4	30.2						35.8
11 Hh. 250-300 Rbl. p.m.									3.6						2.5	22.8						80.3
12 Hh. 300-350 Rbl. p.m.									4.5						3	25.1						91.8
13 Hh. 350-400 Rbl. p.m									4.2						2.8	23.9						98.1
14 Hh. > 400 Rbl. p.m.									19.5						13.1	100.8						382.6
									404.3						92.6							597.7
15 Firms						150.3			49.2						99.4							395.4
16 Government										2.4	3.9	5.9	6.6	47.7	281.1	-115		-4.7	23.1	11.6	-16	435.8
17 Capital										2.7	6.7	11.5	13.9	146.9		307.6	41.7	8	49	47	0.7	288.8
18 Agriculture	66.5																188.9	47	130.1	2.8	173.7	1589.5
19 Mining & ind.	143.2	20.5	180.6														184.3	47.9	622	212.7	4.5	948.8
20 Services			11.5	61.6													20.9	41	269.5	68.8		162.9
21 Rest of world	26.4	2.5	28.4															7.1	63.9	13.7		
Total	236.1	23	220.5	61.6	455.5	150.3	16.1	55.9	488.8	66	72.9	94.1	96.9	459.5	496.9	395.4	435.8	288.8	1589.5	948.8	162.9	6815.3

Bibliography

Adelman, I., Taylor, J.E. and Vogel, S. (1988): Life in a Mexican Village: a SAM perspective, in Jounal of Development Studies, 25, 5-24.
Alessie, R.J.M. and Kapteyn, A. (1986): Consumption, Savings and Demography, working document, Tilburg University.
Bennett, J. (1989): The Economic Theory of Central Planning, Oxford, Blackwell.
Berg, L. van den (1987): Urban Systems in a Dynamic Society, Gower Publishing, Aldershot.
Berg, L. van den, and Meer, J. van der (1988): Dynamics of urban systems: general trends and Dutch experiences, in Environmental Planning, 20, 1471-1486.
Bojo, J., Maler, K.G. and Unemo, L. (1992): Environment and development: an economic approach, Boston, Kluwer Academic Publishers.
Braber, R. and Gavrilenkov, E. (1994): A Social Accounting Matrix for the Russian Federation, Foundation of Economic Research Rotterdam and Higher School of Economics Moscow, working paper 1994.
CBS (1978.2): TheProduction Structure of the Netherlands, input output table, part IX, Central Bureau of Statistics, The Hague (in Dutch).
CBS (1982): National Accounts, Central Bureau of Statistics, The Hague (in Dutch).
CBS/DBO (1978.1): Budget Research 1981/85, National and regional basic figures, DBO, Central Bureau of Statistics, The Hague (in Dutch).
CBS/DBO (1981/85), Budget Research 1981/85, National and regional basic figures, DBO, Central Bureau of Statistics, The Hague (in Dutch).
CBS/WBO (1983): Ciffers inzake Woningbehoefienonderzoek WBO in Statistisch Zakboek 1983, CBS, The Hague (in Dutch).
Chaloupek, G., Lamel, J. and Richter, J. (1988): Beublkerungsrackgang und Wirtschaft: Szenarien his 2051 far Oesterreich, Physica-Verlag, Heidelberg, 1988.
Chenery, H., Robinson, S. and Syrquin, M. (1986): Industrialization and Growth, Oxford University Press, New York.
Civiardi, M.C.B. and Lenti, R.T. (1990): A SAM for Italy paper presented at the conference A SAM for Europe, Universidad Internacional Menendez Pelayo, Valencia.
Cohen, S.I. (1988): A Social Accounting Matrix Analysis for the Netherlands, in De Economist, 136, Nr. 2, pp. 253-272.
Cohen, S.I. (1989.1): Multiplier Analysis in Social Accounting and Input-Output Frameworks, in Miller, R.E., Polenske, K.R. and Rose, A.Z. (eds.): Frontiers of Input-Output Analysis, Oxford University Press, Oxford, pp. 79-99.
Cohen, S.I. (1989.2): Analysis of social accounting multipliers over time: the case of the Netherlands, in Socio-Economic Planning Sciences, 23, pp. 291-302.

Cohen, S.I. and Tuyl, J.M.C. (1991): Growth and Equity Effects of Changing Demographic Structures in the Netherlands: Simulations within a social accounting matrix, in Economic Modelling, No. 8, pp. 3-15.

Cohen, S.I., ed. (1993): Patterns of Economic Restructuring for Eastern Europe Avebury-Ashgate Publishing, Aldershot.

Cohen S.I. and Gupei W. (1995): The construction, modelling and analysis of a SAM for China. working paper, Foundation for Economic Research Rotterdam.

Cohen, S.I., M.C. Braber, T. Révész, Z. Zolkiewski (1996): Policy Modelling under Fixed and Flexible Price Regimes: SAM-CGE Transitional Applications to Poland and Hungary, in Journal of Policy Modelling, 8 (5), pp. 495-529.

Cohen S.I. (Forthcoming 2002): Social Accounting and Economic Modelling for Developing Countries, Ashgate, Aldershot.

Delft, A. van (1995): Spatial Ordering and Regional Policy in the Netherlands, in Velden, W. van der, and Wever, E. (ed.): The economic emancipation of the wider Netherlands, Van Gorcum, Assen (in Dutch).

De Melo, M., Denizer, C., Gelb, A., Tenev, S. (2001): Circumstance and Choice: The Role of Initial Conditions and Policies in Transition Economies, in The World Bank Economic Review Vol.15 No.1, pp. 1-31.

Dervis, K., de Melo, J., and Robinson, S. (1982): General Equilibrium Models Development Policy, Cambridge University Press, Cambridge.

Fox, K. A. and Miles D. G. (1987): Systems Economics: concepts, models and multi-disciplinary perspectives, Ames, Iowa: Iowa Satte University Press.

GSO (1970-86): Input-Output tables (Volkswirtschaftliche Gesamtrechnungen: Ergebnisse der Input-Output-Rechnung 1970 bis 1986), German Statistical Office.

GSO (1983): Budget Survey. (Einkommens- und Verbrauchsstichprobe 1983, Heft 4, 5 & 6), German Statistical Office.

GSO (1989): National Accounts (Volkswirtschaftliche Gesarntrechnungen: Konten und Standardtabellen 1989), German Statistical Office.

Jackson, W.A. (1989): Population ageing, productivit y and unemployment, paper presented at the Third Annual Meeting of the European Society for Population Economics, Bouray sur Juine, France, June 1989.

Kehoe T. et al. (1985): A Social Accounting System for Spain, 1980, working paper no. 6386, Universidad Autonoma de Barcelona.

Kemper, N.J. and Pellenbarg , P.H. (1993,5): Business Mobility in the Netherlands, in Economisch Statistische Berichten, March 1993, pp 249 - 252, and April 1995, pp. 380 - 384 (in Dutch).

King, B. B. (1981): What is SAM? A layman's guide to social accounting Matrices, World Bank Staff Working Papers N. 463. Washington D.C. The World Bank.

Laan, L. van der (1991): Spatial Labour Markets in the Netherlands, Erasmus University, Rotterdam.

Meester, W.J. (1994): Recent Changes in the Locational Preference of Dutch Entrepreneurs, paper presented at RSA European Congress, Groningen.

Nelissen, J.H.M. and Vossen, A.P. (1988): Applying a microsimulation model to project the future structure of families and households, paper presented at the

HASA Conference on Future Changes in Population Age Structures, Sopron, Hungary, October 1988.

Nolan, P. (1995): China's Rise Russia's Fall, Macmillan.

Piggott, J., and Whalley, J., eds. (1985): New Developments in Applied General Equilibrium Analysis. Cambridge, Cambridge University Press.

Priemus et al. (1995): Housing Construction and Spatial Developments, in Velden, W. van der, and Wever, E. (ed.): The economic emancipation of the wider Netherlands, Van Gorcum, Assen (in Dutch).

Pyatt, G. and Roe, A. (1977): Social Accounting for Development Planning, Cambridge University Press, Cambridge.

Pyatt, G. and Round, J.I. (1985): Social Accounting Matrices, Symposium Series, World Bank Publications Department, Washington D.C.

Pyatt, G. (1991): Fundamentals of social accounting in Economic System Research, 3, pp. 315-341.

Round, J.I. (1989): Decomposition of input-output and economy-wide multipliers in a regional setting, in Miller, R.E. et al. (eds.): Frontiers of Input-Output Analysis, Oxford University Press, Oxford.

Shoven, J. B. and Whalley J. (1992) Applying general equilibrium. New York, N.Y. Cambridge University Press.

Silverman, B. and Yanowitch, M. (1997): Winners and Losers on the Russian Road to Capitalism, M.E. Sharpe.

United Nations (1977): Comparisons of the System of National Accounts and the System of Balances of the National Economy, New York, United Nations, Series F 20.

Van Tongeren, F. W. (1993): Corporates in an Economy-wide Model, a Microsimulation Approach, Ph.D. Thesis, Erasmus University, Rotterdam.

Walder, A.G. (ed.) (1996): China's Transitional Economy, Oxford University Press.

Index

Adelman, 195
agriculture, 36-7, 52, 73-5, 112-5, 128-9, 146, 14 9, 153
Alessie, 145-6, 195
Austria, 145

banking, 108, 110, 113, 115, 130-4, 146, 150, 153
Bennett, 59,195
Berg, 126, 127, 195
Braber, 42, 195-6
budget deficit, 67,72-3, 97

capital-intensive, 74, 83-4, 92-3
CGE, 57-61, 67-8, 70, 72-8
changes in multipliers, 27-8, 40, 42, 67-9, 74, 82-3, 96, 102, 108-131, 134-6, 150-3, 156-7
Chaloupek, 145, 195
Chenery, 19, 195
China, 39-41, 43-55, 57, 60-1, 192, 196-7
Civiardi, 176, 195
Clark, 19
closed-loop effects, 32, 104-7
closure, 27, 44, 107
comparative, 20-1, 4 9, 55
construction sector, 68, 83-4, 91, 94, 98, 109, 116, 126-135, 147-8, 154-5
converter, 43, 94, 148-9
cross-country, 2, 27, 48

De Melo, 40, 57, 196
decomposition, 32,104-7, 120-3, 139-142, 169-70
demand injection, 47, 52-4, 108-9, 114, 118, 120, 127, 149

demographic, 152-63
Denizer, 40, 196
Dervis, 57, 66, 196
distribution, 2, 7, 12, 13, 16-7, 20-40, 42, 44, 47, 51-3, 61, 68, 73-4, 82-5, 91, 95, 101-122, 125, 134-5, 137, 141, 144, 159, 163

economic efficiency, 24, 49, 57
equality, 58, 114, 122, 175
equity, 2, 62, 99, 121

fixed-price, 57-8, 61, 66-9, 77-6, 85, 94, 97
flexible-price, 57-8, 61, 66, 70, 85, 94, 97

Gavrilenkov 42, 195
Gelb, 40, 196
Germany, 2, 7, 10, 11, 12, 14, 16, 17, 21, 26-7, 32, 36-7, 183
growth, 2-3, 24-5, 38, 41, 47, 52, 56, 69, 74, 82-6, 90-1, 100, 102, 107, 108, 110-128, 135-8, 140-7, 154, 160-4, 167
Gupei, 42, 196

Hicks, 1, 101
Hungary, 7, 10-16, 21, 26-37, 40-1, 68, 77- 88, 94, 178, 181, 187-8

income multiplier, 21-43, 54-68, 96, 102, 108-136, 142, 150-7
industry, 17, 27, 32, 37, 52-3, 58-9, 108, 115
input-output, 2, 8, 10, 21, 68, 103-7, 120, 128, 138, 147, 163-5, 175-6, 195-6

Institutional transfers, 163, 166
inter-temporal, 2, 163
Italy, 2, 8, 12-7, 21, 26-27, 31-2, 36-7, 176-7, 184

Jackson, 146, 196

Kapteyn, 145-6, 195
Kehoe, 177, 196
Keynesian model, 21, 137, 146
King, 196
Kuznets, 19

Laan, 111, 197
Lamel, 145, 195
leakage, 27-8, 38, 69, 77, 114, 125, 138, 159, 161-2
Lenti, 176, 195
Leontief model, 59, 67, 137

market, 3, 11, 20, 28, 33, 38, 45, 50, 58-9, 61, 66, 68, 86-7, 97, 111
Material Product System, 8, 171-4
Meer, 126, 195
Meester, 110, 197
Miles, 196
M-system, 9, 10-5, 27-8, 32

Nelissen, 152, 197
Netherlands, 2, 11-4, 21, 26, 28, 36-7, 39, 98-101, 104, 108, 117-162, 177, 180, 185
Nolan, 40, 196

open-loop effects, 32, 104-7
output multiplier, 25-33, 40-3, 54-8, 109, 112, 127-9, 131-3, 149, 151-6

performance, 2, 30-1, 46-8, 54, 56-8, 64-6, 93-4, 135, 139, 142, 156-160
Piggott, 57, 197
planning, 3, 17, 30, 43-4, 55, 68-9, 76, 98, 141
Poland, 7, 10-7, 20, 26-9, 32-8, 41-2, 58, 68, 90, 95, 178, 185, 189, 190
population, 27, 42, 48, 53, 91, 111, 127, 146-7, 153-4, 164, 171-3
Priemus, 110, 197
progressive, 36, 108, 164, 167
P-system, 9, 11-5, 27-8, 32
Pyatt, 1, 22, 57, 89, 196

Quesnay, 1

RAS method, 43, 50, 106, 171
redistributionary effects, 41, 51
regional, 122-139, 142, 160, 196
regressive, 33, 36-7, 42-3, 48, 114-5, 180
relative distributive measure 32, 59, 112, 127
remuneration, 20, 63
Richter, 145-6, 196
Robinson, 19, 57, 66, 195-6
Roe, 1, 89, 196
Round, 142, 196
rural, 57, 138, 143, 145-9, 151-5
Russia, 39-41, 43-58, 61, 193, 195

sectoral injection, 25-32, 40, 47-9, 92-3, 97-8, 112-8, 125-129, 132-4, 139, 142, 149, 150-4
services, 10, 16, 20-1, 29, 34, 37-7, 39, 40, 46, 54, 57, 67, 73-4, 78, 81, 83, 88-94, 107-9, 112, 116, 126-9, 133-5, 147-8, 154-5, 158
Shoven, 57, 196
Silverman, 48, 196
social welfare, 24, 26, 49, 57, 69
social security, 10, 12, 14-5, 30, 63, 68, 70-6, 86, 135, 138, 148, 156, 159
Spain, 2, 8, 12-7, 21, 26-7, 31-2, 36-7, 177-8, 186
spatial, 118, 120, 121, 136, 137
Stone, 1, 101
surplus, 76, 91
Syrquin 19, 195
System of National Accounts, 8-10, 171-4

tax, 15, 16, 70-2, 75, 78, 82, 86
Tenev, 40, 196
trade, 17, 27, 32, 37, 108, 110, 112-3, 115, 126, 128, 130, 132, 146, 150, 153
transition, 41
transport, 17-8, 27, 32, 37, 108, 110, 113, 115, 130, 132, 146, 150, 153
transfer effects, 37, 137
transfer injection, 50, 52-5, 58-9, 109, 114, 120-1
Tuyl, 128, 196

unemployment, 120, 133, 137, 158, 159
utilities, 109, 116, 126-7, 129, 130, 134-5, 146-8, 150-1, 154-5, 170
United Nations, 22, 47, 101
urban, 60, 125-7, 140-2, 134

Van Tongeren, 108, 197
Vossen, 152, 197

workforce, 147
Walder, 41, 48, 197
Whalley, 57, 197

Yanowitch, 41, 48, 197